This Land We Do Not Give

a history of Macedonian resistance to foreign occupation

Michael Seraphinoff

Chris Stefou

This Land We Do Not Give

a history of Macedonian resistance to foreign occupation

For information on ordering books in the USA please contact:

website: www.MacedonianLit.com

For orders in Canada please contact:

website: www.oshchima.com

Published by: Nettle Hollow

with the assistance of Aardvark Global

Printed by "2nd of August- S" – Shtip, Republic of Macedonia
 ISBN 978-1-4276-2529-8

cover art: bronze monument at Mechkin Kamen (cover design: Susan C. Prescott and Michael Seraphinoff)
portions of this book first appeared in *History of the Macedonian People from Ancient Times to the Present* and *Oschima- The Story of a Small Village in Western Macedonia.*

...For the world was good
and the ways of invaders evil,
incomprehensible and absurd.
...

Men, animals, all nature's flesh
was never severed from his soul
which flowed like the rapid rush of streams
and rendered a useless wonder
the holy men's talk of sin and salvation.

But the sporadic intrusions
of flashing knives
broke the charm of his paradise.

from "Icon 1: The Macedonian Peasant,"
Fragments of a History, Jim Thomev

Preface

For most people the name Macedonia immediately brings to mind the ancient world conquerors led by their daring and charismatic young warrior-king Alexander, who is the subject of so much legend and lore. However, for Europeans Macedonia is known in modern times as the "apple of discord" among southeastern European nations.

By the late 19th century the Ottoman Turkish Empire had lost nearly all of its European colonies. The bulk of what remained was the Ottoman province that was the ancient land of Macedonia. The people of Macedonia at that time were predominantly of a single ethnic group defined by their language, which is a distinct set of Slavic dialects, and their Eastern Orthodox Christian faith, both of which are clearly documented in church manuscripts dating as far back as the 9th century on the Balkan peninsula.

Thus, the Macedonians were in a position to self-organize to resist the foreign rule. However, that resistance was tragically manipulated by their recently liberated neighbors in Serbia, Bulgaria and Greece. They saw the future liberation of Macedonia more as an opportunity to expand their own nation-states' borders at the expense of that neighbor than an opportunity to help free one more oppressed Balkan people, despite the fact that all three of those states had achieved their own independence only with aid from outside.

That outside aid had come primarily from the Great Powers of Europe, the Germans, the British, the French and the Russians. The Macedonians, however, while they had the sympathy of most of the people of Europe, were unable to gain the support of any of the governments of Europe for their liberation, because those governments shifted positions and alliances in endless pursuit of further power and influence. Thus, Macedonia has a history not unlike that of other "troubled" regions of Europe, such as the regions of Spain and France inhabited by the Basques or the former island colony of the British Empire, Ireland, where the negative consequences of colonialism are still a fact of life.

As we know, the victors enjoy the various spoils of war, and one of these is the opportunity to have their version of the history of the war broadly and boldly disseminated. So it has been for over a hundred and fifty years that Macedonian history has been primarily written and disseminated by those Greek, Serbian or Bulgarian victors in the Balkan wars of liberation of the 19th and 20th centuries. Only in one small part of Macedonia that fell to socialist Yugoslavia after World War Two were the Macedonian people able to begin to tell their own story in their own words, although even there certain political considerations led to censorship.

In the pages that follow you will hear the authentic voices of the people of Macedonia, voices that to this day have been drowned out by the stronger voices of those Balkan neighbors with territorial claims on the land of their Macedonian neighbors. To add to the depth of this tragedy, too many Macedonians in past times and up to the present day have lent their own voices to this anti-Macedonian chorus as the recipients of various "gifts". Those neighbors have at times offered opportunities for social advancement for assimilation into the neighboring linguistic, ethnic, political or religious communities, and, as often, they have meted out punishment to those who refused to cooperate. Centuries ago in the Ottoman Empire one gift took the form of a "torba" or sack of grain during hard times for any Macedonian Christian willing to enter the mosque and receive the Moslem faith. Today it includes such things as new freedom to travel, which the Bulgarian government is offering any Macedonian from the Republic of Macedonia willing to accept Bulgarian citizenship.

While it is possible to understand and even sympathize at times with desperate people who have accepted such offerings, it is the great sacrifice of those who suffered terrible humiliations, hardships, torture, imprisonment, banishment, wounds both physical and mental and even death in order to resist the theft of their land, the denial of their language, their culture or their religion that is the subject of the pages that follow.

Few people in the world have endured the trials of war imposed upon the Macedonian people. They resisted the foreign Ottoman Turkish occupation for nearly five hundred years. They fought in large numbers in the Karposh Uprising in 1689. Then, in more modern times they fought and suffered in major struggles for freedom beginning in 1822 in the Negush Uprising, in 1876 in the Razlovtsi Uprising, and in 1878 in the Kresna Uprising. Macedonians rose up again in 1903 in the well-organized and widespread Ilinden Uprising. After the failure of the 1903 revolt many joined regional armies in the Balkan War of 1912 that finally ended Ottoman Turkish rule over Macedonia. Too many were also drawn into the tragic second Balkan War over division of Macedonia among the neighboring Balkan states in 1913, followed by the First World War from 1914 to 1918. In the Second World War Macedonian Partisans helped defeat the fascist occupiers of Yugoslavia and earned the right to form the first autonomous Macedonian Republic within socialist Yugoslavia in 1945. Macedonian anti-fascist Partisans in Greece would later also fight in the Greek Civil War from 1947 through 1949. Most recently Macedonians were caught up in the wars that accompanied the breakup of Yugoslavia beginning in 1991, leading finally to open warfare in Macedonia in the year 2001. The stories that you will read in the following pages record Macedonian resistance to foreign occupation over this entire period. This record is one answer to those who might otherwise dismiss the entire existence of the Macedonian people with something like: "What the heck is a Macedonian?"

Table of Contents

Introduction

Macedonia endured attack after fierce attack from Rome during the four Roman Macedonian wars. Rome didn't cease until Macedonia was reduced to rubble and even that didn't satisfy them. Macedonia was partitioned into four parts, rendering her incapable of defense. Macedonia was the last state in Europe to fall to the Romans and for her courage and tenacity she paid a heavy price. Roman cruelty and brutality turned Macedonia into a slave state and her people into slaves and "gladiator fodder" for Roman amusement. Life became so harsh that mothers no longer wanted to bear children. No wonder Macedonia was the first European nation to embrace the teaching of the peace loving Christ. C. Stefou

Macedonia is one of the oldest recorded names among European states. Its territory encompasses the northern part of present-day Greece, the southern part of former Yugoslavia (the Macedonian Republic), the southwestern region of Bulgaria and a small portion of southeastern Albania. The ancient kingdom of Macedonia can be traced back to the eighth century B.C. That kingdom reached its height of glory under King Philip who conquered Greece, and his son Alexander, who conquered much of the ancient world in the 4th century B.C.

Today, there are those who, for political purposes, would deny the present-day Macedonian people any relation to the ancient Macedonians. A number of invasions, migrations and conquests occurred there over the centuries, further altering the ethnic cultural make-up of the region. We know that in the 2nd century B.C. Macedonia became a Roman Province. The early Christian apostle Paul preached the gospels there in the 1st century A.D. The Macedonian Christian missionary brothers Cyril and Methodius in the 9th century spread the faith throughout the Balkans and beyond with their translation of Christian writings into their native speech, which also made those teachings available to Serbians, Bulgarians, Slovenians and other Slavic peoples, as far away as the Ukraine and Russia.

Balkan kingdoms that encompassed all or part of Serbia, Macedonia and Bulgaria, and at times Greece, competed with the Byzantine Empire for regional dominance during the Middle Ages. These kingdoms fostered a rich Orthodox Christian culture based on Byzantine art, architecture, music and literature, but with their own distinct features.

Balkan life changed dramatically in the 14th century, when the Moslem Ottoman Turks conquered most of the Balkan Peninsula, slowly extending their influence north and south over the peninsula. The Byzantine capital of Constantinople fell to them in the mid-15th century. Turkish conquest in Europe reached its zenith at the end of the 16th century, when Sultan Suleiman's armies threatened to take the central European capital Vienna.

Macedonia was the last Balkan land to eventually cast off Turkish rule. National liberation movements early in the 19th century freed neighboring Serbia and Greece from Ottoman rule. Macedonia's people thought they might achieve this in 1878, when a treaty concluded between the victorious Russians and the defeated Turks, placed Macedonia in a newly created Bulgarian state. Other European powers, however, overturned that treaty the next year and returned Macedonia to Ottoman rule.

The Macedonians rose up in rebellion against Turkish rule several times in the decades that followed. The largest of these, the Ilinden Uprising of 1903, like those that preceded it, ended in failure, cost thousands of lives and resulted in brutal Turkish repression of the population. However, the Ilinden Uprising created a mythology among the Macedonian people of brave heroes who sacrificed themselves in the struggle for freedom. Songs and stories began to circulate among the people about the courage and sacrifice of a pantheon of martyred leaders.

The aftermath of the Ilinden Uprising through the Balkan Wars of 1912-13, World War One and World War Two were among the unhappiest of periods in Macedonian history. The surrounding Balkan states had joined together in 1911 to drive the Turks out of Macedonia. Macedonia was then partitioned among the neighboring Bulgarians, Serbs and Greeks, but they immediately began quarreling over how to divide the region. Again in World Wars One and Two and the Greek Civil

War of 1947-49, while many Macedonians continued their resistance to foreign rule, Macedonia's neighbors continued their fight for control of Macedonian territory.

By the end of World War Two nearly all of Macedonia's people had rallied around the cause of "Macedonia for the Macedonians" promoted by the victorious communist Partisans of the region. The failure of these Partisans in the Greek Civil War and the Yugoslav break with the Soviet bloc in 1948, however, made the partition of Macedonia among the several neighboring Balkan states a hard fact of life for Macedonians to the present day. It has led to particularly brutal repression of the Macedonians in Greece, and harsh treatment for Macedonians in Bulgaria and Albania, as well.

Only in a small Macedonian republic, one of the constituent republics of post-war Yugoslavia, were Macedonians able to realize their centuries-old dream of freedom from foreign rule. Despite continuing restrictions on the press and political and economic activity, the Macedonians of the Yugoslavian Republic of Macedonia now had books and newspapers and magazines and tv and radio programs in their native language, and the children studied in school in their native tongue, and political and economic life were conducted in Macedonian.

In 1991 this small republic achieved full independence. However, Greek political pressure kept the republic out of the UN for two years and a Greek economic embargo crippled the economy during the same period. As the events of the year 2001 unfolded it became clear that the future of the Republic of Macedonia remained at risk. The Albanian insurgent take-over of the northern Macedonian border settlement of Tanushevci in February of 2001 at first appeared to be just a minor spillover of the continuing unrest in the Yugoslavian province of Kosovo. When in March it came to include street demonstrations in the town of Tetovo, it was clear that something bigger was unfolding, although many people still wanted to imagine that the unrest might be contained before it could spread any further. The rebellion spread, however, to additional settlements just north and east of the capital city Skopje and began to include major acts of sabotage, such as disruption of the drinking water supply to the one hundred thousand inhabitants of the city of Kumanovo. With the expulsion of thousands of ethnic Macedonian inhabitants of very old settlements such as Arachinovo, near Skopje, and Leshok near Tetovo, where Macedonians were a minority in Albanian-dominated districts, it was no longer possible to fool oneself into believing that this was not a war.

As the daily news from all over northern and western Macedonia grew more troubled, world news sources began to report on the fighting in Macedonia, including daily UPI, Reuters, Guardian, and New York Times reporting in English. For the most part, those dispatches could have as easily been extracts from decades of reporting on the conflicts in Vietnam, El Salvador or Lebanon. The descriptions of the guerillas and the armed forces that opposed them, their weapons, their camouflage fatigues and actions, all easily merge into accounts of any of a dozen conflicts that have raged across the globe at century's end. Only the names of the victims and their places of residence seem to change. The subtleties and singularities of these conflicts are easily lost sight of.

What the typical numbed reader, when exposed to such public spectacles, rarely receives is a true heart's journey through real time and space. For that, one must have access to knowledge and experience that world-roving teams of reporters usually have neither the time nor interest to acquire.

Some observers may have wondered why so many journalists adopted certain terminology that particularly suited the Albanian insurgents in this conflict. Did readers ever wonder why this was the only Balkan or East European conflict where the term Slav was attached to the name of the principle ethnic group involved? No one ever referred to Russian Slavs during the war in Chechnya or Serbian or Croatian Slavs in the other Balkan conflicts. Yet, every day we saw the term Macedonian Slavs applied to the Macedonian people of the Republic of Macedonia.

This just happens to be one of the preferred terms used by those who would deny Macedonians the right to their separate and distinct language, culture and national identity. According to hostile neighbors, Macedonians as a people have no right to exist. They are, according to these neighbors, nothing more than a mongrel mix of the neighboring

Slavic peoples, the Serbs and Bulgarians. Therefore, their little republic should be divided up among their neighbors, Serbs on the northern border, Bulgarians on the eastern side, Albanians on the western side and Greeks to the south, thus, once and for all, resolving the "Macedonian question" in southeastern Europe.

There was also far too little recognition of the impressive political and social progress of the Republic of Macedonia in comparison to all of its Balkan neighbors. It is the sole Balkan state that has succeeded in creating functional multi-ethnic institutions and granted full recognition to all ethnic minorities. No other Balkan country has been ruled for the past sixteen years by multi-ethnic coalition governments. Albanian and Macedonian parties have formed parliamentary coalitions from both the philosophical left and right in order to govern. There is also integration of public institutions, of government offices, schools, the army and police, through quotas of ethnic minority Albanians in each. If it is not complete or perfect, it is, however, far advanced of anything to be found in neighboring states.

This one small parcel of earth where the indigenous Macedonian people freely and openly speak their native tongue and pursue their fortunes will always owe a debt to the thousands of their brave ancestors who resisted invasion and conquest. And, now, others, beyond the borders of Macedonia, in the wide world of the Macedonian diaspora, will have this opportunity to learn about the terrible price that Macedonians paid over the centuries for their modern identity and an independent Macedonian state.

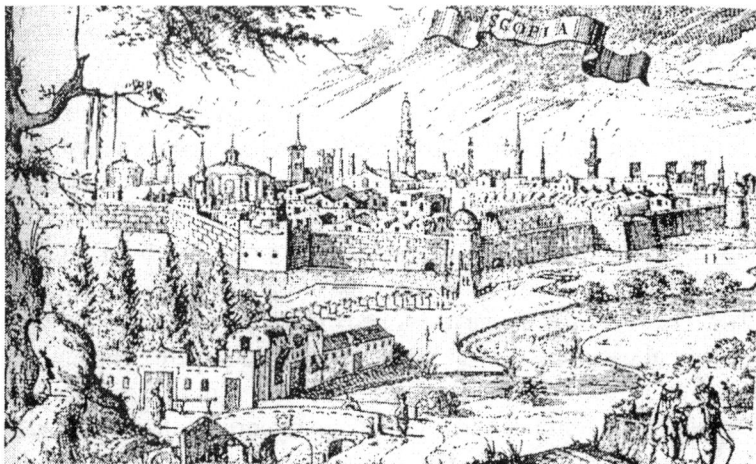

the city of Skope in the 17th century

Chapter One

Ottoman Rule in Macedonia and Early Resistance

Had Greek mythology developed a god of Pathetic Endurance, his likeness must have been that of a Macedonian peasant. You see his hunching shoulders supporting them all: a degenerate ruling race, a corrupt clergy, a breed of vampire landlords and a revolutionary organization, which, though self-imposed, still seemed at times to be holding back its rewards for future generations.

(Albert Sonnichsen, *Confessions of a Macedonian Bandit*, New York, 1909)

The rulership of the Turks in the Balkans marked the beginning of an historical period in which the subject nations hoped to preserve their historical heritage. Naturally, we succeeded in preserving only what it was possible to preserve, i.e. whatever the Turks did not wish to take from us either because they did not need it or because it was not dangerous for them. The Turks took our land and divided it among themselves; we had to reconcile ourselves to this loss. They then began to take our children to bring them up as Turks and to turn them into Janissaries. Even then we kept silent. The Turks felt it would be difficult to subdue Serbia because the name Serb meant much the same as outlaw for them. We bowed our heads and ceased calling ourselves Serbs so as not to anger the Aga. But he did not want us to call ourselves Bulgarians either; so we did not call ourselves Bulgarians. The Turk would come to our house, eat our food, drink our drink and tell us: You there! Bring me this or bring me that! And we would answer: Straight away, master! If a Turk asked us what we were we would answer that we were "giaours", i.e. the unbelievers or 'the Emperor's rabble". In other words we presented ourselves to the Turks in such a way as to avoid angering the Aga; to them we were the "unbelievers" and the "rabble", and we even began to address one another as "giaours". In our epic folk songs the names "giaours" and "rayatin", "land of the unbelievers" and "land of the rabble" are often used in the ethnographic sense.

(Krste P. Misirkov, *On Macedonian Matters, 1903*)

The Ottoman Turks crossed into Europe for the first time around the year 1345 as mercenaries hired by the Byzantine Empire, the medieval Orthodox Christian empire based in Constantinople, to defend their state against invaders. Over the years as this Turkish tribe gained strength and grew in number, they settled in Galipoli, west of the Dardanelles, and later used that place as a staging area for further conquest.

In 1389 the Ottoman Turks met and defeated the combined forces of the Balkan Orthodox Slavic kingdoms in a decisive battle on the plains of Kosovo. Not only did they succeed in destroying the army, but they also succeeded in wiping out much of the Balkan nobility in the process. In 1392 they attacked and conquered geographical Macedonia, including Salonica, but not Sveta Gora (the Holy Mountain). In 1444 while attempting to drive north, through today's Bulgaria, they met and routed Western Crusaders at Varna. Soon after, they recovered sufficiently to lay siege to and finally take the great city of Constantinople in 1453, looting all of the wealth that had been accumulated there over two millennia.

To finally put the war of 1444 behind them, the Ottomans turned northwest and in 1526 attacked and destroyed a large Hungarian army, killing 25,000 knights. After that they unsuccessfully tried twice to take Vienna, once in 1529 and again in 1683. The failure to take Vienna halted the Ottoman expansion in Europe.

In a steady process of state building, the Ottoman Empire expanded in both easterly and westerly directions, conquering the Byzantines and remnants of the Macedonian, Bulgarian and Serbian kingdoms to the west and the Turkish nomadic principalities in Anatolia, as well as the Mamluk Sultanate in Egypt to the south. By the 17th century the Ottoman Empire had grown to include vast areas in west Asia, north Africa and southeastern Europe.

During the 16th century the Ottomans shared the world stage with Elizabethan England, Habsburg Spain, the Holy Roman Empire, Valois France and the Dutch Republic. Of greater significance to the Ottomans were the city-states of Venice and Genoa, which exerted enormous political and economic influence with their fleets and commercial networks that linked India, the Middle East, the Mediterranean and Western Europe.

Initially the Turks may have been ethnically Turkish, perhaps originating from a single race, but by the time they had conquered the Balkans, the Ottoman Empire had become multi-ethnic and multi-religious. The Ottoman Empire built its power base on a heterogeneous mix of people who were added to its population with every conquest.

After conquering the Balkans, the Ottoman Turks immediately started to establish their own administration and, where possible, retained existing administrative and territorial divisions. Macedonia belonged to the Bejlerbejlik, or Elajet of Rumelia. Salonica was administered by the famous military commander Evrenos Beg and served as the oldest military center for the defense of the empire's western frontier. When Skopje fell to the Ottomans in 1392 it became the center of a new region. The first Skopje regional commander was Pashaigit Beg.

In an attempt to create a stable political and social support network in conquered Macedonia, the Ottoman authorities introduced voluntary migration for Turks from Asia Minor. As a result, many Turkish settlements sprang up all over Macedonia and occupied strategic positions such as valleys of navigable rivers and coastal plains. This increase in Muslim numbers, particularly in the larger towns, was at the expense of the Christian population. The semi-nomadic people of Anatolia were best suited for such resettlement because of their unsettled past.

In time and as a result of Ottoman colonization policies, small Turkish livestock breeding settlements were established at Jurutsi and Konjari near Salonica, and in the districts of Nevrokop, Strumitsa, Radovish, Kochani and Ovche Pole. Migration into Macedonia was not restricted to Turks. Late in the 15th century Jews fleeing the Western European Inquisitions in Spain and Portugal also settled in Macedonia. These migrations were of particular significance to Macedonia's economic development. Jewish colonies sprang up and flourished in important urban centers like Salonica, Bitola, Skopje, Berroea, Kostur, Serres, Shtip, Kratovo and Strumitsa. The Jewish colony in Salonica was one of the largest and most significant of all colonies in the entire Ottoman Empire. By the middle of the 16th century Salonica was home to more than three thousand Jewish families.

Besides the colonization of Macedonia by foreign elements, there was also the assimilation of Macedonians into the Islamic fold. The process of converting Christians to Muslims began as soon as Macedonia was conquered. At the outset, a fair number of the old nobility converted to Islam in hope of protecting and even increasing their landholdings. Gradually, greater proportions of the population were converted, sometimes whole villages and districts at once. Macedonians living among the Turks, especially in the larger towns, gradually began to assimilate into the Turkish fold. Even though they outwardly became Turks, a great many of them retained their mother tongue and continued to speak Macedonian, and to practice many of their traditional social and religious customs.

In terms of taxation, the most fundamental and distinguishing feature of the feudal system introduced in the Balkans by the Ottomans was the *Timar-Spahi* system. In the Ottoman system, at the very top was the Sultan, as supreme owner of all lands. At the bottom were the peasants, or *rayah*. Between the Sultan and the peasant were the feudal landlords or *spahi*, who, in return for their military service, received a fief from the state. The spahi had the right to work the land but could not dispose of it. The amount of income derived from the fief in the form of feudal rent from the rayah was standard and controlled by the state. One Macedonian villager, Foto Tomev, described the effects of this Turkish colonial system on the peasantry as follows:

One of the major evils for the people of our village, and for the rest of the enslaved Christians, was the imposed tax, the so-called 'one tenth', or as the people used to call it the 'spahiluk' after the Spahi or tax collectors. This tax was to be paid in produce since there was no money in circulation at the time. Great injustices were committed by the tax collectors in their arbitrary ways of getting the taxes from the people. It was to be one tenth of the produce, but only God knows how much more the spahi took from the people. The trouble was not the amount of tax that had to be paid by each family, but the way in which it was collected. The Turkish government would put the collection of taxes up for auction - the one who would offer the best price had the right to collect the tax from the population. The right to collect taxes was usually purchased from the government either by the Turks or the 'arnauti' (Moslem Albanians). The state took its due, but those who obtained the right to collect taxes charged the people what they wanted. These people went to each house in the village, to the fields, to the pastures and the vineyards, and collected these taxes without any control or scales or measures. These collectors were the masters of the population and no one dared to complain because the people feared the worst. And, if someone dared to complain his voice was a voice in the desert - no one would hear it. People used to say: 'Who is there to complain to? God is high and the Tsar is far away.' The people endured and carried this heavy burden like mute animals. The burden of the yoke was increased by the arbitrary acts of the spahi. Sometimes the spahi would not come in time to collect the produce and the people silently waited for him; they waited without daring to speak. What followed was a sorrowful sight - the fields of grain ripened, and the sheaves were gathered, the rain fell, and everything rotted. The grapes, already spoiled by the rain were gathered, but to what avail? This pitiful situation did not disturb the Spahi. The Spahi were lords and they would get their due by robbing the Rayah (the slaves) anyway. The Spahi would bribe government officials to look the other way. All these people were corrupt - from the lowest to highest officials in office. They conspired with each other and the population in silence carried the burden.

The Macedonian people were never willingly occupied, and they resisted occupation at every opportunity. The first major organized resistance occurred in the middle of the 15th century in the Debar region, where Macedonians, Albanians and Vlahs lived together. Led by George Castriot, the people rose up against the tyranny of the Turks.

George Castriot, who took the name Scanderbeg after Iskander, more commonly known as Alexander the Great, came from a prominent feudal family which, at the time, ruled part of present day central Albania and the greater Debar region in the present day Republic of Macedonia. During the Ottoman conquests in the region, John Castriot, George's father, managed to retain his title and holdings by acknowledging the supreme authority of the Sultan and fulfilling certain obligations as his vassal. As proof of his loyalty, John Castriot surrendered his sons to the Sultan to be held as hostages. One of those sons was George, who quickly became fascinated by the energy and vigor of the Ottoman military and could not wait to join them.

Having accepted Islam, George's first act was to change his name to Scanderbeg. Scanderbeg quickly built a reputation as an able commander and gained the confidence of the Ottoman supreme authorities. When his father died in 1437, Scanderbeg took his father's place as governor of the same district. Even though Scanderbeg was an ally of the Sultan, his real loyalties lay with his people.

When war broke out in the region in 1442 and Janos Hunjadi's armies penetrated the interior of the Ottoman Empire, Scanderbeg decided the time was right to renounce his allegiance to the Sultan and raise a rebellion. When a great battle broke out in 1443 near Nish and the Ottoman front was smashed, instead of attacking, Scanderbeg, his nephew Hamza, and three hundred cavalrymen deserted and fled with the Ottoman soldiers.

On his way Scanderbeg passed through the Debar region, where he received much support and a hero's welcome. In Debar he was joined by local chieftains and a large number of peasant rebels. With his cavalry and new recruits he began the revolt by attacking Croia, present-day Kruje, an important Ottoman military and administrative center. After sacking Croia with ease, he returned to Debar where he began to organize a broad-scale revolt. With Croia in his possession, Scanderbeg, on November 27, 1443, declared his principality independent. Using the Debar region as his base, Scanderbeg's rebels began a campaign to capture a number of fortresses, including the strategically significant fortress of Svetigrad (Kodzhadzhik). The siege of Svetigrad was led by Moses the Great, one of Scanderbeg's loyal supporters, with a three thousand man rebel force from the Debar region. After a fierce battle the fortress fell and the entire Debar region was liberated.

The rebels did not continue their easterly expansion. As a result, the eastern border of the greater Debar region became the border between the Ottomans and the rebels, and an area of continuous conflict for the next three decades.

The next great battle was fought on April 29, 1444 at Dolni Debar. A rebel strike force of insurgents from the Debar region led by Moses the Great crushed the Ottoman army, leaving seven thousand dead and capturing five hundred prisoners. Two years later on September 27, 1446 another battle took place near Debar in which the Ottomans again suffered heavy losses.

Scanderbeg was becoming a legend and a serious threat to Ottoman rule, so in the summer of 1448 Sultan Murat II, together with his heir, Prince Mehmed, prepared a strike force and set out to find him. Their first encounter with the rebels was at the fortress of Svetigrad where a garrison of local rebels, led by Peter Perlat, offered them strong resistance. Unfortunately, after a long drawn out siege the fortress fell. All was not lost, however. Due to more pressing matters elsewhere the Sultan decided to abandon his pursuit, leaving a greater part of the Debar region still in the hands of the insurgents.

Their next encounter came in 1452 when Sultan Mehmed the Conqueror amassed a large army in Ohrid. Upon learning of this, Scanderbeg immediately concentrated his forces at the military camp of Oronic, the present day town of Debar, and together with Moses the Great and his nephew Hamza, launched an attack. The opposing armies met near the fortress of Modrich and Scanderbeg's forces broke through the Turkish lines in a single battle, giving him a decisive victory and forcing the Turkish army to retreat.

Dissatisfied with the outcome, the following spring Mehmed dispatched his general Ibrahim Pasha to launch another attack on the rebels. The armies met in Polog on April 22, 1453. Led by Scanderbeg and Moses, the rebels fought fiercely and gained another victory over the Turks.

Unable to gain any ground against the rebels by force of arms, the Sultan turned to bribery. He paid Moses to look the other way while a large Ottoman force crossed the Debar frontier and approached Scanderbeg's forces in a surprise attack. During this catastrophic battle, which took place in 1455 near Berat, six thousand men, nearly half of the rebel force, were lost. To save himself Moses fled the region and joined the Ottoman army. Despite the heavy losses, the people of Debar did not surrender. They continued to support Scanderbeg. In a very short time, he was able to recoup his losses, rebuild his army and renew the struggle.

The next Ottoman attack came a year later. This time not only was Scanderbeg ready for it, but being aware of the fact that it was led by the traitor Moses the Great, he marched his army in person to meet him. On May 19, 1456 near Oronic, the rebels attacked and defeated the Ottoman army of fifteen thousand, giving Scanderbeg another victory. Thoroughly satisfied with this result, Scanderbeg even forgave Moses for his treachery and welcomed him back to the rebel camp. Upon their return home, Scanderbeg reinstated Moses to his former position, entrusting him once again with the defense of the Debar region.

When it seemed like Scanderbeg's troubles were nearly over, a new set of problems arose. The Sultan convinced a number of powerful feudal lords to support him, and they in turn began to attack the rebels, leading to the loss of large areas of territory. One such territory was the fortress of Modrich, which, like the fortress of Svetigrad, was of strategic importance.

By gaining Modrich the Ottomans gained a safe route to the rebel camps. Losing no time, an Ottoman army was dispatched and reached the town of Lesh in the summer of 1457. Sensing their vulnerability, instead of waiting for an attack, the rebels took the offensive and met the marching Turkish army head-on in a fierce battle. Surprised by the attack, the Ottoman army scattered, giving Scanderbeg another decisive victory. With the success of this battle the rebels were able, through diplomacy, to regain all previously lost territories.

The prolonged struggle with the rebels convinced the Sultan that Scanderbeg could be subdued and the rebel territory freed only by a large-scale military campaign. Led by the battle-hardened, experienced commander Balaban Pasha from Mat, a massive campaign was organized and unleashed upon the rebels in 1465. A fierce battle ensued near Debar, but the Turkish force was much too strong for the rebels to overcome. Besides losing much of his force, Scanderbeg also lost many of his experienced commanders, including Moses the Great, who was captured, sent to Constantinople and put to death in the cruelest manner. Both sides suffered heavy losses, but Balaban succeeded in quelling the rebellion, though only in the Debar region. The rebellion moved into the interior of Albania and continued on for a decade after Scanderbeg's death.

Scanderbeg died of illness on January 17, 1468. Ten years later, after the fall of Croia, the last rebel stronghold, on January 16, 1478, the rebellion came to an end. This, however, was not the last rebellion against the Ottoman Empire on Macedonian territory. In time, and with the erosion of the empire, resistance would grow.

With the breakdown of the Timar and Spahi systems and the decline of the Ottoman state, exploitation of the population of Macedonia increased. Violence, especially on the part of certain officials within the Ottoman state, rose dramatically. Life for the average Macedonian was almost unbearable, and frustration began to express itself in various forms. Peasants who could no longer afford to pay their taxes were fleeing to the mountains and settling in remote places where the tax collectors could not easily find them. Others, without peaceful means of relieving their suffering under the Ottoman yoke, had no choice but to turn to violence.

The next significant uprising took place in 1564/65, in the Mariovo region and spread to the Prilep plains and from there to the town of Prilep. It is not known how the Prilep and Mariovo revolt began, but it is clear from Ottoman documents that three peasants and two priests from the Mariovo district initiated the rebellion. The Sultan issued a decree, dated October 3, 1564, ordering that these leaders of the revolt be put to death, while their followers were to be sent to serve as oarsmen on Turkish galleys. Before the decree could be enforced, however, the rebel leaders fled, causing the Sultan to issue another decree for their capture:

'*To the Skopje beg and to the Kadiya in Prilep:*

A command.

The Kadiya has written us a letter, naming the following as the ringleaders inciting revolt among the Christian peasants of the Prilep region; Dimitri Stalev of Satoka, priest Dimitri, Mate Nikola from the village Peshino, Stoyan Pejo and priest Yakov of Staravina. These lawbreakers were the subjects of an earlier royal decree calling for their arrest, but they have reportedly fled.

Recently we have been once again informed that these rebels continue to disturb the peace in the aforementioned land. I have concluded that the aforementioned Christian peasants must be captured.

Therefore, you are hereby notified of my command, to take all measures necessary to achieve their capture and put an end to their activities. You are to execute some of the rebels, and send the others to the capital to serve as galley slaves on our ships. You will give the conduct of this campaign to capture the aforementioned rebels the highest priority.

Given in the hand of the Vizier Mustafa on 26 Sefer in the year 973 (1565)

Prilep was the scene of revolt the same year after the Ottoman court ruled in favour of a pasha in a dispute with the peasants. According to a document dated December 1565 a revolt broke out inside the town of Prilep when the Prilep Court, in settling a dispute between the peasants and Mustapha Pasha, ruled in favour of the pasha. When the news reached the streets, more than a thousand rebels from the surrounding villages, armed with sticks and stones, assembled and stormed the court. It is not known for certain how this revolt ended, but in one popular modern account of the uprising, the author of the historical novel, *Kalesh Ang'a,* Stale Popov, described the final days of the revolt in the following way:

The Skopje begler-bey was also a pasha, a commander of the Skopje garrison, so he had a troop of two hundred paid professional soldiers to lead on this expedition, and in Kavadartsi five hundred additional men awaited him from the estates of the Tikvesh beys, with Yashar-bey in command. Men had volunteered from all over Tikvesh province at the prospect of plunder in Mariovo.

Five days before the Easter holiday, four heavily-armed Ottoman war parties made their way to Mariovo by four different routes, each party burning and looting every Christian village in their path. But the leaders of the expedition kept their forces directed toward their main objective, the villages of Gradeshnitsa and Staravina.

The Kadiya, with the first party, and Selim, Fazli and Daut with the second party, arrived at the Tsrna River after two days- the first party at the Chebrenski Bridge, and the second at Svetets- while Mehmed, Muarem and Feta had already crossed the Konyarka River above Skochivir and had ascended the rocky slopes to Budimirtsi and Gurunishta, arriving at the very approaches to Staravina.

The Kadiya ordered an attack across the Chebrenski Bridge, but priest Yakov, with his village guard-force from Staravina, Gradeshnitsa, Bzovich and Satoka, held his forces on the opposite shore of the river for two days. Though on the third night, the Turks took the bridge and stormed up the steep rocky slopes, where the rebels had their positions. And other Turks, on the other side of Bzovich, had already taken the high ground, and they were about to make another charge on Baba, on the outskirts of Staravina.

Many Turks fell in the battle here, just as they had at the Tsrna, but there were so many attackers, well over 500, that the rebels, along with all of the inhabitants of Staravina, were forced to take refuge in the old roman fortress at Peshta. The kadiya's men swarmed into Staravina. They plundered the houses and burned down the homes of known rebels. Then, they re-crossed the river above the village to reach Gradeshnitsa.

Most of the people of Gradeshnitsa had also managed to escape to the fortress at Peshta or into the mountains, and only a few ancient grandmothers and grandfathers remained in the village. Since Gradeshnitsa had offered them no resistance, and the kadiya's forces would need shelter for the night, they looted the houses, but they didn't destroy any except the homes of the two rebel leaders, Petre Mitre and Riste Naide.

While the Kadiya had waged his campaign to take these villages, Selim Fazli and Daut had forded the Tsrna above Svetets, since the bridge had been destroyed earlier, and with only minor losses, they attacked the rebels beyond it. The rebels, upon seeing the great size of the enemy force, hurried off to report the approaching peril to their home villages, so that the elders, women and children could seek safety in the thick forests. In this way this party advanced and took the hamlets of Manastir and Melnitsa, plundered them, and when they reached Vitolishta, they discovered the Skopje bey already there with a thousand-man force that had carved a similar path through the villages.

Coming up from the south the third party under Mehmed, Muarem and Feta, after plundering Budimirtsi and Gurunishta, joined the kadiya's party in Gradeshnitsa and prepared for the assault on the Peshta fortress.

The Skopje pasha pacified Vitolishta, Zhiovo and Vrpsko. They bound the young men and women, and some were butchered or beaten. Then, they plundered and burned many of the houses, and after passing through Polchishta, they reached Satoka.

Here, many Turks fell in battle with the rebel forces of Mate Nikola and Dimitri Stale, but they were eventually overwhelmed, and the two leaders, along with those villagers who were still alive, fled from their village, which was then burned to the ground and destroyed. And so, already by Easter day all four Turkish forces met in Gradeshnitsa and Staravina, and together they laid siege to Peshta.

Almost every rebel leader who was still alive had assembled with his people in the Peshta fortress, and they had sealed the heavy iron gates. Here were: priest Yakov, Dimitri Stale, Mate Nikola, Stoyan Peyo, priest Dimitri, priest Peyo, Vasil Petko, Risto Naide, Stoyan Traiko and all of the armed peasants...

Eventually the rebels were no longer able to hold the fortress and the rebellion was crushed, but the memory of their resistance lives on among the people of Macedonia in history book, story and song.

Since Christians by law were not allowed to carry arms, they had no effective defense against mistreatment, particularly from the corrupt legal system. The only recourse available to them was to become outlaws. Although unpopular, outlawry was one of the oldest forms of armed resistance engaged in by the Macedonian people. It reached epidemic proportions over the course of the 17th century. The outlaws, or *haiduks,* as they were known, lived secret lives known only to other outlaws or trusted friends. When it came to defending their homes and properties, they came together in bands or *druzhini* of twenty to thirty people. Occasionally, for defensive purposes a number of smaller bands combined together to form a large band usually numbering no more than three hundred people. The leaders or *voivodi* were elected by members of their bands and were usually chosen for their military skills and leadership abilities. The ranks of the outlaw bands came mostly from the feudally oppressed peasants, but it was not uncommon to find priests and monks among them. Women too were known to have joined outlaw bands. The oldest record of a woman outlaw dates back to 1636. Her name was Kira and she was from the village Chapari. Kira was a member of Petar Dundar's band from the village of Berantsi near Bitola. There were also documented cases of women who led outlaw bands.

A major concern of the haiduks was the defense of their oppressed people, and in times of trouble they would come to their aid. In retaliation for Turkish wrong-doing the outlaws were known to attack feudal estates and even burn Spahi harvests. They also ambushed and robbed merchant caravans and tax collectors. Bands are even known to have attacked some of the larger towns. On several occasions outlaws banded together and overran Bitola, Lerin, Ohrid and Resen. Twice they looted the stores of Bitola, once in 1646 and again in 1661.

To curb outlaw activities, the Ottoman authorities frequently undertook extreme measures. These included organizing posses to hunt down outlaws, burning down villages that were known to be sympathetic to outlaws and imprisoning and sometimes executing relatives of outlaws. When all of these measures failed to stop them, the Ottomans introduced the services of armed guards known as *derbendki*, to provide safe passage through the countryside to important functionaries, merchants, tax collectors and travelers.

Outlaws who were captured were usually tortured, sent to prison for life, or executed. The lucky ones were executed outright. Their dead bodies were then impaled on stakes or on iron hooks for everyone to see. Those less fortunate were skinned alive, had their heads split open and were left to die a slow and painful death. Those sent to prison were usually chained to galleys and spent the rest of their lives as oarsmen on Turkish ships.

Despite the extreme measures used against them, the outlaws were never eradicated and were always a part of every conflict. The outlaws were the nucleus of the armed rebel forces and provided the experienced leaders and commanders of most revolts and uprisings. They were the first to raise the banner of resistance and the first to stand for the people. That is why the haiduk outlaw is so widely revered in Macedonian folklore.

The Ottoman noose continued to tighten on the peasants, Christian and Muslim alike. A moment to strike back, however, came when the Ottomans became engaged in a war that led to an Austrian invasion of Macedonia in 1689. What came to be known as the Karposh Uprising, after its leader Karposh, was a Macedonian people's revolt against the economic, social and political injustices perpetrated by the Ottoman overlords.

In 1683 the Ottomans, for the second time, had tried to take Vienna, but failed after a two-month siege. The city was saved with the assistance of the Polish army led by King John Sobiesky. The Ottoman army suffered a catastrophic defeat, resulting in enormous losses of territory, material and manpower. To prevent further expansion and keep the Ottomans in check, the Holy League of Austria, Poland, Venice, and later Russia was created.

Once they gained momentum in the war, the Austrians continued to drive the Ottomans southward, eventually reaching the northern boundaries of Macedonia. Led by General Piccolomini, the Austrians entered the Skopje plain on October 25, 1689 and were met by a jubilant crowd, there to celebrate their triumphant arrival.

The Austrians continued to march southward until they arrived at the town of Skopje only to find it empty. Skopje had been evacuated and left with plenty of food and all kinds of merchandise. Feeling that it may have been a trap, Piccolomini withdrew his forces at once and set the town on fire. The fires raged for two whole days and consumed the greater part of Skopje.

The Austrians continued to move through the Macedonian interior and set up camp in the village of Orizari near Kumanovo. One detachment was sent to the town of Shtip, which arrived there at dawn on November 10, 1689, where they met fierce Ottoman resistance. A battle broke out, which ended when the Austrians managed to force the Ottomans out, leaving about two thousand of their dead behind. After setting the town on fire, the Austrians left for their camp, but on the way they encountered another Ottoman company of three hundred soldiers. Another battle ensued, but the Ottoman force eventually scattered in confusion.

During mid-November the Austrians organized a unit of Albanian Catholic volunteers and sent them to Tetovo, where they succeeded in routing a garrison of more than six hundred Ottoman troops. On December 20 an Austrian detachment, with Serbs led by Captain Sanoski, was sent from Prishtina to Veles, where it succeeded in capturing and burning down the town. Unfortunately, upon their retreat, the company was ambushed by janissaries, and Sanoski was mortally wounded.

The destruction and mayhem caused by the Austro-Turkish War led to harsh economic and political conditions in the region. The need for further military operations forced the Ottoman state to increase its purchases of grain, fodder, livestock, timber and other agricultural products far below normal prices. Also, to pay for the military campaigns, a series of new taxes were imposed. During this difficult period the rayah also suffered violence at the hands of deserters from the Ottoman army and from state government defectors.

Among those who abandoned their military posts was the notorious General Jegen Pasha, the former Bejlerbej of Rumelia. With ten thousand deserters in his ranks he ravaged the Balkan Peninsula until he was finally defeated and put to death in February of 1689.

The military defeats and the chaotic situation inside the Ottoman Empire again created suitable conditions for widespread lawlessness and rebellion in all parts of Macedonia, especially in the Mariovo, Bitola, Tikvesh, Veles, Shtip and Mt. Dospat regions. All of this led up to the famous Karposh Uprising.

Sometime in the middle of October of 1689 the famous outlaw Arambasha Karposh led an uprising which began in the region between Kustendil and Skopje. Immediately after declaring the revolt, Karposh attacked and captured the town of Kriva Palanka. Kriva Palanka was an Ottoman stronghold built in 1636 to house Ottoman troops. After capturing the town, Karposh declared it liberated rebel territory and made it his center of resistance. Among the items captured in the stronghold were six cannons, a real prize for the rebels. After securing Kriva Palanka the rebels built and manned a new fortress near Kumanovo.

It is not known whether the rebels were assisted by the Austrians, but it is possible. According to contemporary Ottoman chronicles and local legends, Karposh was known as the "King of Kumanovo". This could have been a title conferred upon him by the Austrian Emperor Leopold I, who sent him a busby (a tall fur hat worn by hussars and guardsmen) as a gift and a sign of recognition.

Unfortunately for the rebels, the current situation did not last long and a reversal in military and political fortunes played a decisive role in the fate of the uprising. The Ottomans had by now had enough time to take countermeasures to reverse the military occupation of their state. The first step taken in Macedonia was to send a force to put down the rebellion and drive the Austrian army out of Macedonian territory. To do that the Ottomans employed the services of the Crimean Khan, Selim Giray, along with a detachment of fierce Tartar warriors.

A war council convened in Sofia on November 14, 1689 decided to attack the Karposh rebels through Kustendil. But before they could do that they had to secure Kriva Palanka. Upon finding that they were about to be attacked, the rebels set fire to Kriva Palanka and concentrated their forces in the new fortress in Kumanovo. No sooner had they prepared their defenses than the Ottoman and Tartar detachments arrived. The rebels stood their ground and fought gallantly, but they were quickly overwhelmed by the numerically superior Ottoman force. A large number of rebels, including Karposh, were captured early in the battle. When it was over, all rebels who had resisted to the end were killed. Karposh and a number of others were taken prisoner. After subduing Kumanovo, the Ottomans left for Skopje, where they executed Karposh and his fellow prisoners.

According to one story, (there are several versions of how he was executed) Karposh was brought before Selim Giray, who at the time was standing on the Stone Bridge over the River Vardar in Skopje. Selim used him for target practice and impaled him with Tartar lances. He then had his body hurled into the Vardar River. Karposh died early in December of 1689 and with him died the revolt.

For the rebels who had survived the battles there was no salvation from the Ottomans except in leaving Macedonia. Many fled north beyond the Sava and Danube Rivers. Some even went as far north as Russia and joined the Russian military. There they formed the "Macedonian regiment" which became part of the regular Russian army. The failed Karposh Uprising drastically reduced the local population of northwestern Macedonia, opening the way for large-scale Albanian immigration.

Just as the Karposh revolt was winding down in Macedonia, on April

6, 1690, Leopold I issued a manifesto inviting "all peoples of Albania, Serbia, Moesia, Bulgaria, Silistria, Illyria, Macedonia and Rashka to join the Austrians in taking up arms against the Turks." Then on April 26, 1690 he issued a letter declaring Macedonia and her people under his protection. It has been said that Leopold acted on the advice of the Macedonians Marko Krajda of Kozhani and Dimitri Georgija Popovich of Salonica. Among other things, the letter stated that "we graciously accept the Macedonian people, in its entirety in every respect, under our imperial and regal protection." Another letter was issued on May 31, 1690 extending Austria's protection to Bulgaria, Serbia and Albania. Unfortunately, these were no more than well-meaning gestures, too little, too late for Macedonia, which by 1690 was back under strict Ottoman control.

Macedonian peasants in the Turkish Empire

Chapter Two

Macedonia and the Ottoman Empire in the 18th Century

"...why do we suffer in this life, why do we fast, why are we baptized, why do we have Christian burials, why do we offer food for a departed person's soul, why do we endure the suffering inflicted upon us by other faiths, why do we step off the paved roads, why don't we wear the green [of the moslems], why don't we wear beautiful things, why do we speak less about the Turks, why when they ride over us and trample us down, why do we endure it, if not for Christ?"

(excerpt from Macedonian priest Kiril Pejchinovich's book, *Ogledalo,* 1816)

After the Treaty of Karlowitz in 1699 the frontiers of the Ottoman Empire were withdrawn as far south as the Sava and Danube Rivers. By this treaty, the Ottoman Empire lost Hungary to the Habsburgs (Austrian rulers) and parts of the Ukraine to Russia. The Ottoman Empire began to lose its economic and political independence and became more and more dependent on the rapidly developing Western European states. With the annexation of Hungary, the Habsburg Empire became ruler of Catholic Eastern Europe while the Ottomans ruled over the Orthodox Christians of the Balkans.

The 18th century witnessed renewed conflict, with several new wars breaking out, resulting in further negative consequences for the Macedonian people. Internally, the Ottoman Empire was plagued by feudal anarchy, caused by the powerful feudal lords. Some were so powerful that they openly defied the central government by not submitting taxes and by using state money to fund their own private armies to maintain their independence.

One such feudal lord was Mahmud Pasha Bushatlija, who ruled the districts of Ohrid, Debar and Skopje. Another was Ali Pasha Tepelen of Ioannina who controlled the southwestern districts of Macedonia. Yet another was Abdul Aga Shabanderoglou, whose family estates were scattered throughout Doiran and fourteen other kazas. Shabanderoglou attacked a neighboring beg and ally of the Sultan, Beg Hasan and took over his estates. With this and other wealth that he had accumulated, he built himself an army and attacked and took over the estates of other feudal lords in Petrich, Melnik and Demir Hisar. Eventually, however, the central government caught up with Shabanderoglou and destroyed his power base, though by then he was an old man.

Ali Aga and Ismail Beg of the Serres district also defied the central government when together they raised a combined army of six thousand Albanian recruits. The Tetovo Pashas took control of the Skopje, Tetovo, Gostivar and Kichevo districts and Dzheladin Beg took over Ohrid. All of these feudal lords built up their military power base with Albanian mercenaries and terrorized the local population in their districts.

Besides the renegade begs, the 18th century also gave rise to a new breed of bandits who found it easier to rob innocent people than to work. At times these groups numbered as high as five hundred roaming the Macedonian countryside, robbing and looting entire villages. Most of these marauding bandits were of Turkish and Albanian ethnicity. They often collaborated with the defiant feudal lords and corrupt state officials, often doing their dirtier jobs for them. There was an incident in 1709 when Kadizade Mustapha, the Tax Lessee of Prilep, hired a group of these bandits and through sheer terror exerted pressure on the peasants to pay their taxes. On several occasions in 1711, the Deputy Lieutenant Governor and Tax Collector from Ohrid hired a gang of one thousand bandits from Mat and attacked the town of Bitola.

By 1715 banditry had become a profitable profession and, for some, robbing and looting became a way of life. Some of these gangs were even bold enough to attack larger towns like Prilep and Veles. An Albanian band damaged the Slepche Monastery and looted its furnishings and livestock. When complaints from Turkish merchants and businessmen began to arrive, however, the Ottoman state had no choice but to intervene. In 1779 the Bejlerbeg of Rumelia himself took action against Suljo Starova's gang.

At times even the Martolozes, who were hired to protect the population, also contributed to the anarchy. Instead of upholding the law, they held up villages, taking food and materials without paying. Some even committed atrocities under the pretext of pursuing outlaws. One of the more powerful gangs which, among others, employed the services of two hundred ex-Martolozes, led by deserter Martolobasha Hibetulah, roamed, looted and pillaged the Lerin, Bitola, Kostur and Voden districts for nearly half a century.

During the Ottoman war with Austria and Russia, which lasted from 1787 to 1792, a new group of bandits, known as the Krcali, appeared in Macedonia. The Krcali were a large group who used various mountains throughout Macedonia for refuge. The Krcali were organized in bands of about two thousand. Their ranks consisted of peasants and army deserters, and even included women. People of all faiths and nationalities joined them. They rode on horseback and were extremely mobile. They were known for their surprise attacks and ability to loot whole villages and towns in a few hours time. Many districts were devastated by the

Krcali, who were hunted down by the Sultan's army for over a decade before they were eradicated.

The principal victims of this anarchy were the defenseless Christians, whose only way to obtain justice was to become outlaws. As in the 17th century, lawlessness flourished again in the 18th century, forcing the Ottoman State into crisis. Unable to deal with outlawry on its own, the central government made it the responsibility of the general population. A special budget was set aside dedicated to the pursuit and extermination of outlaws. The Ottomans raised this money by imposing additional taxes on the general population. In 1705 the surrounding villages of the Bitola kaza were taxed 103,800 Turkish akcis just for the pursuit of outlaws in their own region. For that period, this was an enormous amount of money.

Unable to stop the outlaws by conventional methods, the Ottoman authorities proposed various schemes, including the idea of employing Martolozes (protectors) with a regular monthly income. The bands that agreed to the terms were pardoned for past crimes. This inability to deal with the outlaws on its own was a clear sign of the Ottoman central government's growing weakness, which encouraged a further escalation of the lawlessness.

Attacks on the Macedonian peasant population in both villages and town occurred on a regular basis. The pressure of violence caused people to leave the dangerous countryside for the safety of larger towns. Macedonians who left their rural homes for the urban setting thus created opportunities for foreign infiltration. It was mostly Albanians who filled this void. With more Macedonians flooding the towns the economy began to shift from agriculture to craftsmanship and commerce.

On the international stage, the military balance continued to shift away from the Ottomans as they continued to lose their edge in technology and modern weaponry. While Western economies continued to improve, Ottoman economic development remained stagnant. A century of military defeats suffered at the hands of the Western Europeans had severely weakened the Ottoman Empire. More recently, the emergence of Russia as another powerful Ottoman foe had added to Ottoman woes.

Ottoman-Russian wars began as early as 1677. Russia attacked the Crimea in 1689 and in 1695 captured the strategic port of Azov. Russia, up to this point, had been completely cut off from the Black Sea and had suffered both economically and politically due to Ottoman domination of the southern trade route.

Faced with multiple war fronts, the Ottoman Empire began to shrink, and for the first time since its invasions of Europe it began to permanently lose conquered lands. By the year 1700 the Sultan had surrendered almost all of Hungary, as well as Transylvania, Croatia and Slovenia to the Habsburgs while yielding Dalmatia, the Morea and some Aegean islands to Venice and Padolia, and the southern Ukraine to Poland. Russia had gained some territories north of the Dniester River, lost them for a while, only to regain them later.

Another significant event for the Balkans occurred in 1711 when one of the Moldavian *gospodars* (princes) was accused of collaborating with the Russian army and was held responsible for the Russian invasion of Romania. As punishment the Ottomans replaced all Romanian and Moldavian gospodars with *Phanariots* from Constantinople.

Ottoman losses were not limited to Europe alone. On the eastern front, in a series of unsuccessful wars between 1723 and 1736, the Turks lost Azerbaijan and other lands to the Persians. A decade later in 1746, after two centuries of war, the Ottomans abandoned the conflict with Iran, leaving their Iranian rivals to face political anarchy in the new territorities.

The agreement signed at Kuchuk Kainarji in 1774 with the Russian Romanov dynasty, similar to the 1699 Karlowitz treaty with Austria, highlights the extent of the losses suffered by the Ottomans during the 18th century. The 1768 to 1774 war, the first with Empress Catherine the Great, ended with the destruction of the Ottoman fleet in the Aegean near Chezme. Russian ships sailed from the Baltic Sea through Gibraltar, across the Mediterranean Sea and sank the Ottoman fleet at its home base. By this victorious engagement Russia forced the Sultan to break ties with the Crimean Khan. Without the Sultan's protection, the Khans were left at Russia's mercy, and this meant that the Sultan could no longer count on the Khans for help.

The 1774 Kuchuk Kainarji Treaty gave Russian ships access to the Black Sea, the Bosphorus and Edirne (the Adrianople region). By this treaty Russia built an Orthodox church in Constantinople and became the self appointed "protector of Orthodox Christians" inside the Ottoman realm, which also included Wallachia (Romania) and Moldavia at the time. Also, for the first time, the Ottomans allowed Russian (outside) consular agents inside their empire. Russia at the time did not have enough ships to fill all the shipping demands, so that many of the shipping contracts went to Phanariot captains who were on friendly terms with both the Russians and Ottomans. Russian gains at the expense of the Ottomans began to cause some alarm among the Western European states, particularly since Russia had appointed herself protector of all Orthodox Christians.

The next event to shake the world was the French revolution and Napoleon Bonaparte's rise to power. Bonaparte invaded Egypt in 1798, which marked the end of Ottoman domination of the strategic and rich lands along the Nile. The Ottoman central government never regained Egypt, which later emerged as a separate state under Muhammad Ali Pasha and his descendants. After Ali's death his successors kept close ties with the Ottomans in Constantinople but remained independent.

Despite the many losses the Ottomans also experienced some gains. In the 1714 to 1718 war with Venice the Turks took back the Morea.

Toward the end of the 18th century and in the early part of the 19th century, Macedonia, like other parts of European Turkey, was a hotbed of resistance and revolt. Trouble was stirred up by military deserters and by local feudal lords who, in the absence of the Ottoman military, had declared themselves independent and were fighting with one another for greater dominion. Ismail Beg of Serres, Ali Pasha of Ioannina, the Debar Pashas, Redzhep Pasha of the Skopje Pashalik and Dzheladin Beg in the Ohrid and Prespa district were but a few who had gained notoriety in this way.

The political and economic insecurity created by this anarchy and by the central government's inability to cope, forced another large migration of Macedonians from the villages into the towns. The sudden growth in the urban population caused an increase in the production of crafts and agricultural products, which became trading commodities for the Central European and Russian markets. The fairs in Serres, Prilep, Doiran, Struga, Enidzhe Vardar, Petrich and Nevrokop became commercial trading posts for both domestic and foreign trade. The newly created market network enabled Macedonian businessmen to develop trading ties with the outside world. Businessmen from Veles, Bitola, Serres, Bansko and Ohrid set up their own agencies in Vienna, Leipzig, Trieste and Belgrade. Along with trade also came prosperity and exposure to the outside world. Macedonian merchants became the bearers of progressive ideas, education, culture and Macedonian national sentiment.

artist's version of an 18th century Macedonian rebel

Chapter Three

Macedonia from 1800 to 1878

"No sooner had I heard the sound of Ares's bugle and the weeping call of my beloved fatherland for the protection of its rights, then I scorned my tranquility, wealth and glory, took arms against the tyrants and managed to stay near Negush during the entire war. There I fought long and blood-shedding battles until the destruction of Negush, where my beloved children and my wife were taken prisoner, but, thank God, they are now alive, although in a hostile country, exposed to the will of the barbarians.

(Angel Gacho, 16th September 1824)

The Negush (Naussa) Uprising is a little-known event, even though it was the first Macedonian popular uprising of the 19th century.

Macedonia's neighbor to the south has ignored this history, because it took place on what is now considered Greek territory.

For the oppressed peoples of the Balkans, the dawn of the nineteenth century marked the beginning of new national struggles for liberation from the centuries-long domination of the Ottoman Empire. The first was the Serbian Uprising of 1804, followed by the Phanariot Uprising of 1821. Macedonians, in an effort to liberate their Christian brothers from the oppressive Muslim Ottoman Turk, and advance their own cause, took part in both uprisings. In the first Serbian uprising a Macedonian named Volche was instrumental in building the Deligrad fortifications and distinguished himself as a great fighter. Petar Chardaklija was another Macedonian who also distinguished himself as a fighter in the Serbian resistance. Petar Ichko, another Macedonian, led a delegation that concluded the Ichko Peace Treaty of 1806 with the Ottoman government. When news of the Serbian uprising reached Macedonia the Macedonian people were stirred to action. Unfortunately, the Ottoman authorities were ready and concentrated large numbers of troops in Macedonia, quelling any spark of rebellion before it had a chance to spread.

Macedonians participated in the Phanariot Uprising of 1821. Immediately after the outbreak of the Morea revolt, Macedonians formed their own bands, particularly in the Voden district and joined up with the Morean rebels. Among the leaders of such rebel bands who fought side by side with the Moreans were the brothers Ramadanovi, Dimche Minov, Dincho Drzhilovich and Demir Trajko.

Strongly influenced by the ideals of the Phanariot freedom fighters, who were calling on the entire Balkan population to take up arms against the Ottoman yoke, many Macedonians, particularly those in the Voden and Negush districts, did take up arms. In early March 1822, under the leadership of Atanas Karatase and Angel Gacho, a revolt broke out in the town of Negush. The rebels quickly overwhelmed the Turks and declared Negush liberated. The revolt quickly spread towards Voden, involving a significant number of villages. Unfortunately, effort and determination alone were not enough to stop the numerically superior Ottoman army. Isolated and besieged from all sides, the rebellion was soon suppressed. After a fierce battle the Turks recaptured the town of Negush and retribution and pillaging followed. To discourage future resistance, the population of Negush was either enslaved or resettled in other parts of Macedonia.

The following is part of a letter written the 16th of September, 1824 by Angel Gacho that reveals some of his participation in the Negush Uprising.

"No sooner had I heard the sound of Ares's bugle and the weeping call of my beloved fatherland for the protection of its rights than I scorned my tranquility, wealth and glory, took arms against the tyrants and managed to stay near Negush during the whole war. There I fought long and blood-shedding battles until the destruction of Negush, where my beloved children and my wife were taken prisoner, but, thank God, they are now alive, although in a hostile country, exposed to the will of the barbarians."

(*Documents*, 1985, 183)

The Kuchuk Kainarji Treaty bolstered Russian expansionism in the Balkans, which alarmed the Western Powers and initiated the "Eastern Question": What will happen to the Balkans when the Ottoman Empire disappears? The Eastern Question of the 1800's later became the Macedonian Question of the 1900's.

At about the same time as Russia was making her way into the Balkans, the West was experiencing changes of its own. The industrial revolution was well underway, spreading from England and making its way around the world. France was the economic superpower of the time, but it was quickly losing ground to England. The French Revolution (1789) gave birth not only to new ideas and nationalism, but also to Napoleon Bonaparte. As Napoleon waged war in Europe and the Middle East, French shipping in the Mediterranean declined, only to be replaced by Phanariot and British traders. French trade inside Ottoman territory also declined and never fully recovered. Austria, due to its extensive mutual border, dominated overland European trade with the Ottoman Empire, exercising its own brand of influence on the Balkans, especially on the Serbian people.

With the beginning of the 19th century came rapid economic development to Europe, and the Balkans became a last frontier for capitalist expansion. By the 1800's Europe's political, economic and military institutions were rapidly changing. Western governments and exporters were aggressively pursuing Balkan markets on behalf of their Western manufacturers. This aggressive pursuit smothered Balkan industries before they had a chance to develop and compete. As a result, Balkan economies began to decline, causing civil unrest and nationalist uprisings. While Western countries were left in peace to develop economically and socially, external forces prevented Balkan societies from achieving similar progress. Mostly regulated by guilds, Balkan trades could not compete with Western mechanization and went out of business. Without jobs, many city folk became a burden on the already economically strained rural peasants. The economic situation in the Balkans deteriorated to intolerable levels and, as in the previous two centuries, people began to rebel.

Serbia was the first among the modern Balkan states to rebel. The first revolt took place in Belgrade in 1804, the same year that Napoleon became emperor of France. The immediate causes of the armed uprising were political and economic oppression and a further deterioration of the Ottoman system. When Napoleon invaded Egypt in 1798 the Sultan took troops from the Balkans and sent them to fight the French in Egypt, leaving the region unguarded. In 1801 Belgrade became a sanctuary for bandits and unruly Janissaries. Robbery and murder became commonplace. Then in February of 1804 a group of bandits murdered seventy prominent Serbian village leaders and priests. They did this to frighten the population and to stop the Serb leaders from complaining to the Sultan. Fearing further murders, some of the Serb leaders fled to the forests and organized the villagers into armed units. They attacked the Janissaries in the countryside and fought them until they were pushed back to Belgrade. The war, however, ended in a stalemate.

The stalemate was broken in 1806 when the Serbs decided to no longer seek help from the Sultan and took matters into their own hands. At about the same time the French and Turks became allies. Since France was already an enemy of Russia this alliance made Turkey an enemy also. Now, as an enemy of the Turks, the Russians intervened

on behalf of the Serbs and in 1807 helped them take Belgrade. The Sultan offered the Serbs full autonomy, but the Russians advised against it. They insisted on negotiating for full independence instead. Unfortunately, when the war between Russia and France ended in 1807 Russia made peace with Napoleon and became allied with both France and Turkey. Russia, more concerned with its own self-interests, left the Serbs on their own. The Serbs lost Belgrade to a Turkish army attack in 1808, and many Serbs fled into exile while the rest continued guerilla warfare from the forests.

The revolt began again in 1809, when Russia renewed its campaign against Turkey, and ended in 1813 with a Serb defeat. The Serbs failed to win because Russia wavered in its commitment to Serbia. Russia had a lot more to gain by appeasing Turkey, especially when war with France became imminent. When Napoleon invaded Russia in 1812, the Russians abandoned the Serbs and in 1813 an Ottoman army invaded Serbia, forcing many of her people to flee as refugees into the Austrian Empire.

Relations between the Serbs and Turks turned from bad to worse when the Turks extorted provisions from the Serbs by force, tortured villagers while searching for hidden weapons and increased taxes. A riot broke out at a Turkish estate in 1814 and the Turks massacred the local population and publicly impaled two hundred prisoners inside Belgrade. The Serbian leaders decided to revolt again and fighting resumed on Easter in 1815. This time Serb leaders made sure that captured Turkish soldiers were not killed and civilians were released unharmed. To further ease Turkish fears, the Serbs also announced that this was a revolt to end abuses, not a war to gain independence. After the Russians defeated Napoleon in 1815, the Turks feared that Russia would again intervene on Serbia's behalf. To avoid this, the Sultan gave Serbia autonomy.

After the Russian-Turkish War of 1829-30, a new treaty was signed which put an end to most abuses in Serbia. All Muslims, except for a small military garrison, left Serbian territory. Serbs took control of the internal administration, postal system and courts. Individual taxes and dues paid directly to the Sultan were replaced by a single annual

tribute payment from the Serbian state to the Sultan. Serbia remained autonomous until 1878 when she gained full independence.

Next to rebel against Ottoman rule were the Phanariots. The Phanariot uprising was far more limited than the Serbian. Unlike the Serbs, most Phanariots were wealthy and already enjoyed substantial privileges in Ottoman society. Rebellion did not have the same appeal for them because they had much to lose and little to gain.

When the Ottomans imposed the *millet* system, organizing the population according to religious affiliation, the Phanariots began to gain economic and other advantages over other Balkan Christians. In time the Phanariot-controlled Patriarch appointed his own clergy and took control of administering the entire Christian *millet*. Patriarch-appointed clergy had religious, educational, administrative and legal power in the Ottoman Balkans. In other words, Phanariots were already more or less running all political, civil and religious affairs in the Christian millet.

The Phanariots were the upper class, or the blue blood of the Christian world. Even though they were of varied ethnicity they were distinguished by their status, material wealth and the power they wielded within the Ottoman administration. They were also distinguished by their use of the Koine language of the eastern Mediterranean , a tradition from the time of the Byzantine Empire.

By the 1700's, Phanariot ship owners in the islands dominated Balkan commerce. As Christians, Phanariot traders were exempt from Muslim moral and legal restraints (particularly those dealing with money) and were permitted to engage in commerce with non-Muslims. Westerners who did business in the region used local Jews, Armenians and Phanariots as agents. Different branches of the same Phanariot family often operated in different cities. Ties of kinship reduced certain risks of trade.

Between 1529 and 1774 only Ottoman ships were allowed to navigate the isolated waters of the Black Sea. Phanariot trade grew without competition from the Venetians or other Western traders. As mentioned earlier, the 1774 Treaty of Kuchuk Kainarji opened the Turkish straits to Russian commerce. There were not enough Russian ships, however, to meet all shipping demands, so Ottoman Phanariots

filled the void. Also, the Napoleonic wars between England and France created new opportunities for the neutral Phanariot ships and by 1810 there were 600 Phanariot trading vessels conducting commerce.

For the Phanariots, especially the more well-to-do, Ottoman rule provided many advantages in comparison to other Balkan groups. Rich ship owners, agents, prosperous merchants, important officials in the Christian Church, tax collectors, *gospodars* or lords in Romania, primates in the church in Morea and members of the interpreters' service all had much to lose and little to gain by rebellion.

How then can one explain the movement that led to the revolution in 1821? Although the poor peasants, village priests, sailors, etc. who lived in Morea had no investment in the Ottoman status quo, they were without a clear sense of purpose or leadership. Such people were mostly preoccupied with their own poverty and reduced to preying upon each other merely to survive. Under such circumstances only outside forces were capable of fomenting rebellion.

The original instigators were members of the "Filiki Eteria" a secret society founded in 1814 in the Russian port of Odessa. The Filiki Eteria sent representatives into Morea to recruit fighters. A number of important *klefts* (Greek outlaws) and district notables answered their call by organizing peasants and forming armed bands.

Because Morea was so poor, most of the countryside had no Turkish presence and Christian primates or *kodjabashii* virtually ruled themselves. Christian militia or *armatoli* kept the peace, while the bandits known as *klefts* roamed the hills, robbing and plundering their neighbors.

The 1821 revolution began as a planned conspiracy involving only selected elements of the population. At that time the idea of "nationality" remained very elusive, even for the most enlightened revolutionaries. The intent of the uprising was to liberate all of the Balkan people from Turkish tyranny and unite them in one Christian state.

The Filiki Eteria planned to start the uprising in three places. The first was Morea, where a core group of klefts and primates supported the idea. Second was Constantinople, where the Phanariot community was expected to riot. Third, Phanariot forces were expected to cross the Russian border from Odessa to invade Moldavia and Romania. However, the conspiracy did not go as planned. When 4500 men of the "Sacred Battalion" entered Moldavia in March 1821, the Romanian peasants ignored the Turks and instead attacked the Phanariots. The Phanariot invasion of Romania was a complete failure. At the same time, class divisions in Phanariot society worked against the planned uprising in Constantinople. The Turks ended any revolt there by hanging the reigning Patriarch. Their only success was in Morea, and then mainly because Christian leaders there feared the Turkish Pasha's retribution in the event of failure.

Fearing arrest or even execution, the Christian primates joined the klefts, who massacred the Turkish population of Morea. Turkey was unable to quell the uprising and the conflict remained a stalemate until 1825. The stalemate, in part, was due to internal problems among the Phanariots, reflecting pre-existing class differences, i.e. the armed peasants and klefts in Morea were loyal to Theodoros Kolokotronis, a kleft. Opposing them were the civilian leaders in the National Assembly, which was made up mostly of religious primates and well-connected Phanariots. By 1823 the two sides were locked in a civil war. The stalemate was also due, in part, to interventions from Britain, France and Russia. Each of these states had strategic political and economic interests in Turkey and each wanted to make sure that the results of the war in Morea would be in their best interest. The British were sympathetic to the Phanariot cause, but at the same time they wanted a strong Turkey to counter Russia. Initially, the British were prepared to support Turkey to prevent Russia from gaining control of the Turkish Straits and threatening the Mediterranean trade routes. Later as Britain gained control of Cyprus plans changed. The Russian Tsar, in turn, had sympathy for the Christians but feared the possibility of a Morean state becoming a British ally. French investors held large numbers of Turkish state bonds, which would be worthless if Turkey collapsed. France was also anxious to re-enter world politics after her defeat by Russia in 1815.

The Great Powers, given the stalemate, could see that the Morean revolt would not go away. So they were prepared to intervene to make

sure that the final result was acceptable to their own interests. Foreign intervention continued from 1825 until 1827. It began with a blockade to stop the Egyptian navy from invading Morea in 1825 (after the Egyptian Mehmet Ali's capture of the port of Navarino) and ended in 1827 when the British, French and Russians sank the Egyptian navy. The European Powers sent a combined fleet of 27 ships to Navarino Bay to monitor the Egyptian navy, but things got out of hand when musket shots were fired and the observation escalated into a battle. When it was over the European fleet had sunk 60 of the 89 Egyptian ships. The loss of the Egyptian navy left the Sultan without sufficient armed forces and the inability to reclaim Morea or resist the Great Powers. Turkey was forced to make concessions over the Morea, but the Ottomans kept stalling. To put an end to their delaying tactics, the Russians invaded Turkey in 1828 (Russian-Turkish War of 1828-1830) and almost reached Constantinople by 1829. The Sultan gave in to Russian demands. Russia too gave in to Western Power demands and agreed to British and French participation in the peace settlement through the London Protocol of 1830, which gave birth to a small, independent Greek kingdom. Prince Otto of Bavaria, a German prince, and a German administration were chosen by the Great Powers to rule this new Greek kingdom. The choice was a compromise acceptable to all three powers.

Two overwhelming forces came into being in the 19th century, which transformed the Balkans. The first was the Western economic revolution, which cast the Balkans into social and economic upheaval. The second was increased intervention from non-Balkan political forces. As the century advanced these developments merged, working not for the interests of the Balkan people, but for the benefit of Europe's Great Powers.

Before continuing with internal Balkan developments, it would be best to explore the "external forces" and their political desires in Balkan affairs. Besides Turkey, there were six Great Powers during the nineteenth century. They were Russia, Great Britain, France, Austria-Hungary, Italy and Germany. From time to time the Great Powers expressed interest in the Balkan population, but, in crisis situations, each followed its own separate interests. When the Great Powers made compromises, they did so to avoid war with each other and often failed to address the real issues that caused the crisis in the first place. This is quite similar to what the Great Powers are doing in the Balkans today.

Russia tended to be the most aggressive and was usually the cause of each new Turkish defeat. The 1774 Kuchuk Kainarji Treaty allowed Russia access to the north shore of the Black Sea, gave her power to act on behalf of the Orthodox *millet* and to conduct commerce within the Ottoman Empire. Russia's goals in the Balkans were to gain exclusive navigation rights from the Black Sea to the Mediterranean Sea for both merchant and military ships and to annex Constantinople and Edirne for herself, both of which were unacceptable to the Western Powers.

After the end of the Crimean war in 1856, with the Treaty of Paris, the Western Powers made efforts to rein in Russia's expansionist ambitions. First, all Russian warships were barred from the Black Sea and second, the Black Sea was opened to merchant ships from all the other states. After that, all the Great Powers, not just Russia, became the guarantors of the Balkan states.

From 1815 to 1878 Great Britain was Russia's strongest rival for Balkan influence. British interests led her to intervene against the Turks in the Morean revolution of the 1820's, but she went to war against Russia in 1853 (Crimean War) on Turkey's behalf.

The British goals in the Balkans were to maintain access to the eastern Mediterranean and to secure shipping lanes to India. Most of the trade routes passed through Turkish controlled waters. Turkey was too weak to be a threat, so Britain was inclined to oppose France, Russia and Germany when they became a threat to Turkey.

To bolster her claim to the Eastern waterways, in 1878 Britain took control of the island of Cyprus and in 1883 occupied Egypt and the Suez Canal. After that Britain kept a close watch on Morea and Russian access to the Straits, interfering less in Ottoman affairs.

Britain also had important commercial interests inside the Ottoman Empire, and later in the successor states. Investors in railroads and state bonds took as much profit as they could, as soon as they could, which in the long term contributed to the Ottoman Empire's instability.

France, like Britain, had both political and economic interests in the Balkans. During the Napoleonic wars, France was a direct threat to Ottoman rule (Napoleon invaded Egypt in 1798) but after her 1815 defeat she lost military and political clout. France had commercial rights in Turkey dating back to the Capitulation Treaties of the 1600s and relied heavily on trade with the Ottoman Empire.

In the 1820s France joined British and Russian intervention on behalf of the Moreans. France did this mostly to protect her commercial interests but also to counter-balance Russian-British domination in the region.

More so than the British, French investors played a key role in Balkan policy. During the Eastern Crisis and the war of 1875-78, the Turkish state went bankrupt and French bondholders were the biggest potential losers in case of default. So when the Ottoman Public Debt Administration was created to monitor Turkish state finances, French directors were directly involved in the management of Ottoman state finances. Like the British investors, French investors forced Turkey to maximize their returns and ignored the needs of the Ottoman people.

Austria had been the main threat to Ottoman rule at one time, but after 1699 Russia replaced her in that regard. Austria retained a major interest in the Ottoman Empire, mainly because the Turkish Empire neighbored its Hungarian territory. In other words, Vienna had no desire to replace a weak Ottoman neighbor with a strong Russia or with Russian allies like Serbia or today's Bulgaria.

Austria's goal was to have access to a western Balkan economic resource and a potential market. Control of the Adriatic coast was key to Austria's foreign trade through the Adriatic Sea. Austria made sure she exerted sufficient influence to keep the hostile Great Powers away and to prevent the growing new Balkan nations from annexing further Ottoman territory. Austria had no desire to annex the western Balkans for herself. The ruling German Austrians, or the Hungarians had no ethnic or religious ties to the Slavs in the region.

After 1866 Germany (not Austria) became the leader in Central Europe. Austria now had only southeastern Europe where she could exert influence. Austria was too weak to absorb the Balkans by herself so she preferred to sustain a weak Ottoman Empire instead of Russian controlled states. This explains why Vienna took an anti-Russian position during the Crimean War and why it became allied with Germany later. Germany was an ally of both Russia and Austria, but Austria turned on Russia, so Germany had to abandon the Russian German alliance to please Austria.

Serbia and Romania created problems for Vienna, which she unsuccessfully tried to manage through political alliances and economic treaties. Romania feared Russian occupation and Bucharest generally accepted alliances with Austria. Serbia, however, had fewer enemies and less incentive to bend to Austrian wishes. The two states (Austria and Serbia) found themselves on a collision course, which resulted in the war in 1914 (World War One).

Italy became a state in 1859 after fighting a successful war against Austria. In 1866 the Kingdom of Piedmont united the Italian peninsula and took its place as a new Great Power. Italy lacked economic and military might in comparison to the other Powers but made up for it in influence at the expense of the weaker Ottoman Empire.

Italy viewed the western Balkans, especially Albania, as her natural zone of influence and her leaders watched for opportunities to take the area away from the Turks. Italy's Balkan goals were not only a threat to Turkey but also to Serbia and Greece, who both had designs on the Adriatic. Italy was too weak to seize Balkan territory so she followed a policy of "lay and wait" until 1911 and 1912 when she took the Dodecanese Islands and Tripoli (Libya) from the Ottomans.

Germany, like Italy, became a Great Power at a later time after the German state unification of 1862 to 1870. Due to her strong military and economic might, Germany had more influence in Europe than Italy, but no direct interest in Balkan affairs. For the new German Empire the Balkans were only an economic outlet.

After defeating Austria in 1866, Germany made Austria-Hungary an ally and to retain loyalty, Germany had to support Austria in Balkan matters. After 1878 Germany could no longer reconcile Russian and Austrian differences over the Balkans and by 1890 Germany and Austria strengthened their alliance and pushed Tsarist Russia into a conflicting partnership with Republican France. After that, German policies in the Balkans supported economic and military investments in Turkey. This made Germany a rival not only of Russia but also of Britain. The Great Power alignments of 1890-1914 established a pattern that dominated affairs through the two world wars.

Germany had no stake in the development of any of the successor states, which left her free to support the Sultan (and later the Young Turk regime). German officers trained Turkish troops and German marks built Turkish railways.

The Ottoman Empire of the 19th century was the weakest of the Great Powers, especially after the Crimean War. At the 1856 Treaty of Paris, Britain and France granted Turkey "legal status" in the Balkans that was far beyond her ability to administer. The Western Powers desperately wanted the Ottoman Empire stable and intact.

The Ottomans, on the other hand, mistrusted the other Powers, partly because they were infidels and partly because of bad past experience. Russia was clearly Turkey's greatest enemy, bent on dismantling her empire. To keep Russia at bay, Turkey cooperated with the other Powers but was always wary of falling under the influence of any single Power. From the 1820's to the 1870s, Britain was Turkey's guardian. After 1878 Germany replaced Britain as economic and military sponsor. Turkish relations with the new Balkan states were poor at best. Any gains for them usually meant losses for Turkey.

The Western Great Powers believed that if corruption, crime and poverty could be eliminated, Balkan unrest would end and the Ottoman Empire could remain intact. After all, they didn't want anything to happen to their goose that laid the golden eggs. So instead of kicking the "sick man" out of Europe, they pushed for reforms. However, it was one thing to draw up reforms and another to make them work. Ottoman efforts in Macedonia, for example, made it obvious that the Turks lacked the resources and the will to carry out reforms. Also, Europeans failed to grasp that mere suggestions and wishes alone could not replace five hundred years of Ottoman rule. The Ottomans believed their way of life was just and proper.

However, unrest began to grow within Turkish society as well.

In 1865 a group of educated Turks formed the secret Young Ottoman Society. Their aim was to revitalize old Islamic concepts and unite all the ethnic groups under Islamic law. Threatened with arrest, the Young Ottoman leaders went into exile in Paris.

In 1889 a group of four medical students formed another secret Young Turk Society. They rejected the "old Islamic aims" and embraced a new idea, "Turkish nationalism". Turkish nationalism became the foundation for a secular Turkey in 1908 after the Young Turks came to power and again in 1920 after the collapse of the Ottoman Empire in Turkey proper.

The next important event in Balkan history was the Crimean War of 1853 to 1856, which pitted Russia against Turkey, England and France. The crisis ignited over the issue of who was in control of Christian Holy Places in Turkish-ruled Jerusalem. Orthodox and Catholic monks quarreled over insignificant issues, such as who should possess the keys to locked shrines. By old treaties Russia and France were the international guarantors of Orthodox and Catholic rights respectively, but in 1852 Napoleon III tried to undo that. He needed to distract French Catholic public opinion away from his authoritarian rule, so he instigated the dispute.

Because the issues in dispute involved the highest levels of the Turkish government, to the nations involved it became a symbolic struggle for influence. The Russians badly misjudged the other Powers and failed to see that Britain could not accept a Russian victory. Tensions arose as all sides prepared for conflict. A Russian army occupied two Romanian Principalities, failing to see that this threatened Austria's Balkan interests. Russia expected help and gratitude from Vienna for her help against Hungary in 1849, but Austria refused her. With support from the Western Powers, the Turks refused to negotiate and in 1853 declared war on Russia.

The Crimean War pulled in the Great Powers even though none of them wanted to go to war. In 1854 Austria forced the Russians to evacuate the Principalities and Austria took Russia's place as a neutral power. In 1856 the allied Western Powers took Sevastopol, the chief Russian port on the Black Sea, by force. After that Russia agreed to their terms at the Treaty of Paris.

As a result of the Treaty of Paris, the Danube River was opened to shipping for all nations. Russia lost southern Bessarabia to Moldavia. She also lost her status as primary protector of Romanian rights. The two Romanian principalities remained under nominal Ottoman rule. However, a European commission was appointed and, together with elected assembly representatives from each province, was responsible for determining "the basis for administration" of the two Principalities. Also, all the European powers now shared responsibility as guarantors of the treaty.

On the surface it appears that Turkey won and Russia lost the Crimean War. In reality however, both Russia and Turkey lost a good deal. The Crimean War financially bankrupted Turkey. As for Russia, she lost her shipping monopoly on the Black Sea that allowed capitalism to enter into Eastern Europe. Russia not only lost influence in Romania and Moldavia, but she was also humiliated before the entire world. This set the stage for future conflicts including the recent "Cold War".

As mentioned earlier, Turkey's financial collapse opened the door for Western governments to manipulate internal Ottoman policies as well as divert needed revenues to pay foreign debts. On top of that the Ottoman Empire was forced into becoming a consumer of Western European commodities. While Western Europe prospered from these ventures, Ottoman trades and guilds paid the ultimate price of bankruptcy. Lack of work in the cities put more pressure on the village peasants. They were now being taxed to near starvation in order to care for unemployed city dwellers, as well as maintain the status quo for the upper class. The Ottoman Empire became totally dependent on European capital for survival, which put the state past the financial point of no return and marked the beginning of the end of Ottoman rule in Europe.

By 1875 the Ottomans entered a crisis situation, owing 200 million pounds sterling to foreign investors with an annual interest payment of 12 million pounds a year. The interest payments alone amounted to approximately half the state's annual revenues. In 1874, due to some agricultural failures, military expenses and worldwide economic depression, the Turkish government could not even pay the interest due on the loans. On the brink of bankruptcy, to preserve Ottoman stability and to make sure Turkey paid on Western European debts, the Great Powers in 1875 took over the management of Turkish revenues. This was done through an international agency, called the Ottoman Public Debt Administration (OPDA). To continue to receive credit, the Sultan had to grant the OPDA control over state income. Therefore, control of the state budget and internal policies fell into foreign hands. The agents in control were representatives of rich capitalists and their only interest was in profit, and very little else. This certainly did not prove to be of any benefit to the local people.

traditional Macedonian peasant folk costumes and dance

Chapter Four

Macedonia from 1878 to 1903

"During the whole period of the Turkish rule, the Macedonian Slavs did not cease to wage an aware and persistent struggle, first for their independence, and after they were finally subjugated by the Turks, for their liberation from the Turkish yoke. They organized a large number of insurrections and often defeated the Turks, but, of course, at the end of it all, the insurrections were always suppressed in streams of Macedonian blood. They also took part in the liberation struggles of their neighbours - the Serbs, Greeks and Bulgarians - whose freedom was attained with the endeavours and help of the Macedonians, as well. Thus, at the time of the Russo - Turkish War of 1877/78, two thirds of the volunteers from the Balkan Slavs were Macedonians. The names of Georgi Pulevski, Stojan Vezenkovski, Popot Bufski and a whole pleiad of others who took part in the struggle of the cross against the crescent, meant a lot and still mean a lot to the hearts of the South Slavs. And although Macedonia, after the unhappy Congress of Berlin had to remain under the rule of the Turks, it was only because it was closer than any other Slavs to the administrative centres of the Ottoman Empire, like Constantinople, Adrianople and Salonika; Macedonia

could be freed only alongside the final ruin of Turkey in Europe.

The Congress of Berlin which offered the Macedonian people as a sacrifice to the revenge of the shattered Turks, who knew what role the Macedonian detachments had played in the war that had been a Turkish defeat, caused an explosion of despair and discontent throughout Macedonia. The whole people.as one man, rose up and started an unequal struggle against the Turks for their liberation. This uprising lasted for more than a year and ended. of course. with the triumph of the embittered Turks, who finally devastated that unfortunate country. Many villages, and even towns, were burnt down, many people were butchered, and some of the Macedonian intellectuals were killed while others found salvation in fleeing to the free states.

Regardless of this bloody suppression of the uprising, the idea of liberation did not leave the Macedonians. All these 35 years which have passed from the Congress of Berlin up to the present war are one bloody page of continuous gigantic struggle of the Macedonian people for their liberation . . . The hundreds of thousands of victims they have offered at the altar of their fatherland have redeemed the right of Macedonia to freedom . . .In just five years - from 1898 to 1903 - there were more than 400 confrontations between the Macedonians and Turks.

The persistent rebellious struggle against the Turks was guided by the so-called Internal Organization, which over 10 years (up to the well-known uprising of 1903) achieved a marvelous feat: it turned the elements which had until then been disorganized and inspired only by the spirit of protest and rebellion. into a powerful disciplined army, which was able to offer resistance to the tyrants. The most prominent activists of that organization were Gotse Delchev and Damjan Gruev.

Apart from the Internal Organization, there were two other revolutionary committees in Bulgaria, the most serious role being played by the Supreme Macedonian-Adrianople Committeee. This committee was founded by the Bulgarian government with a special aim - to take over the leadership from the Internal Organization, which had set itself as its aim the principle ,,Macedonia to the Macedonians ", which, of course, was not very pleasant for the Bulgarians, who aspired to Macedonia.

Those who are acquainted with the history of the revolutionary movement in Macedonia know about the many excesses of the Committee, which were contrary to the tasks of the Internal Organization and thus weakened the power of the popular movement.

Following the Macedonian uprising of 1895 (led by Trajko Kitanchev) and the (Armenian) slaughter in Asia Minor, the European states succeeded only in forcing the Sultan in 1896 to proclaim his famous "trade" for reforms in the whole of European Turkey. But this trade did not help the Christian population of Macedonia in the least.

The Internal Organization, however, vigorously prepared itself for a new uprising under the slogan, "Macedonia to the Macedonians", and the people, exhausted by the Turkish atrocities, were glad to join the revolutionary movement. Of course, this did not suit the wishes of other Balkan states, which dreamt of grabbing Macedonia themselves. They only awaited a suitable moment to declare war on Turkey, and such an event was a result of the difficult position of the Osmanli state, caused by the Macedonian and Albanian uprisings, internal turnovers, and primarily, by the Italo-Turkish War. Even before the end of that war, the Balkan states united in an alliance and came out against Turkey under the slogan of liberation of the Christians from the Turkish yoke."

(Dimitrija Chupovski, *Makedonskij Golos, 1913)*

Russia's rash attempt to gain access to the Mediterranean, by creating a "Greater Bulgaria" (under the San Stefano Treaty), gave the Bulgarians rationale to make territorial claims on Macedonian territory. In addition to Greeks forcibly trying to Hellenize Macedonia, the Macedonian people now faced a new enemy, Bulgarian chauvinism. At the hands of the Turks, Greeks, Bulgarians, Albanians and Serbians, Macedonian misery multiplied, as if all the evil in the world was unleashed on Macedonia, striking repeatedly with all its fury. What makes Macedonia's misery even more tragic is that the entire world stood by and watched the horrors unfold and did nothing.

While the Greeks employed brutality, the Bulgarians adopted intrigue to sway Macedonians to their side. The Bulgarians were publicly calling for Macedonian autonomy while they were promoting a Bulgarian nationalist agenda. In the decades after 1878, nationalist fever gripped the Balkans. The new nations (Serbia, Greece and Bulgaria) were making exclusive claims not only on Macedonian territory, but also on the Macedonian people, each claiming that Macedonians were Serbs, Greeks, or Bulgarians. Each new nation desperately tried to prove its claim by propaganda campaigns, coercion and forcible assimilation. Here is what Brailsford (1971, 101) has to say on the subject:

Are the Macedonians Serbs or Bulgars? The question is constantly asked and dogmatically answered in Belgrade and Sofia. But the lesson of history is obviously that there is no answer at all. They are not Serbs, ... On the other hand they could hardly be Bulgarians... They are probably what they were before a Bulgarian or Serbian Empire existed...

As for the Macedonian's being Greek, this is what Brailsford (1971, 91) has to say:

The Greek colonies were never much more than trading centers along the coast, and what was Greek in ancient times is Greek today. There is no evidence that the interior was ever settled by a rural Greek population.

During the period immediately following the Berlin Congress Balkan chauvinist intent was not merely to occupy, govern and exploit Macedonia, but to eradicate the Macedonian culture and impose its own culture upon a people alien to it.

A Macedonian could not rise out of his tragic conditions of existence on his own, because every time he did so he was either killed for his education, robbed of his wealth, kicked out of his home for his lands, murdered for defending his family, or humiliated for his existence. This is not what Macedonians wanted for themselves, but those powerful enough to help refused to do so. The Greek clergy, who were responsible for the well-being of the Macedonian people were the first to condemn them. Their first priority was to Hellenize them so that they could steal their lands. The Greeks, with their "superior attitude", despised the Macedonians because of their race (the Slavs were the enemy) and because of their agrarian way of life (which the Greeks looked down upon).

The Great Powers, in their zeal to dominate the Balkans, found themselves at odds with each other and by 1878 were either content with doing nothing or, overcome by frustration, they turned their backs on the mess they had created. Turkey, for Western capitalists, was also the goose that kept on laying golden eggs.

No excuses or apologies from the English and the French can make up for unleashing Turkey and Hellenism on Macedonia after 1878. No Macedonian, nor any other human being for that matter, could easily forgive the Western Powers for putting profit ahead of humanity and intentionally turning their backs on the Macedonian people.

Labeling people "Slav" and "barbarian" because they were not educated does not make them less human and certainly does not excuse the "civilized" Western societies for adding to their torment. Here is what Pandora Petrovska (1997, 167) has to say about these "uneducated" Macedonian peasants in her book *Children of the Bird Goddess*:

It is erroneous to dismiss peasant culture as backwards, simply because they are not literate cultures. Indeed the opposite is the case. Children were educated by way of story telling and folklore, which contained morals and lessons about life, relationships and their places in the world.

One has only to examine Macedonian traditions, customs, dress, folklore and attitude towards life to find an "old race" full of vigor, enduring hardships, living as it always lived, close to nature, always craving peace. Macedonian songs are timeless records of sorrow and of hope that "someday this too will pass." They have survived to this day because they have a capacity to care about others and to give and to forgive, usually demanding little in return. Anyone who has visited a Macedonian home or has lived among Macedonians can attest to this.

Macedonia had done no ill against any nation to deserve her punishment by the Turks and the Greeks. Macedonians did not desire to be labeled "barbarian Slavs" or choose to be illiterate. It was pure prejudice on the part of Western societies that degraded the Macedonian people to barbarian status and created the conditions for the Turks and the Greeks to abuse them. The West's artificial creation of Greece and Hellenism and the Greek quest for purity and national homogeneity is what upset the "natural balance" in the Balkans. Macedonia, since Alexander's time, had been a "worldly" nation and had maintained her multi-ethnic, multi-cultural pluralistic character. If you take the Turks out of Macedonia in the 19th century, you will find a society of several peoples working and living together in relative peace, each doing what comes naturally. Anyone who has lived in Macedonia can attest to that. It has always been "outsiders" who shifted the balance and disturbed the peace in the Balkans. While Western Europe slept through her "dark ages", the people of the Balkans enjoyed relative harmony for over a thousand years. Each people played an important role in maintaining the social and political balance and the economic self-sufficiency of the region.

During the 19th century almost all Macedonians lived in village communities. There were no Greeks living in the Macedonian heartland and only a small minority lived in the coastal towns, islands and larger cities. The majority of the villages were Macedonian with the odd Vlach village nestled here and there in the mountains. Macedonians spoke the Macedonian language and lived an agrarian life working the land. Among the Macedonians lived some Vlachs who spoke both Vlach and Macedonian. Their main occupation was retail trade, running the local grocery stores and retail businesses.

In addition to the Vlachs, there were roving Romas (Gypsies) who traveled from village to village trading their wares. They traded pack animals such as horses, mules and donkeys, repaired old and sold new flour sifters, loom reeds and other craft items. They bartered with the village women and traded beads, string and sewing needles for beans and walnuts. To those who could afford it, they sold silk kerchiefs, handmade baskets and purses. With those who couldn't afford to pay, they traded their wares for vegetables, eggs and a few bales of hay. Among themselves the Gypsies spoke their Romany dialect, but with their customers they spoke Macedonian.

Another group that frequented the Macedonian countryside were the "panhandlers" from Epirus and Thessaly who performed magic on old copper pots and pans and made spoons and forks shine like mirrors. In addition to their own language, they too spoke Macedonian and were open to bartering for their wares and services.

Carpenters, stonemasons, barrel makers and woodcutters were a common site. They came from as far away as Albania or as nearby as neighboring poor Macedonian villages. For a fair wage, some rakija, home-made alcohol, sometimes spiced with anise during distillation, and three meals a day, they built fences, porches, staircases and entire houses. For the Macedonians the soil provided most of life's necessities. For the rest they bought, traded, or bartered.

The only desire Macedonians had in the 19th century was to rid themselves of the tyranny of the oppressive Turks. This is most evident in the communiqués, appeals and manifestoes of the legendary Macedonian Revolutionary Committee.

While Macedonia suffered the Turkish yoke, was tormented by Hellenism and frustrated by Bulgarian deception, the Greek army in 1881 annexed Thessaly and in 1885 the Bulgarian army (with Russia's support) annexed eastern Rumelia. While the Ottoman Empire was crumbling at the edges, it was tightening its grip ever tighter on Macedonia. Looting, burning of homes and murder were on the rise. More and more Macedonians were made homeless and forced to become outlaws. The brave ones took up arms and fought back, only to see their actions cause more death and misery. The Turks and their Albanian allies behaved as brutes. If one Turk or Albanian died in battle, the army took revenge on the next village they encountered. Thousands of innocent women and children were murdered in revenge killings, not to mention the rape assaults on young girls. Homes were torched and the inhabitants were gunned down for target practice as they ran out to save themselves from the fire. Those too old or sick to move quickly enough died a horrible, fiery death. Many of the survivors from the burned out villages joined the outlaws in the mountains, and as their ranks swelled they began to organize and fight back.

Western Europeans and Russians, on the other hand, were visiting the Ottoman Balkans in ever greater numbers on vacation, or to do business or lend a helping hand as missionaries or relief workers. They enjoyed all manner of freedoms and privileges as honorary citizens of the Ottoman Empire, under the protection of their country's flag, and they paid little or nothing for the privilege, not even taxes.

Soon after the Turks conquered Albania, Albanians began to convert to Islam. As Muslims, the Albanians, to a large extent, enjoyed the same privileges and advantages as their conquerors. The advantages of becoming a Muslim as opposed to staying Christian were obvious. Those who wanted to retain title to their lands did not hesitate to convert. In fact, many realized that by converting they could amass wealth and increase their own importance at the expense of their Christian neighbors.

By the 19th century about two-thirds of the Albanians had embraced Islam and served in almost every capacity in the Ottoman administration, including the Sultan's palace guard. Also by the 19th century much of the Ottoman services had become corrupt and self-serving. Being Muslims, the Albanians were protected from prosecution for crimes committed against the Christians. This encouraged them to engage in predatory acts such as kidnappings for ransom, illegal taxation, extortion and forceful possession of property.

There are two documented methods that describe how Albanians of the 19th century came to live in Macedonia, among the Macedonians. One way the Turks kept the Macedonians in check was by creating and strategically positioning Albanian villages inside Macedonia among the Macedonian villages. Another was by expelling or killing a few families in a Macedonian village. Albanian bandits could then claim squatter's rights and move in. By the next generation, the children of the squatters would become the "begs" of the village, which made them legitimate landowners. Being in charge of the village, they then appointed their own family members and trusted friends in positions of authority such as tax collectors and policemen. In this manner they could rule unchallenged.

Forceful occupation of villages was most prevalent during campaigns in the absence of the Turkish army. When the Turks were sent to fight against Russia in the east or against Napoleon in Egypt, the Albanians saw their chance and moved in unchallenged. Here is an excerpt from Brailsford's (1971, 224) book about the habits of some Albanians:

> *He will rob openly and with violence but he will not steal...He will murder you without remorse if he conceives that you have insulted him...*

To be fair, it should be said that Albanians have their good qualities as well. Brailsford speaks very highly of them when it comes to loyalty and honesty. Of course, under the right conditions Albanians can peacefully co-exist with other ethnicities and be a contributing factor to the wealth of a nation. The Macedonians have always co-existed side by side with Albanians. Also, the Albanians who fought to liberate Greece in Morea did not fight for Hellenism, they fought for the good of all the people of the Balkans, including the Macedonians. There was also that one-third of the Albanian population who remained faithful to Christianity that equally suffered the injustices of the Greek clergy and the Ottoman authorities that deserve mention.

flag of the Macedonian rebels of 1876

Chapter Five

Macedonian Rebellion Against Turkish Rule from 1876-1881

In Asia, in the bosom of our tyrant, there is a wild place called Bodrum, which, to the southwest, borders on a sea, and, to the northeast, is surrounded by high mountains. In that barren, rocky and sparsely populated land, there is a fortress, surrounded by high stone walls. Here is where our worthy sons are living! It was with great trepidation that we approached the ugly facade of the fortress, which boasted, as it were, that it held our dear children within its cold stone walls. The profound silence inside and outside the fortress filled our hearts with sadness and our eyes with tears. After long pleading, an order was given to let our patriots out to see us. In the tomb-like stillness, a great noise was made by the rattling chains. It was then that we beheld a bunch of people that tottered along, led by a man covered in a black tattered cassock. We recognized the reeling black figure of Father Kozma, the Abbot of the Lesnovo Monastery, and his group of disciples, who had chosen the way of Christ, our rebels, not by their faces, but by the few words they said in Bulgarian. They came towards us calmly, but their faces were withered and we lost heart and burst out sobbing. Then the unfortunate martyrs smiled at us in orda to console us. It was a smile not caused by joy, but by suffering, and by the rueful realization that their appearance had brought on our sorrow and our sobbing.

What a mournful spectacle! Half-naked and clad in tatters, these Macedonian lions told us about the suffering they had gone through and about the barbarous tortures (the vice, the splinters, the hot eggs under the armpits, the gallows, and the red-hot irons under the armpits and in the mouth) as they stamped the earth with their feet. But that was not stamping, but the thumping of dry legs! Their heart-rending voices were hollow, despite their efforts to speak more loudly and forcefully, and sounded more like the voice of a man drowning in the depths of the sea, becoming fainter and fainter, stifled, as it was, by the waves of salty water.

These martyrs, far away from their own beds and their own country, imprisoned in that wild land and in a hole walled in on all-sides, walk about naked and barefoot, they are in chains and suffer so many privations! They are almost starving! Bread and leeks is their daily food! Appalling! All these privations were recounted with such accuracy, and in such a low and quiet voice, that we were filled with even greater emotion, and, after the sobbing we had been trying to contain for a long time, we could no longer hold back our tears which had hardly stopped. Woe! Had Nero himself seen and heard all this, he would have been moved! Even his callous heart would have been moved by this piteous sight, by the woeful tale of their sufferings and privations! Miraculously, however, their spirit had not been completely broken! 'We are dying for the people, and we are suffering for freedom!' they told us.

(excerpt from a letter by Spiro Stoloyan to the Bulgarian Diplomatic Agent in Istanbul, Nov. 3, 1898, from *Macedonia- Documents*, 1978)

Encouraged by the Russian success in war against the Ottomans that had led to an independent Bulgarian state to the east, Macedonians quickly seized on the opportunity to seek to gain their own freedom. The first organized revolt in this period occurred in 1876 in the Maleshevo region, led by a teacher named Dimitar Pop-Georgiev Berovski from the village of Razlovtsi. He, along with a number of local village priests, secretly planned and organized an uprising of the local peasantry that they firmly believed would spread and would also elicit the aid of sympathetic outsiders. To further the cause, Berovski sold his property in the village of Berovo and used the money to buy weapons and supplies, and he also had a silk banner made with the image of a lion and the word Macedonia embroidered on it for the revolt. Although the Maleshevo district uprising of 1876 failed to achieve more than local village control, it proved to be only the first in a series of local revolts in that period, and it served to stir others in nearby Kresna, and eventually as far away as Prilep and Ohrid in western Macedonia two year later in 1878.

The Kresna Uprising of 1878 took its name from the village of Kresna in eastern Macedonia that, along with the nearby villages of Vlahi and Oshtava, was at the center of the rebellion. The fighting began on October 5th of that year, when a rebel force composed of local peasants and seasoned *haiduti* and their *vovoidi* attacked a Turkish military post on the Struma River where it passes through the Kresna Gorge. After a fierce battle lasting for many hours the Turkish forces surrendered and over a hundred were taken prisoner.

From there the rebellion quickly spread to neighboring villages and regions along the Struma and into the valley of the Mesta, until it included the districts of Melnik, Petrich, Razlovtsi and Nevrokop. While there were plenty of volunteers from among the Macedonian villagers, a lack of arms, supplies and organization soon led to problems for the rebels. The leadership of the revolt consisted of an assortment of local outlaw chieftains, including the seasoned fighter Ilyo Voivoda, Macedonian volunteers from the victorious Russian army and a number of foreign adventurers, including Serbs, Montenegrins, Greeks, and others such as Adam Kalmykov, an ex-Cossack officer, and Luis Voitkewicz, a Polish teacher working in Veles, Macedonia.

During the winter lull in hostilities, the local Bishop Natanail, with help from a Herzegovinian officer by the name of Miroslav Hubmayer, and a member of the Turnovo revolutionary committee in Bulgaria, Stefan Stambolov, who saw the future of the rebellion in the organization of a series of similar committees after the successful model employed by the Bulgarian rebel leader Levsky, tried to prepare the rebel forces to defend against a spring offensive planned by the Turks. However, by May of 1879 Russian troops withdrew from the nearby town of Gorna Dzhumaya to fulfill a provision of the Treaty of Berlin signed by the Russian government. By the early summer of 1879 a well-armed and numerically superior Turkish force, with material assistance from Britain and other European allies, then recovered Kresna and the villages of the Karshiyak region of the Struma Valley, which put an end to the local rebellion. The rebels had pinned much of their hopes on foreign, mainly Russian assistance, which was not to be.

This was not, however, the end of rebellion in Macedonia. Other would-be rebels in the Ohrid, Debar, Kichevo, Krushevo and Prilep regions continued preparations for an uprising. These included active rebel bands in the Prilep region under the command of the voivoda Spiro Tsurne, in Kichevo a cheta led by Mihaile Todorov, and a band led by Dimo and Mihail Chakrev which roamed Mariovo, Selechka, Pelagonia and Krushevo. A number of these leaders met at the Slepche Monastery in January of 1881 in order to plan the uprising in more detail.

Unfortunately, a Greek church leader alerted the Turks, who began searching possible suspects. Eventually, in March of 1881, they caught one of the conspirators, Hristo Popov, transporting hidden guns in a cart. He resisted Turkish torturers, but another member of the group, Yane Samardzhiyata, who was arrested after him, revealed all he knew.

Soon the jails began to fill with members of the conspiracy as well as many innocent people who simply had the misfortune of being associated with members of the group. Some of those arrested suffered terribly. Mercia McDermott in *Freedom or Death* (1978, 56-57) described the cruel treatment of one rebel:

Hristo Popov was incarcerated in a dolap - a tiny grave-like cell, the low ceiling of which did not permit a man to stand upright. There was no window - only a small hole in the lower part of the thick iron-bound door - and the wretched man spent eight day and nights kneeling by the hole in his own filth, struggling to avoid suffocation. The conditions under which the rest of the prisoners were kept were not much better. ..

While most of those arrested were eventually released for lack of solid evidence to convict them, others such as Hristo Popov and the unfortunate brother of Bishop Natanail (Unlike the bishop, he had not managed to flee in time and suffered such abuse that he was forever after mentally unbalanced.) were sentenced to life in prison. Other conspirators received lesser sentences of five years each.

The rebels in the mountains also suffered heavy losses in battles with the Turks later that year. The vojvoda Spiro Tsurne was killed near Kumanovo, and the Chakrev Brothers were surrounded by a detachment of Turkish soldiers and bashi-bozouks while on a visit to Prilep at Easter time and burned to death in the house where they had taken refuge. Other rebel leaders, such as the voivodas Mihail and Angel, were also killed in battles with the Turks. The remaining rebels had no choice but to abandon the fight.

Macedonian rebel leader Dimitar P. Berovski

Chapter Six

Lead up to the Ilinden Uprising of 1903

"This people must be roused from the five-century-old sleep that has made the Macedonian rather thick on the subject of human rights. And, if not the whole people, then at least part of it; and then, instead of Mr Chakurov looking for forty men, four hundred would be looking for him, to put themselves under his banner. If this doesn't happen, and a rising is proclaimed, it will be tragic for the people, and woe betide the person responsible. It is tragic because the youngest forces will be lost to no purpose (some in prison, others on the gallows), innocent Macedonian women will be abandoned to the bestial and cruel passions of savages, and, finally, children of five and old men of seventy will be abandoned to the yataghans of Asiatics, and for all this the person responsible will be answerable to his own conscience, and to the people and to history. Is the Kyustendil Committee of the same mind as Chakurov? I am addressing myself to you as well, because, according to Chakurov's statements, he was sent by your committee (and, in addition, he told other people that he was sent by the chief one) He came over to proclaim a rising - and with whom, and with

what?! With 30 guns, seven bombs, and three boxes of dynamite! Did his Lordship - in the event of his finding 40 people and carrying out his task - think about the consequences? Did those who sent him foresee that they would be spattered, if not drowned, in the blood of their enslaved brothers? What kind of witticism is this? What kind of idea for liberation? One man with forty people to proclaim a rising!... What kind of a plan is this? Can it be that some Bulgarian Odysseus has been born? Or are we to deceive one another, to deceive the ordinary people until they despair and lose the people's confidence? Did His Grace believe his own words, what he said verbally and in letters to G. Ivanov: "I'll raise an internal rebellion, and as soon as the banner is unfurled, then Russia, Oh glorious Russia, will fly into Macedonia on the spot, and there you are - we're free"??!! Is that what he thinks, is that what you think and finally, is that how we have to educated the rebels? If you feed rebels with such empty hopes, then you must realize that even the most outstanding hero will at times fall into utter despair. No, lies don't help at all - especially not this one. Try to root out this weakness (this waiting for help from the Russian tyrant) from even the most deluded coward, then in its place the unconquerable power of self reliance and resolve will be reborn, and then, believe me, every single person will fight to the finish with the greatest eagerness. Work, work, gentlemen, only let it be a little more in line with common sense."

(Gotse Delchev, in a letter dated October 17, 1895)

While emigre Macedonian students were fighting Greek and Bulgarian propaganda and shoring up Western support, an historic moment inside Macedonia was about to unfold. It was October 23rd, 1893 in Salonica when two high school teachers, Damjan Gruev and Anton Dimitrov, together with Petar Pop Arsov, a former editor of the political journal *Loza* and Hristo Tatarchev, a doctor, came together in bookshop owner Ivan Nikolov's house for an informal meeting. The main point of discussion was the plight of the Macedonian people and what to do about it. As word got around a committee was formed, more Macedonians became involved and a second, more formal meeting was held on February 9th, 1894. The topics of discussion included the drafting of a constitution to guide the committee. By the end of the meeting the committee made the following resolutions:

1. The committee will be revolutionary in nature and will remain secret.

2. Its revolutionary activities will be confined to inside Macedonia's borders.

3. Irrespective of nationality or religion, any Macedonian can become a member of the committee.

The committee also set the following objectives for itself, which were later ratified at the first Revolutionary Congress held in Resen in August 1894:

1. Destroy the Ottoman system of government.

2. Remain an "independent" organization.

3. Seek Macedonian autonomy.

The organization became known as the *Vnatreshna* (Internal) *Makedonska* (Macedonian) *Revolutsionerna* (Revolutionary) *Organizatsia* (Organization), VMRO (IMRO). Being clandestine in nature, IMRO had some difficulty recruiting new members, but within a year or so its influence extended beyond Salonica and into the rest of Macedonia. Initially the organization was more ideological and less practical, the majority of its recruits being teachers, most of whom taught at the Exarchate schools inside Macedonia. To rally the population at large the organization needed to educate the people so that they would understand and support IMRO's objectives. For that they needed charismatic leaders who would be able to explain the cause in terms that the people could understand, and leaders who were free to travel without too much interference from the authorities. The man who answered that call was Gotse Delchev, a man of remarkable vision, a father to the Macedonian revolution and the soul of the movement. (To learn more about the IMRO leadership, read Michael Radin's book, *IMRO and the Macedonian Question*).

Gotse was a realist and at the same time an idealist, who loved people, hated tyranny and saw the world ideally as a place of many cultures living together in peace. Gotse was convinced that in order for a revolution to be successful it had to be a "moral revolution" of the mind, heart and soul of an enslaved people. People needed to recognize that they were human beings with rights and freedoms and not slaves. With that in mind Gotse set out to build a revolutionary consciousness among the Macedonian people, and thus set the revolutionary wheels in motion. Gotse's role as undisputed leader of the IMRO was established during the Salonica Congress of 1896, after which the IMRO began mass organizing. Gotse's ability to "listen and learn" brought him close to the problems of ordinary people who wanted freedom but who also wanted to preserve their religion, culture and way of life. With Gotse's practical understanding of this, the IMRO's strategy became one of "giving the people what they want" to win them over. Initially the strategy worked well and won the IMRO much of the support it needed.

By 1896 the IMRO was able to exert such influence that it acted as a state within a state, taking over administrative positions from the Ottomans, leading boycotts against Ottoman institutions and offering isolated villages protection from brigands. In time IMRO operatives were able to penetrate Ottoman economic, educational and even judicial functions. The downside of "giving the people what they want" was that it opened the doors for Bulgarian infiltration. By their arrogant attitude and the use of the Greek language, it was easy to recognize Greek influence. However, Bulgarian influence was not as easily recognized. While the Greeks cared nothing about Macedonian affairs and loathed the Macedonian language, the Bulgarians were a part of Macedonian affairs and spoke the Macedonian language readily. By far the greatest Bulgarian infiltration into Macedonian affairs took place in Sofia among the pechalbari or migrant workers.

As mentioned earlier, the cosmopolitan lifestyle in Sofia, a far cry from life in the village, seduced some Macedonians, so that they fell prey to Bulgarian propaganda, which resulted in the formation of the "External Macedonian Revolutionary Organization"; better known as the "Supreme Macedonian Committee." This organization was formed in Sofia in March of 1895. Gotse Delchev called it the "Trojan Horse" of the IMRO. The initial membership consisted of emigrant Macedonian nationalists, but in time officers from the Bulgarian State

Army took over the leadership. The objective, on the surface of this devious organization termed "Vrhovist" (Supremacist) by IMRO, was to fight for Macedonia's independence, by armed intervention in an aggressive revolutionary manner. It's true nature, however, concealed from the people was to undermine the IMRO by subordinating its central committee to its own "Supremacist" directives. This, and the fact that Vrhovism masqueraded itself as "Macedonian patriotism" in the eyes of the Macedonian people, very much disturbed Gotse Delchev. True to his nature of keeping an open mind, Delchev, along with Gruev, took a trip to Sofia in hopes of reconciling their differences with the Vrhovists, but came back thoroughly disillusioned. Instead of receiving a handshake on March 20th, 1896, Gotse was informed that Bulgaria would no longer support the IMRO and all finances and arms would be cut off. From here on the Vrhovists would decide what actions the IMRO would take inside Macedonia. This was indeed an attempt by the Vrhovists to usurp control of the IMRO. Disappointed, but not discouraged, Gotse turned to "Mother Russia" for assistance, but there too he found no welcome reception. Russia had no interest in helping the IMRO, because there were no advantages to gain from liberating Macedonia, given Russia's current relations with the Western Powers.

Due to IMRO's popularity, strength and ability to recognize a "Trojan Horse", the Bulgarian-led organization failed to achieve its true objectives. After that it resorted to violent attacks and assassination attempts with the aim of eliminating the entire IMRO structure and its leadership. It used armed interventions in order to provoke Ottoman reprisals against innocent village peasants and put the blame on IMRO. By selective propaganda to villify the Ottomans in the eyes of the world, the Bulgarian-led organization hoped to provoke a Great Power intervention to weaken the Ottomans and at the same time create a climate for a Bulgarian invasion ro "liberate" the oppressed Macedonians.

In the meantime both Delchev and Gruev were promoted to the rank of "District Inspector of Schools" in their employment, allowing them to travel more freely and with less suspicion by the authorities. Using inspection tours as cover, they were able to find new ways to purchase and smuggle arms into Macedonia. They also had more opportunities to address the Macedonian villagers and establish personal contacts with the village chiefs. Many people flocked to hear what these patriots and potential saviors had to say. Unfortunately, lecturing out in the open placed IMRO leaders at greater risk from spies. As a result, on one occasion Gotse was arrested by the Turkish authorities and spent 26 days in jail in May of 1896. When the Turks couldn't find anything to charge him with, Gotse was released.

Bulgarian influence was not limited to Vrhovist actions alone. Bulgarian undercover agents were dispatched to Salonica to spy on IMRO activities and report back to the Bulgarian state authorities. The Bulgarian Exarchate Church also had its own agenda and continued to rally the Macedonian youth to its own cause. When it seemed like the IMRO was unassailable, the Vrhovists attempted to infiltrate the IMRO leadership itself, which in time brought them some success. Bulgarian interference in IMRO policies caused hardships and internal squabbles among executive committee members and eventually caused the organization to split into hostile factions. This undermined the IMRO's credibility within and outside Macedonia.

The Vrhovists badly wanted to provoke Turkey, so that they could "liberate" Macedonia, but the Great Powers, especially Russia and Britain didn't accept that and saw their actions as provocative and dangerous. While the Vrhovist leadership claimed it would reduce its activities, its armed wing, however, penetrated into and captured parts of eastern Macedonia. This adventure only lasted about two days, and it became clear as to "who was who" and the true Vrhovist agenda was exposed. After that the IMRO gave the Vrhovists a stern warning to stay out of Macedonia. To use Delchev's words, "Whoever works for the unification with Greece or Bulgaria is a good Greek or Good Bulgarian but NOT a good Macedonian." After that, while the IMRO worked for a "Macedonia for the Macedonians" the Bulgarian Supreme Committee openly worked for a "Macedonia for the Bulgarians". The IMRO leadership strove to purge the IMRO of the Vrhovist infiltration. The IMRO constitution was rewritten to exclude Vrhovist demands but it was still able to give the Macedonian people what they wanted. The IMRO leadership, without much success, made its own attempts to challenge the Vrhovist Supreme Committee at home. During frequent trips to Sofia, attempts were made to rally dissident emigrant forces inside Bulgaria to the IMRO cause.

While the Vrhovists were plotting against the IMRO and its work for the Macedonian people, a new menace was brewing from the south. On April 9th, 1897 armed Greek bands began to aggressively cross into Macedonia. The Turks protested this action to the Great Powers, but the Greeks denied responsibility, insisting that they were not Greek soldiers but the Macedonian cheti. It wasn't long before the Turks took the offensive, drove the Greeks out and pursued them inside Greece. When the Turks were about to overrun the entire country the Great Powers intervened on Greece's behalf to once again save her. The Greek government responsible for the invasion fell from grace, and when a new government was elected, it agreed to pay a hefty fine, which consisted of four million Turkish pounds, as well as giving up Thessaly to the Turks. In addition to losing land, Greece had to relinquish control of her own finances to the Great Powers to ensure prompt payment of the fine. The Great Powers, without German support, forced the Sultan to accept the offer and sign a peace agreement. The Germans never forgave the Greeks for lying to them about their actions in the Ottoman Empire. The Germans at that time were responsible for certain government functions of the Turkish Empire. Outside of Greek brigand actions, for the moment at least, Greece was not a direct threat to the IMRO.

The IMRO demonstrated its leadership capability by organizing Macedonia into seven revolutionary districts (Salonica, Serres, Strumitsa, Shtip, Skopje, Bitola and Edrene (the Dardanelles). It also demonstrated certain weaknesses. Having allied itself with the poor village peasants and striving to refrain from outside obligations and debts, The IMRO found itself lacking needed resources. The IMRO committees were unable to raise all the funds necessary to finance their campaigns. While the leadership turned a blind eye, the local commanders resorted to kidnapping rich landowners, merchants and even foreign dignitaries for ransom. Kidnappings did not exclude foreign missionaries, such as the American Miss Stone, who fell into the hands of Yane Sandanski's cheta. Moved by the plight of her captors, Miss Helen Stone voluntarily made sure that the ransom was paid in full.

This lack of financial resources, mostly due to unfriendly relations with the Vrhovist Supreme Command in Sofia, meant that the IMRO continued to lack the necessary arsenal to wage war. Subordination to Bulgarian demands was out of the question, so Gotse had to look elsewhere to get his weapons. Efforts were made to purchase weapons from Greece, Albania and even from the Turks themselves, but without much success. By 1897 the situation was getting desperate, so the IMRO leadership resorted to purchasing from the black market, and even stealing weapons. One such purchase was made from the Bulgarian military. The military allowed the sale of outdated guns, but later refused to sell cartridges, fearing the weapons might be turned against them. In October 1900 Vasil Chakalarov, a local chieftain in the Lerin/Kostur regions, who spoke Greek, dressed up as an Albanian pretending to be from Ianitsa. He was successful in purchasing some weapons from Athens. Later attempts by others, however, were not so successful. On one occasion a translator betrayed the purchasers to the Turkish consul on the advice of a Greek priest. After that the Turks trusted this translator and made him a sergeant in their gendarmerie. He served the Turks well and brought them considerable success in their "search and destroy" missions, until he discovered he could make even more money by taking bribes before turning people in. As a result of this man's actions many band members, from a number of villages, were killed.

The lack of sufficient arms brought home the realization that the struggle for liberation was going to be a long one. Here again, Gotse and the IMRO leadership proved their worth by adopting a policy of self-arming. With a little bit of skill in weapons manufacture, learned from the Armenian Revolutionaries, IMRO set up a number of munitions factories in remote areas, capable of producing homemade bombs and other explosives. Unfortunately, in 1900 during a Turkish raid on one of these factories, Damyan Gruev was arrested by the authorities and imprisoned in Bitola. He was not released until April of 1903.

Despite all their efforts to obtain weapons, the Macedonian cheti never had enough guns, but they did have plenty of courage to make up for it, which in time put fear in the Turkish hearts. As IMRO grew beyond its formational stage, it began to recruit, equip and train fighters.

Volunteers were recruited mainly from the villages, young men who were willing to fight for freedom. Especially those who were in trouble with the law were armed and recruited into active duty. Such men were already eager to attack Turks and steal from them.

Experienced outlaws were already actively engaged in attacks on Turks in order to steal from them. They were also admired for their courage and their ability to live as free men. Many were highly skilled in the art of war, knew how to live in the open, how to ambush and how to hide. They were the men who taught the young Macedonian recruits to fight and win. The remainder of the IMRO recruits were reservists who lived at home, only called to duty as required. Each reservist was expected to purchase and secure his own rifle and ammunition. Recruitment was carried out in utmost secrecy. Women were also enlisted into the Macedonian revolution, but their role was usually limited to cooking, washing, mending and nursing the wounded. Many, however, took on dangerous assignments, acting as couriers, carrying messages and even arms and ammunition, and some extraordinary few even joined chetas as armed combatants.

The primary role of a fighter was to defend the people from Turkish and brigand attacks. The cheti consisted of about five to ten men, organized for rapid mobilization and quick response. The goal was to have one cheta responsible for a village, preferably their own. The leader of each cheta was chosen for his ability to lead men, and more so, for the people's confidence in him to protect their village. To respond quickly, the cheta had to be familiar with the village's terrain and escape routes. To maintain secrecy, all orders were given by word of mouth.

The IMRO organizing campaign managed to elude the Turkish authorities for a long time. However, an unfortunate discovery of some explosives eventually led the Turkish military on a series of "search and destroy" missions. Their conduct, unfortunately, was less than honorable when the soldiers began torturing innocent people and burning properties in order to obtain confessions. The chetas responded by ambushing these Turkish units in guerrilla raids designed to meet the enemy before they could enter villages and thus prevent them from doing harm. This, however, did not always work, so some of the chetas engaged in retaliatory activities for crimes already committed. Although poorly armed and vastly outnumbered (sometimes there were as few as one Macedonian for every ten Turks), the cheti fought fierce battles and gained legendary reputations among both the Turks and the Macedonians.

Unfortunately, as the Ottoman authorities became more aware of IMRO's intentions the Turkish army and militia units were reinforced. At about the same time the Exarchate, suspecting IMRO affiliation, began to dismiss Macedonian teachers in large numbers. Even though most Macedonian teachers were not happy working for the Exarchate, they had used the schools as a means of promoting IMRO's aims. They frequently gave lectures, taught Macedonian patriotic songs, canvassed among the people, etc. This was a blow to the IMRO. A more severe blow, however, came in April of 1897 in what was termed the "Goluchowski-Muraviev Agreement." This was an agreement drawn up by Tsar Nikolas II of Russia and Emperor Franz Joseph of Austria concerning the future of the remainder of the Ottoman Empire. In part, the agreement stated that at some future time the Macedonian territory would be divided equally between Greece, Serbia and Bulgaria. In other words, when the Great Powers got their fill of Turkey and abandoned her, Greece, Serbia and Bulgaria were welcome to Macedonia. This indeed was bad news and, as history has show, it was devastating for IMRO and disastrous for the Macedonian people as well.

In about 1898 the Bulgarian Exarchate, instructed by the Bulgarian Prime Minister, created the Vrhovist or Supremacist organization inside Macedonia. Based in Salonica, and known as the "Revolutionary Brotherhood", it in turn began to form its own cheti. While pretending to be part of IMRO, the purpose of this organization was to carry out terrorist activities and, in the eyes of the world, discredit the real IMRO. By the year 1900 IMRO's enemies were growing in number and expanding their activities. To add to IMRO's woes it was discovered that the Vrhovists had dispatched six assassins to attempt to murder Delchev and Sandanski (a legendary cheta chieftain affectionately known as the "Tsar of Pirin").

The Vrhovist cheti were actively sowing terror in the Macedonian coutryside, provoking the Turk to act. Although never proven, it was alleged that the Vrhovist leaders were also giving the Turks information to have members of the IMRO arrested, destroying munitions depots, and often leading to the torture, rape and murder of people who fell into their hands.

The Turks themselves also used subterfuge. Several Greek spies were killed in one incident and the IMRO was blamed. As a result of this, many organizers we rounded up and arrested. In reality, however, it was Turkish begs who had committed the crimes, as was later discovered. The same begs were seen attacking Turkish tax collectors. Failing to assassinate Delchev and Sandanski the six assassins, in frustration, turned to attacking people, burning down village homes, stealing money and claiming it to be the work of the IMRO. Several important leaders, including the famous "Marko Lerinski" (the "Tsar of Lerin"), were attacked by Vrhovists during this period.

The IMRO, however, responded. Yane Sandanski and his cheta were ready when a group of Vrhovists entered his region in September 1902, and he sent them scurrying for home. The Turks did the rest by dispersing the remaining Vrhovist insurgent bands in Macedonia in November of the same year. The disturbances and civil strife were enough to convince the Ottoman Turks that yet another uprising may be imminent and that they should take action to prevent it. As usual, violence was answered with more violence. The Turks initiated a wide-scale campaign of "search and destroy" missions, causing serious damage and sowing terror among the villagers. In addition to regular Turkish troops, the Ottomans now enlisted reserves from their Albanian Muslim allies. Every bridge, railway grade and tunnel was guarded. Villages often had troops garrisoned in them. While the Turkish troops would engage in direct combat with the cheti, and then would retire to their barracks, the Albanian reservists avoided direct confrontations and preferred to join the *bashi-bozouks* (armed Muslim civilians) in pillaging and plundering the villages.

The local police, recruited from the Albanian Gheg Muslim community, had a vested interest in disorder. They thrived on lawlessness. It was crucial to their employment. They rarely engaged in policing and their meager pay was always in arrears, so they readily accepted bribes to supplement their income. Both the Patriarchate and Exarchate were known to bribe the local police in order to allow Greek and Bulgarian brigands to function freely.

To make a bad situation worse, at the end of August 1902, the Vrhovists again showed up in Macedonia uninvited and began to issue orders directly to the local voivodas to commence the rebellion. According to Vrhovist plans the rebellion was ordered to begin September 20th, 1902. This was news to the IMRO leadership. This latest bold Vrhovist drew an immediate response from respected local leaders, including Vasil Chakalarov in the Lerin/Kostur region. Chakalarov was a respected chieftain who managed to dissuade people from joining the Vrhovists.

The Vrhovists, however, were not so easily put off. They began a campaign to publicly discredit Chakalarov and others, accusing them of cowardice for not wanting to fight. When that still didn't work, Chakalarov was personally called a thief, alleging that he had stolen a fortune from the Vrhovist money allocated for purchasing arms. Fortunately the Macedonian people knew that Chakalarov was an honest man. They also knew that the Vrhovists didn't contribute any funds for the purchas of arms. Isolated, unable to start a rebellion, the Vrhovists tucked in their tails and went off elsewhere to stir up trouble.

This latest Vrhovist action did not go unnoticed by the Turks, however, and put the IMRO in a difficult position. The Vrhovists had wanted to get the IMRO into a fight with the Turkish army for a long time, but so far were unsuccessful. It would not be long, unfortunately, before their wishes would come true. The Vrhovists believed that an all-out fight with the IMRO would weaken Turkey enough to make a Bulgarian invasion possible. They encouraged the leaders of the cheti to "start the insurrection and Bulgaria would finish it" for them. "Bulgaria has hundreds of thousands of troops standing by and will come to your rescue as soon as the first shot is fired," is what the Vrhovists were preaching to the Macedonian chieftains and people.

The IMRO knew that its fighters were not ready for direct

confrontation with the Turkish military. They also knew, however, that, fight or not, the Turkish military was going to destroy Macedonia village by village over time. The Vrhovists, on the other hand, could not be trusted for their help, because they had no intention of honouring their promises. Their actions had made that very clear in the past. In either case, the IMRO had no choice but to act soon. The "search and destroy" missions were putting many innocent people in harms way, including women and children. Local informants, and Greek and Bulgarian brigands did not hesitate to inform on the villagers, especially if they had old grudges against them. On many occasions Patriarchate and Exarchate brigands (essentially hired goons) were put out of action by the cheti, which made their benefactors angry, who in turn informed on the villagers.

Brigands were hired to harass and sow terror among the villagers to get them to change allegiance from one church to another. The local *cheti* were fierce fighters and fought gallantly when it came to protecting their villages, but they were always undermanned and poorly armed. As much as they may have wanted to, they were not capable of standing up to the large, well-equipped Turkish military. The Turkish forces, on the other hand, were often savage and brutal and were open to bribes. The poor people who couldn't afford bribes fared the worst. Some say it was cause for less punishment to produce a rifle than not to have one at all. Some resorted to purchasing rifles and turning them in just so that they could receive a lesser punishment. On many occasions the houses of those suspected of aiding the cheti were burned to the ground. The Turks did not hesitate to even jail old women accused of that crime. Historical accounts show that during the height of the search and destroy activities the jails in Macedonia were filled beyond capacity. In fact, a Salonica jail with a capacity for 500 was holding 900 prisoners during this period. (Some were held in the infamous White Tower). There is an old Macedonian saying: "There is nothing worse than being locked up in a Turkish jail."

On January 31, 1903 the Turks declared the IMRO illegal and sought to destroy it completely. This bad news for the IMRO gave the Vrhovists the necessary momentum they needed to become a wedge between those in the IMRO who wanted an immediate uprising and those who believed that an uprising at this point in time would be suicide. Gotse Delchev was against this "willing sacrifice" and was hoping to find a better solution, but time was running out.

A second Salonica Congress, dominated by the Vrhovists, was organized in February of 1903. Delchev and most of the IMRO's loyal supporters did not attend. A resolution was reached, but not ratified by the regional committees, that an uprising would take place on Ilinden, on the 2nd of August, 1903. To further weaken the Turks, the Vrhovists staged or encouraged a number of bombings and terrorist attacks during this period. The Salonica to Istanbul (Constantinople) railway line was bombed on March 18th, as was the Salonica Ottoman bank a month later. This did not weaken the Turks as expected, but instead brought more Turkish troops into Macedonia and further escalated the violence against innocent civilians. If that was not enough, the sudden rise in violence against Ottoman institutions was not well-received by European investors and businessmen, who had viewed Ottoman Macedonia as a safe place for investment. The few lone voices in London, calling for Macedonian support, were quickly drowned out by the many voices calling for the detention of the terrorists.

Tragically, the Turks killed Gotse Delchev in the village of Banitsa on May 4th, 1903, a day after the IMRO Smilevo Congress began. The purpose of the Smilevo Congress was to review the resolutions from the Vrhovist dominated Salonica Congress held earlier the same year. Damjan Gruev (a native of Smilevo) chaired the Congress and tried hard to present the situation realistically by presenting the arguments for and against an early uprising. When the matter was put to a vote, however, the majority declared themselves in favour of an uprising. With these words, "better an end with horrors than horrors without end," Gruev also voted in support of the Ilinden planned rebellion. From here on there was no turning back.

A general staff was elected with Gruev as the head and preparations for the uprising were begun. In due time plans were made, a military strategy prepared, weapons, medical supplies and foodstuffs were requisitioned and stock piled. Cheti were further organized and trained. On July 26, 1903, by a dispatch to the Great Powers via the British vice-consul in Bitola, the General Staff formally announced the uprising. Then, on July 28, 1903 IMRO dispatched mounted couriers to all the sub-districts with the message: "Let the uprising begin". On the same day the General Staff informed the Ottoman Director of Railways to warn travelers to choose a different mode of transportation in order to avoid being hurt. Despite the odds against them, the brave people of Macedonia courageously rose up against their oppressors. They knew all too well that the fight that they had been forced into might not bring them what they wanted. They chose to fight, in any event, for their freedom. Freedom, after so many centuries of slavery, was valued above life itself. That, however, did not convince the Great Powers to aid the rebels. Macedonia, for a second time within a quarter century, was to be left on its own in its fight against the Ottoman Empire. The betrayal of their cause in1878 would appear minor in comparison to what was to come.

a Macedonian rebel band from Enidzhe Vardar- 1903

Chapter Seven
The Ilinden Uprising

Lo, a dark cloud came appearing
From the land of Macedonia,
Came from Banitsa near Serres.
There three hundred guns have thundered,
There three hundred men have fallen.
And the first gun when it thundered
Pierced the heart of Gotse Delchev.
Falling, cried he to his cheta: '
O druzhina, true, united,
O druzhina, true, assembled,
When, my comrades, you are passing,

When through Kukush you are passing,

And my mother comes to meet you,

And she questions you about me:

"Where, oh, where is my son Delchev?"

You will answer, you will tell her:

"Granny dear, thy son has married,

He has married Macedonia,

Married Banitsa near Serres,

With the black earth as his chosen,

Slender rifles as his sisters,

Two twin pistols as his brothers,

And black ravens as his kinsfolk."

(Macedonian folk song)

A few miles outside of the picturesque central mountain town of Krushevo there is a small rocky knoll known as Mechkin Kamen (the Bear's Rock). This lovely, peaceful forested hillside is sacred ground to all Macedonians. For it was on this site in mid-August of 1903 that a group of Macedonian rebels chose to fight to the death rather than surrender to the advancing Turkish army. While that day signaled the beginning of the end for the rebellion against Turkish rule that has become known as the Ilinden or St. Elijah's Day Uprising, the brave actions of the men who died there and in similar combat all around Macedonia that month and in the month's to come, will never be forgotten. It will forever after serve as a reminder of what Macedonians are capable of sacrificing for their freedom.

With the tragic death of the movement's guiding light, Gotse Delchev, in a skirmish with Turkish troops in the village of Banitsa on the 4th of May, 1903, the clamor for action, for a rebellion, for an end to the unacceptable conditions of life in Turkish occupied Macedonia at that time became more than the leadership of the Internal Macedonian

Revolutionary Organization could withstand. Young men all across the land were volunteering to follow the example of Gotse Delchev and risk all in a bid for freedom. And one group of young patriots, just days prior to Gotse's death, had fulfilled a solemn pledge they had made to each other, to demonstrate their desperate desire for freedom to the whole world; Europe, the Turkish Empire and their own enslaved people through the most desperate of acts.

They carried out their plan at the end of April of 1903 in the city of Salonica. Here is a brief account of the actions of "the Gemidzhi" or "Boatmen", a group of Macedonian "suicide bombers", young men whose fanatical suicidal actions can rarely be found elsewhere in European Christian history. Mercia McDermott (1978, 354-355) describes the rather spectacular first attack of the "Gemidzhi":

On the morning of April 28, Pavel Shatev bought a ticket, and boarded the [French ship] Guadalquivir with a suitcase full of dynamite, which he exploded as the ship left port. The result was eminently satisfactory: all the passengers and crew, including Pavel himself, were saved and ferried ashore, together with their luggage, but the ship was a total loss and continued to burn all day and all night in a most spectacular manner, watched by the entire population of Salonika.

The attacks continued as later that same day Dimitar Mechev, Iliya Truchkov and Milan Arsov, set off explosive charges on the railway line on the outskirts of Salonica. Fortunately, again, no one was killed, but they managed to derail and damage in inbound train.

On the evening of April 29 Kosta Kirkov set off charges that succeeded in destroying the main water and gas lines into the city, causing a citywide blackout and leaving the citizens without water. At this sign Dimitar Mechev and Ilija Truchkov attempted to blow up the main gasworks, but they were caught in the act by a guard and were forced to flee into town. As they made their way they threw dozens of bombs in every direction until eventually Turkish troops and police surrounded and killed them.

Other members of the conspiracy also leapt into action when the city was plunged into darkness by the destruction of the gas main.The conspirator Ortse detonated huge dynamite bundles buried under the

Ottoman Bank that sent the building tumbling. At the same time Milan Arsov and Georgi Bogdanov tossed bombs into an open-air theatre and a cafe, and Vladimir Pingov attempted to set fire to an inn. Pingov was killed by police, but Arsov and Bogdanov escaped.

The attacks continued the next day as Kosta Kirkov attempted to blow up the telegraph office, and Tsvetko Trajkov made an attempt to assassinate the mayor. Both died in the attempt, and the Ottoman Bank bomber, Ortse was killed that same day by Turkish troops who surrounded him in his rooming house. By the end of the day six of the conspirators lay dead and the remaining for were all under arrest.

Mercia McDermott (1978, 355), however, describes the remarkable response of one Turkish officer when Ortse's body was carried out of the house:

...some enraged soldiers wanted to mutilate it with their bayonets, but their commander who had earlier besieged Mechev and Truchkov, stopped them, and, pointing at the corpse, said: 'This is the way to die for your country. Let this dead man be an example to you of how one should sacrifice oneself and die for one's country. ...

The IMRO leadership met in the eastern Macedonian town of Smilevo at the end of July of 1903 in order to finalize plans and preparations for the rebellion that could no longer be delayed. The course of events had reached a point of no return. Wisely or foolishly, ready or not, the organization that had begun with a meeting of a small group in Salonica in October of 1893 and that had grown to include organized groups in nearly ever village and town of Macedonia, was no longer able to delay a general Macedonian uprising against the Turkish Empire. And so, the date was set at the meeting in Smilevo and a proclamation was sent out, announcing this. It read in part:

Death is a thousand times better than a life of misery. The day has been decided when the people of all Macedonia and Odrin must come out gun in hand to meet the enemy, and that day is 20th July 1903 (2nd August according to the new calendar)... Down with tyranny! Long live the people, long live freedom!

The rebellion took the Turkish authorities completely by surprise.

The network of couriers and communication that had been set up by the IMRO effectively delivered the proclamation issued by the Smilevo meeting to committees throughout the land. Secrecy was strictly maintained and final preparations carefully made. Final instructions were sent out on August 1st from the General Staff of the IMRO, and on August 2nd action commenced. The element of surprise proved itself to be one key to the initial success of the rebels.

Some of the fiercest fighting on the 2nd of August took place in the Bitola region of central Macedonia. The region had been divided into a number of revolutionary committee districts. These included the Krushevo, Gjavato, Bitola Plain, Demirhisar, Resen and Lower Prespa districts. Each saw fierce combat in the opening days of the uprising.

Eight well-armed and organized chetas or bands under the command of Nikola Karev staged a full-scale attack on the central mountain town of Krushevo. After a two day battle the Turkish troops in Krushevo retreated; they fled their posts to carry their unhappy news back to their superiors in the lowland towns.

The people and the rebels danced and sang and celebrated in the streets, and when they were through they established a provisional government. They proclaimed the formation of what has come to be known as the "Krushevo Republic" and they named the respected rebel chieftain, Nikola Karev, as its acting head.

For ten days the flag of the rebel republic flew over Krushevo. For the first time in nearly five centuries the people of the town, the mixed ethnic population of Vlahs, Macedonians, Greeks, and Albanians tasted life without pashas, begs and agas. To the everlasting credit of the revolutionaries, the nearby villages of poor ethnic Turks, settlers from Turkey centuries ago, were assured that they were not the enemy, but were acknowledged as being distinct from the despotic and corrupt Turkish state. In fact, they would be welcomed as citizens in a new, more just and democratic society if the revolution succeeded.

The revolutionary leaders issued the following proclamation to that effect, which became known as the Krushevo Manifesto:

Brothers, countrymen and dear neighbors: we, your known and trusted neighbors from lovely Krushevo and its pleasant villages, of all races and faiths, being no longer able to endure the tyranny of the bloodthirsty inhuman predators who have driven us and you to a beggar's life, today raised our heads and resolve to defend ourselves with guns from our common enemy and to secure our liberty. We wish to make it clear that we are not evil-doers and want to have you understand that we risk our lives because of our tragic circumstances. We will live as free men or die a hero's death.

We do not raise our guns against you. That would be wrong. We will never raise our guns against the peaceful, industrious people who, like ourselves, give their blood away... We have not come to butcher and burn, to pillage and plunder... We have risen up against tyranny and slavery... We sorrow for you as brothers who we know to be slaves like ourselves; slaves of the emperor and the emperor's effendis and pashas, slaves of the rich and powerful, who consume everything in our land... If you are one of us who have not and love the good, if you would share this land with us in the future as worthy sons of our mother Macedonia together, you can aid our cause in some small but important ways, if you will not collaborate with the enemy, nor raise guns against us and if you will cause us no harm.

The holy blessing on our struggle! Long live justice and freedom for all the sons of Macedonia! Long live Macedonia!

After issuing their proclamation, the rebels of Krushevo prepared for battle. They knew that the Turks would return, and there would be a terrible struggle. Ten days later a Turkish army of twenty thousand men arrived at Krushevo. For several days the twelve hundred men in the rebel force held the town until it became clear that further defense would be a costly, futile gesture, and then they retreated into the mountains to fight another day. All retreated, that is, except the band under the command of a Macedonian Vlah chieftain named Pitu Guli, who chose to make a final stand at the Bear's Rock, Mechkin Kamen. His entire band of some forty men would perish that day at Mechkin Kamen, but their memory would live on in stories and songs of the people:

Come brothers, along with me

Over the Vardar to Veles,

From Veles on to Prilep,

From Prilep to Krushevo.

There among the Krushevoans,

Weeping, mourning and suffering

For the loss of homes and loved ones,

There high up on Mechkin Kamen

Stands the warrior Pitu Guli,

Leader of his rebel band.

The Turks cry out allah, allah!

And the komitas ura, ura!

The Turks are falling

And the komitas are singing,

God be with our brave voivoda,

Pitu Guli, valiant hero,

And our pride and glory!

(Macedonian folk song)

The Gjavato district included the villages of Capari, Gjavato and Smilevo and the Bigla mountain; with the village of Smilevo at its center. On the night of August 2nd about two hundred rebels attacked a garrison of about eighty Turkish soldiers in Smilevo, while elsewhere the rebels burned all the houses of the Turkish begs, cut the telephone lines and destroyed the bridges on the road between Bitola and Resen; In the Bufkol region, which was closest to Bitola, they set fire to haystacks to let the people of Bitola know that the battle had begun.

The district of Demirhisar fielded a force of nearly a thousand well-organized and armed men. They attacked the Turkish garrisons in a number of villages and fought a major pitched battle in the village of Karbunica near Kichevo. After this there followed a period of calm that was also a time of intense preparation for future battle.

Prespa was divided into two districts: the Resen (Upper Prespa) and the Prespa (Lower Prespa) districts. Prespa was well-organized, which made it easy to form up a significant number of detachments. One of the major actions of the uprising was the attack on the town of Resen, which was aimed at throwing the enemy into panic and confusion. Most of the Resen area and Lower Prespa was liberated from the Turks by mid-August.

The citizens of Ohrid awoke on the morning of August 2nd to discover street posters written in Turkish, warning the Turkish inhabitants to remain neutral, because the battle which had begun was not directed against them but against the Turkish regime, words to the effect of:

We are taking up arms against tyranny and inhumanity, we are fighting in the name of freedom and humanity... And so for us - all those who suffer in the dark empire of the Sultan - are brothers. Today all the Christian people, and the Turkish peasants as well, are suffering. Our enemy is only the Turkish government . . .

The Ilinden uprising in the Ohrid region was also well-prepared and well-organized. There were secret food stores, secret bakeries, and bullet-casting workshops, as well as a medical aid service and a field hospital. The region was divided into several sub-districts, and the fiercest action took place in Malesia, Upper and Lower Debar, and in Ortakol.

For the first ten days of the uprising skirmishes were frequent in the Ohrid region. Turkish troops were constantly coming in from Albania and Debar and attempting to destroy the villages. Local rebel detachments came to the defense of these settlements. While Albanian outlaw bands, bashi-bazouks, traditional allies of the Turkish authorities, spread terror in the Macedonian villages, the rebels did all they could to defend against them.

On the 2nd of August a force of about five thousand attacked the town of Kichevo, captured it and then left it. One of the bloodiest battles in the Kichevo region took place in the village of Karbunica. Here, instead of guns, the fighters used knives and bayonets in hand-to-hand combat. Thirty rebels and over a hundred Turkish soldiers were killed in the battle. After this fight the Turkish troops no longer used their strength to attack, and most of the Kichevo region was liberated by early September.

The Kostur revolutionary district rivaled Krushevo in the scale of revolt. The region was divided into a number of military sub-districts. Each was composed of village units with their own command and flag. In addition to the central detachments, two regional ones of a hundred and fifty men each were formed. A special unit was also formed, under the command of the district chieftains Lazar Poptrajkov, Vassil Chakalarov and others. These regional commanders issued the following call to arms to the people:

"Today the uprising has been declared. Macedonia has entered the open battle against tyranny... We call on all those who are able to bear arms to join the ranks of the fighters according to constitutional order. Long live Macedonia in its fight for freedom and autonomy . . ."

The following is a report of the leaders of the Ilinden Uprising in the Kostur region sent to all foreign consulates in Bitola, and containing information about rebel operations in Kostur, August 30th /old style/, 1903:

Until July 20 there were between 100 and 150 troops permanently stationed in the villages of Zagorichani, Visheni, Konomladi, Pozdivishta, O Gabresh, Roulya, Dumbeni, Kossinets, Ketram and Kondorabi to hunt down the hitherto small rebel units supporting the Revolutionary Committee. The troops in Visheni were attacked by the leaders V. Chekelarov and Klyashev, together with the village leaders. There were 350 rebels under the leadership of the above-mentioned leaders and commanders. The attack was carried out from all sides, and after a 3-hour battle the troops left the village and took to flight, the darkness of the night saving them from complete extermination. The rebels captured a rifle, cartridges and some food. Five soldiers were killed, while there were no rebel losses. Forty agas from the Turkish village of Zherveni, among whom was a Turkish woman with several children, were captured during the attack against the troops in Visheni. 20 of the worst were killed, while the good ones and the woman with the children were set free. The soldiers who had fled from Visheni spread panic in the town of Kostour with their stories about the red flags, the thunderous cheering, the loud battle songs, and the number of the rebels which they multiplied a hundredfold. The Turks who had hitherto been used to hunt down individuals and small detachments of up to 5-10 men and not big ones of several hundred men each, were startled and frightened. The attack against the troops in Visheni took place about 9.30 p.m., and on the following day ail soldiers from the above-mentioned villages fled to the towns; this was the reason why the rebels did not find a single Turk when they encircled the village of Prekopana in order to defeat the troops stationed there. The rebels from Koreshtata (the western part of the Kostour region) did not manage to attack any troops either, because the latter had fled from these places before the rebels had rallied to the banner. Just a few volleys fired at a distance were enough to confuse and drive the soldiers out of the village of Konomladi.

On July 23 the rebels attacked and captured the small town of Vlaho-Klissoura in the following manner: at 5 o'clock the centre leader Ivan Popov with 80 rebels attacked a force of 150 soldiers coming along the road from the village of Sourovichovo to Klissoura. The soldiers under attack took to flight, leaving 4 cartloads of food and uniforms behind, which were captured by the rebels. They also seized three horses loaded with tents which the rebels burnt. The rebel leaders Chekelarov, Klyashev and Rodov with 300 men, after scattering the 50 soldiers who had held a defensive position at Klissoura, captured it and attacked the troops who were fighting against Popov from the rear. The soldiers, attacked on all sides and frightened by the loud cheering and the singing, beat a disorderly retreat, accompanied by the mayor. So the small town of Klissoura and the mayor's office which was guarded by some 350 soldiers were captured by the rebels. All the government papers in the mayor's office were burnt, and the mayor's own horse was taken. On July 23 the Klissoura pass (Daoula) was closed to the Turks and to postal communications until it was recaptured by the Turks on August 15 which will be described later. In seizing Klissoura the rebels suffered no casualties; on the previous day (July 22) the centre leader Nikola Andreev had lost five men in an attack on the same town. More than 10 Turks had been killed there and the rebels had captured a Mauser rifle with cartridges as well.

On July 24 Lazo P. Traikov (a leader) with 400 rebels from the Dumbeni and Smurdesh centres, attacked the Mohammedan Turkish village of Zherveni. Its location among many Bulgarian [Macedonian] villages was inconvenient because its inhabitants informed the Turkish authorities about the movement of rebel detachments and operations. They also joined the bazhibazouks in their plunder in the Shesteovo and Visheni affairs on February 12, 1902, and on August 3, 1902, respectively. After little resistance the village was set on f~re and burnt down. Before that the Zhervent villagers had been asked to surrender peacefully their own weapons and those given them by the authorities, and to leave the village. The Turks did not surrender their weapons, but turned them against the rebels, and that was why fire was opened, and the village was burnt. Only one rebel fell in that operation. After Zherveni had been burnt, Lazo gathered all the rebels from all the centres in the Koreshtata, a total of over 800 men, and toured the villages and mountains without running into a single Turk.

On July 26 a 700-strong Turkish force left Kostour, set the village of Shesteovo on fire, and on Shesteovo peak encountered a small peasant detachment of 30 men led by Nikola Kouzinchev. The two sides engaged in fighting which lasted an hour, after which the detachment retreated without any losses. The losses on the Turkish side are not known. On the following day the same troops set fire to two or three houses while passing through the village of Chernovishti. On July 28 Lazo, Vassil and Pando, together with four centre leaders (I. Popov, Mitre Pandjarov, Steryo Steryovski and Vassil Nikolov) and many village leaders, more than 800 rebels in all, attacked the purely Turkish small town of Bilishta, the centre of the Albanians in Dyavolta. The southwestern part of the Kostour region borders on villages inhabited by Moslem Albanians and called Dyavoltsi after the river Dyavol. When the village of Smurdesh was burnt on May 9 of this year, they distinguished themselves by the. most brutal plundering and violence; that is why it was necessary to strike Bilishta so as to make them feel the strength ~of the rebels and teach them not to seek easy prey. As the rebel forces were being concentrated at the village of Smurdesh, it occurred to the Albanians to reinforce Bilishta with troops and bashibazouks, and to await the attack from strong positions. The attack was carried out simultaneously on

Bilishta and Kapeshtitsa (the native village of the notorious cut-throat Kasam Aga who had been killed by the Committee). The attack started at 9 o'clock, and after a 4-hour battle, the rebels withdrew without capturing Bilishta. The Turks lost 10 dead (soldiers and bashibazouks), while the rebels suffered one death at Kapeshtitsa, and one wounded at Bilishta who died soon afterwards. The attack on Bilishta struck horror in the Albanians who no longer dared go on looting raids. On the same day, July 29, a Turkish force of 800 soldiers set the village of Dumbeni on fire, but when a 40-strong unit of village rebels opened fire on them, the troops set out in the direction of Lokvat a place up in the mountains. They were met by 500 rebels, and fierce fighting broke out. After a 6-hour battle the soldiers withdrew, and beat a hasty and disorderly retreat to the village of Dumbeni, while the rebels chased them for 2 hours until they disappeared from dead, and a bugler was captured alive by the rebels together with his bugle. A rebel was killed. This bugler was the first captive soldier in the hands of the rebels. This battle showed the Turks that they could not attack us in the mountains with less than a thousand troops.

On August 4, 300 rebels, together with the Lerin unit of Georgi P. Hristov, decided to attack the tower near the village of Psoderi where there were 50 soldiers in addition to the troops stationed in Psoderi (100 men). But at dawn, when the rebels were taking the heights overlooking Psoderi, they ran into Turkish advance patrols. Fire was suddenly opened, and the rebels realized that they would have to deal with many soldiers who had just arrived at the tower' from Lerin. A fierce battle broke out which lasted from morning till almost nightfall. The soldiers numbered more than 1,500, while those from Psoderi and the reinforcements were up to 2,000 men. It took the Turks enormous efforts to capture a single rebel position, and in so doing, they suffered more than 100 dead and some 50 were wounded. The Turks attacked with both mountain and field artillery, while the rebels used bombs before abandoning the abovementioned position. The position was being held by the centre leader Mitre Pandjourov with an insuffficient number of rebels, mostly inexperienced ones, and after he was wounded, the position was abandoned, the rebels leaving behind 6 dead and 3 wounded. All the other positions held out heroically under a shower

*of bullets and frequent grenade explosions. The Turks made a last
big effort to capture the other peaks, sparing no cartridges, but they
did not succeed in advancing a step further. The defeat of the Turks
was stunning and their losses enormous, and that is why on their way
back to Lerin, the troops took their revenge on the innocent village of
Armensko. The bulk of the Turkish force fell back as early as 8 o'clock,
but the Turks kept firing from the tower and the bushes till the evening
so as to prevent the rebels from advancing and from chasing the soldiers
towards Lerin, as they had done at Dumbeni. Since the Turks' cannons
and Mauser rifles could do nothing to the rebels at Psoderi, they were
turned on the innocent village of Armensko.*

*That same day, August 4, the Turks set fire to the villages of
Kossinets, Lobanitsa, Zhoupanitsa and Orman where they killed many
old people and women and took girls, married women and children into
captivity. While all these events were taking place in the western part,
in the eastern one the rebels burnt down several Turkish farms around
Vrabchinsko lake, and attacked th Circassian village of Sveti-Todori
where they killed 3 Turks, while one of th rebels was wounded. For a
long tims the soldiers did not dare attack the rebel who moved about
freely and controlled the whole region of Kostour with th exception of
the towns of Kostour and Hroupishta. The rebels from th Kostour region,
together with those from the Lerin area, launched an attack o the small
town of Neveska in the latter region, where soldiers had bee stationed;
permanently in big and solid barracks for many years. On August
1 the leaders V. Chekelarov, P. Klyashev, M. Rozov and M. Nikolov,
together with the centre leaders I. Popov, V. Kotev, Marko Kochovski,
S. Steryovski, N. Andreev and P. Kakalev and several village leaders,
a total of 400 rebels, attacked the Neveska garrison which numbered
205 men. The rebels encircled Neveska unnoticed under the cover of the
bushes, and carried out a surprise attack on the troops from three sides;
some of the soldiers were camped in tents by the fortifications around
the town, the rest were in the barracks. As soon as fre was opened, the
Turks lost their wits, abandoned their rifles as they had been in stacked
up, and fled unarmed. All these rifles fell into the hands of the rebels.
After an insignificant amount of fighting outside the town, the rebels
entered it, and surrounded the barracks. After several bombs were*

thrown into the barracks and shots fired through the windows, the Turks abandoned the building, and many of them escaped under cover of the night. Thus, the barracks, ignominiously abandoned by the troops, fell completely into the hands of the rebels. The mayor managed to escape, and the government off~ce was also seized by the rebels who captured 7 soldiers alive and found three killed there. A total of 31 Mauser rifles, 5 Greek ones, 1 Martin rifle and 6,000 cartridges were taken from the killed, captured and escaped soldiers. About dawn on August 14, a large force of over 6,000 soldiers from Kostour clashed with several village detachments numbering 150 men, and fighting broke out at Kainak, near the village of Chereshnitsa. The rebel units retreated in an orderly fashion before this big force, and when I. Popov and V. Kotev arrived to help them, a fierce battle broke out in the folds of the Vich mountain, above the village of Prekopana. Thanks to this help, the retreating units escaped a total defeat. The fighting lasted till the evening. The same Turkish force was on its way to attack Vurbitsa peak north of Klissoura, where another 400 rebels had taken up positions. The rebels retreated without fighting. In this way the Turks captured Vurbitsa and Klissoura on the following day. During the battle at Kainak, the Turks burnt down Chereshnitsa and whatever houses were left in Prekopana. In that battle the rebels lost 27 dead, while the soldiers lost at least 250 dead and many wounded. On the following day, August 15, the Turks burnt the big and rich village of Zagorichani, Bobishta, Kotori, Bomboki and Kondorabi, as well as several houses in the village of Olishta. A few days later the Turks burnt also the village of Mokreni, after the rebels around N. Andreev's house had engaged them in several clashes. There are heavy losses in the village, but definite reports are still lacking. Having realized that they could not hold out against the rebels with a 7,000-8,000-strong force, the Turks called in as many for the Kostour region. In this way the Turks, with a big force of more then 15,000 men, blocked the Kostour region and took their will with the women, while they slaughtered the old people, but did not find the thousands of rebels. The troops did not leave a single mountain or valley uncombed, and after setting almost all the remaining villages (Blatsa, Visheni, Gorno and Dolno Drenoveni, Chernovishta, Pozdivishta and Vumbel) on fire, they withdrew to the towns and to the fortified heights. During the raid on the Kostour region by this big force, which lasted 10 days, the

Turks inflicted very great damage on the villages and on the property of the population. They slaughtered many innocent people, mostly old men and women who could not escape. Almost all the cattle and small livestock have been taken away, everything hidden in the ground has been dug out, and most brutal acts of violence and dishonour have been committed by the soldiers and bashibazouks against the poor women and girls. The beautiful girls and young wives have been captured, and now fill the Turkish harems. Everything that the Turks have done makes the rebels become desperate fighters, and eternally implacable enemies of the Turkish authorities. The rebels from the Kostour region have lost everything: the villages have been utterly devastated, the property stolen, the crops burnt and the families robbed and scattered to wander about without food or clothes. The honour of their mothers and sisters had been trampled upon and violated by the Turks, and they seek retribution by continuing the unequal struggle, and by taking revenge on the Turkish brutes. The rebels' guns which disturbed the ease of the Turks and which sought freedom for the slave, and the screaming and suffering of the helpless women and children, are enough to stir human hearts in the free states and to move them to come to their rescue. The Turkish government and the commanding pashas already think that after the big search in the mountains and the burning of the villages, the rebels have scattered afar, and will lay down their arms. During the search on August 26 the soldiers ran into a 60-man detachment in the Dumbeni mountain, without the rebels losing a single man, and into another one in the Vumbel mountain. During the search of the Vumbel mountain 18 rebels from the Vumbel village detachment remained trapped in the caves because they had no chance of escaping through the thick cordons of troops, and of joining the rebel units, and were killed to a man. The rebels, after a skilful retreat before the big force, did not suffer many casualties, and now that the Turks believe that they have cleared the Kostour region of rebels, the latter have returned to their bases more experienced, more thirsty for revenge, and more ready to die for the freedom of their land.

from *Macedonia- Documents* (1978, 516-521)

As described in the preceding narrative, on the 5th of August about six hundred rebels took the small town of Klisura after a brief fight. The liberation of the town was a time of great celebration among the local inhabitants. The town remained in the hands of the rebels until the 27th of August. The revolutionary government functioned, people came to market from the surrounding villages and life went on as usual.

The rebels from Kostur, unlike those of other districts, were in constant movement, always on the attack. On the 25th of August, together with detachments from Lerin, about seven hundred men in all, they surrounded the town of Neveska and liberated it. Revolutionary authority was established in that town as well and general celebrations followed.

Only in the revolutionary region of Lerin did the uprising take on a partisan character. The inhabitants remained in their homes. The district provided about five hundred men, who, as elsewhere, began by cutting telephone lines, destroying rail and road bridges, attacking the towers of |the Turkish begs, etc.

In the Salonica region (Salonica and Serres) there was no mass participation in the uprising. Those districts were poorly supplied with arms and the fierce clashes with the pro-Bulgarian Vrhovists in the district of Serres were a heavy drain on the resources of the IMRO. The assassinations in Salonica also had serious consequences for the district of Salonica. All the same there were a number of armed clashes between rebels and Turkish troops in the districts of Kukush, Enidzhe-vardar, Voden and Tikvesh. The railway lines between Salonica and Bitola and Salonica and Skopje were also attacked.

Rebel activity in the revolutionary district of Skopje was also subdued. In the entire district there were fifteen skirmishes in the districts of Kratovo, Kochani, Skopje and Shtip, Maleshevo and Preshevo. Part of the railway line between Skopje and Salonica, together with thirty-two railway trucks, was blown up, and other acts of sabotage were also carried out. The rebel action in the Salonica and Skopje revolutionary districts, however, forced the Turkish authorities to maintain a strong military presence in those regions, and this proved of benefit to the rebel forces in the Bitola region during the early days of the uprising.

Dr. Krste Bitoski, in an article entitled "The Course of the Ilinden Uprising" in the book *The Epic of Ilinden* (1973, 100-105), tells how the rebellion spread to other districts but was eventually brutally crushed:

At the beginning of September, when the Bitola district was already full of Turkish troops, which were spreading terror throughout the Macedonian villages in their attempt to quell the Uprising, the revolutionary district of Ceres held a congress at which it was decided to begin action in this part of Macedonia on September 27th, Krstovden (Holy Cross Day), without the participation of the inhabitants. At the congress a commanding body was elected and a plan of action drawn up.

After considerable negotiations the District Command decided to allow the Supremacist detachments to join in the uprising. Unfortunately, however, the distrust between the revolutionaries of Ceres, led by Yane Sandanski, and the Supremacists was so great that closer co-operation was not possible. Sandanski, as one writer says, "received the Supremacist detachments, which were entering an unfamiliar region, not only without warmth and friendliness but also without the courtesy to be expected". One of the detachments had come from Bulgaria wearing Bulgarian military uniform and the insignia of the Bulgarian army; Sandanski ordered the men of his detachment to strip off their insignia. Most of them complied with his command.

There were several fights in this district—in Nevrokop, in the Melnik region, in Gorna Dzhumaja, Ceres, Drama and Demirhisar. The area actively covered by the Revolutionary Organization also included the district of Odrin, which did not belong to Macedonia. The uprising in Odrin began on l9th August, 1903, and met with a good deal of success. In addition to the Bulgarian inhabitants of this area, a number of Macedonians also took part.

The Turkish authorities did not manage to discover the date of the uprising, although they were already in possession of many facts indicating the likelihood of an uprising in the near future. The Turkish officials in positions of responsibility did not pay sufficient heed to these warning indications and did not want to believe that such an explosion might occur. This is why the Uprising of Ilinden caught them by surprise.

Shortly after the outbreak of the uprising, however, the Grande

Porte (the Turkish Supreme Command) correctly concluded that the uprising in the Bitola district could only be stamped out with far larger forces than those available on the spot at that time. But a fair amount of time would be needed to concentrate such a military force, and, until this was done, the initiative lay with the rebels, who had liberated not only three towns but also great stretches of mountain territory together with the mountain settlements.

Preparations for moving into a general offensive against the rebels were completed by 25th August. In addition to equipping the regular army, the Turks also armed a great number of Muslim civilians who were to be attached as bashi-bazouks to the regular army or to give help in some other way to the troops.

The prime task of the Turkish command was to take Krushevo. But even after they had set out for Krushevo the initiative still remained in the hands of the rebels despite the fact that Rudzhi Pasha, the commander in chief, had fifty thousand soldiers behind him. Dissatisfied with Rudzhi Pasha, the Turkish government had him removed and set Nazir Pasha in his place. At the end of August the Turkish troops set out under his command on a general offensive. The discrepancy in strength between the two forces, both in men and arms, was so great that comparison is impossible. It should be sufficient to mention only that some boroughs such as Demirhisar, were attacked by twenty thousand soldiers. On 26th August the Turks set out to crush the uprising in the Kostur region. Over five thousand soldiers in Kostur, supported by the Greek Metropolitan of Kostur, Karavangelis, moved in with fire and sword to put a stop to this rebellion of the oppressed. By the beginning of September the army force had been increased to fifteen thousand. The battles were fought all over with the same ferocity. The bloodiest fight in the rebellious region of Ohrid occurred at a place called Grmeshnica, where there was a camp with one thousand seven hundred women, children and old people. The rebels were unable to withstand the pressure; the Turkish troops stormed in among the women and children, and in the terrible massacre which followed a hundred and sixty civilians were shot or slain.

By the second half of October 1903 the uprising in the revolutionary district of Bitola, and in all of Macedonia, had been bloodily crushed.

It is well known that every nation that strikes out for its own freedom is liable to reprisals and torture. With the Macedonian people, however, these reprisals went far beyond "normal" bounds and turned into genocide. It is not possible to describe all that was done ' by the regular army and the bashi-bazouks to the noncombatants; we shall give only a few examples, which may help us to gain a general picture of the methods used by the Grande Porte in quelling the uprising, or to be more precise, the horrors to which the Macedonian Christians were exposed.

A Serbian consul in Bitola described the suffering of the people:

Every conceivable form of torture, murder, hanging, tearing children from their mothers' wombs and flinging them to the dogs, seizing women and girls, breaking into homes and burning them—all this, I think, is every bit as terrible as the violence and bestiality to which the Turkish lords and governors resorted, as the book describes, before our first and second uprisings.. ." And he continues: "The facts we have to hand indicate that the plan they are preparing is not to crush the uprising, nor to destroy the guerilla detachments—for such as they are they cannot be put down—but to wipe out the people in hiding . . .

As did the Austro-Hungarian consul to Bitola, writing of the massacre in the village of Armensko (Lerin):

It is quite impossible to describe in detail the acts of bestiality. Women have had their wombs ripped open, their eyes torn out or their breasts cut off, the heads and bodies of small children have been brutally stabbed with ordinary pocket-knives, infants have been torn apart and flung-to the dogs, nineteen women have been hanged and three girls savagely butchered.

Macedonian Professor Krste Bitoski (1973, 103) goes on to explain some of the strategy behind the reprisals:

The well-known von Gaben alleges that a Turkish colonel told him: "The rebel detachments fight like the Boers and we should follow the example of the English in putting them down. We shall burn their villages and their estates, and when they no longer have anywhere to hide they will be forced to scatter or give themselves up." During the time when the Uprising of Ilinden was being crushed, von Gaben was acting as advisor to the Turkish commanding forces. It may be believed that von Gaben's experience from fighting on the side of the Boers was, in fact, used in Macedonia. Nevertheless, the dreadful acts carried out against the non-fighting part of the population did not help greatly. The longing for freedom was so great that in most cases the people were ready to bear everything.

Krste Bitoski (1973, 104-105) offers several further insights into the nature and failure of the uprising:

Despite instructions from the revolutionary command that the uprising was to be conducted along partisan lines, it had the character of a mass uprising in the area where it was started (the district of Bitola). It was an uprising of the people because the Macedonian masses took part in it, determined to make the highest sacrifices in order to win their freedom. The liberation movement was led by the Macedonian intelligentsia, who mostly belonged to the petite bourgeoisie, but it was the peasant masses who were the striking force behind the Uprising of Ilinden. In essence, the uprising was a bourgeois-democratic revolution.

Right at the very beginning of the uprising the tactics of the General Staff turned out to be at variance with the aims of the people who had risen in revolt. That is, the instigators of the Uprising, and the General Staff, held that the object should be to force the European states to intervene and oblige the Turks to grant autonomy to Macedonia. The people, however, thought differently. They had taken up arms and set out to fight in order to free their country. They liberated several towns and established their own authority, driving out the Turkish troops and organs of government, and showing in fact an initiative and determination which were all unplanned and unforeseen by the high command. Nevertheless, the instructions of the high command, which had served to determine the character of the Uprising, could not help having a harmful influence on the planning and action of the individual regions and on the results of the fighting. We have seen that Kichevo and Resen were not liberated, simply because this was not part of the plan, although the liberation might easily have been achieved.

There were undoubtedly several basic reasons for the failure of the Uprising. It had not been properly prepared and therefore could not cover the whole of Macedonia. Even in the district of Bitola, which was somewhat better equipped, there were few guns, and those available were extremely primitive. It did not take long after the start of the Uprising for the Grande Porte to realise that the main rebel force was in the district of Bitola and that this was where the bulk of the Turkish troops should be sent; and this it would certainly not have been able to do if the Uprising had been carried out with the same intensity all over Macedonia as it was in the Bitola district. On the other hand, the Macedonian people were placed in a situation in which they themselves had to fight against the Turkish Empire. It is well known that the Serbs, Greeks and Bulgarians, when fighting against Ottoman rule, won their freedom largely thanks to the fact that they received military and diplomatic aid from some of the great foreign powers, chiefly from Tsarist Russia...

a Macedonian rebel chieftainess- Kostadinka from Izvor

Chapter Eight

The Legacy of Ilinden

We should also show this favor to our native language if we wish to remain faithful to the spirit of our forefathers. Favor towards our native language is our duty and our right. We are duty-bound to love our language, because it is ours, just as our fatherland is ours. The first voices which we heard were the voices of our fathers and mothers, the sounds and words of our native language. Through them we received our first spiritual nourishment, because by this means we put into thought all that we saw with our eyes. Through our native language we absorb the psychology of our fathers and forefathers and become their spiritual descendants, as we are in the physical sense their bodily continuations. If we turn with disdain upon our native language, we only act thanklessly towards our parents in return for their spiritual care and upbringing. - It is our right, as well as our duty, to defend our native language, and this is our sacred right. He who attacks our language is as much our enemy as he who attacks our faith.

(excerpt from Krste P. Misirkov's *On Macedonian Matters, 1903*)

A Macedonian friend once remarked that: "the Bulgarians cannot let go of their attachment to Macedonia because the most glorious and heroic moments of their modern history really belong to the Macedonians." What he was referring to were the heroic actions of the Ilinden revolutionaries. The conditions of that period in Macedonian history evoked a courage and self-sacrifice among the rebels and the people generally that is rarely seen in our world. When the fighters of Ilinden took the oath on a Bible with a crossed dagger and pistol on it, swearing themselves to secrecy and loyalty unto death to the cause and the organization, the vast majority of them truly adhered to the chief slogan of their cause: "freedom or death." Nearly all of the leadership of the rebel bands and many of the fighters were dead by the time of the Young Turk revolt of 1908 and many others either died in the Balkan Wars of 1912-13 or went into exile by the time of the First World War.

To appreciate the meaning of the Ilinden Uprising to the Macedonian people one only has to spend a brief time among Macedonians. One soon begins to hear songs about Ilinden, to hear stories of the heroes of Ilinden and to learn of the national holiday dedicated to the heroes of Ilinden that occurs every year on the second of August. While most nations create national myths that become associated with major holidays that reinforce a sense of national pride and unity, few such holidays can claim origins in such well-documented collective heroism as one finds in the Ilinden Rebellion.

No doubt it was the very fact of brutal Turkish repression and treacherous foreign intervention, the sources of so much misery in the form of betrayal, murder, torture, plunder, rape and theft during that period, that created the conditions for so many to display a courage and self-sacrifice that we normally associate with figures of myth rather than flesh and blood men and women. All the same, the men and women who fought the soldiers of the Ottoman Empire during the period of the Ilinden Uprising indeed did exist. We have ample proof of their existence and that the course of their lives was indeed consistent with the deeds ascribed to them.

Georgi Delchev, or as he is better known, Gotse Delchev, was born on February 3rd of 1872. He was the son of an innkeeper named Nikola and his wife Sultana from the eastern Macedonian town of Kukush. He attended high school in nearby Salonica, where he became a member of a small fledgling group that would become the leadership of the nation-wide Internal Macedonian Revolutionary Organization, with members in nearly every village and town of Macedonia. He later trained at a military academy in Sofia and then went on to become a teacher at a school in the eastern Macedonian town of Shtip. From that time until his death in a battle with Turkish troops in the village of Banitsa on May 4, 1903, Gotse Delchev devoted himself to the cause of Macedonian liberation through the creation of the IMRO and its work to plan and carry out a successful nationwide rebellion against Ottoman rule. From all of the documents and first-hand accounts of Gotse and his activities, we know that he was selfless in his devotion to the cause and that no one among his peers inspired the movement through speech and action they way Gotse did.

He is perhaps best known as an IMRO organizer, who traveled at great risk throughout the land meeting with individuals and groups of people, to spread the message that their liberation could only be won by a disciplined, organized mass rebellion. This work earned him the title of the "new apostle of freedom." Besides his exceptional courage and unwavering devotion to the cause, he demonstrated a remarkable ability to bring people together to work for the greater good.

Stories abound of his exploits as an organizer of the IMRO's network of committees throughout Macedonia. There are stories of his travels in disguise as a Turkish merchant, in which his perfect command of the Turkish language and his sharp wits fooled the Turkish authorities on more than one occasion. Another time, when he was in danger of discovery during a police search in the town of Bitola, the local people improvised a mock funeral in order to transport him safely outside the city in a casket.

He would die three months before the start of the national uprising that he had worked so tirelessly to plan. Many observers believe that he would have urged further delay of the mass rebellion in order to continue the much-needed work of weapons procurement, further recruitment of fighters and further organization of the revolt. However, he would not be present to argue his position at the Smilevo Meeting later that year. He and a small group of rebels were discovered, some think that they were betrayed to the Turkish troops, while staying in the village of Banitsa in eastern Macedonia.

Gotse had come to the village in the company of the rebel leaders Dimitar Gushtanov, Georgi Brodlijata and Dimo Hadzhi-Dimov and a group of some seventeen others. It was the early morning of May 4th, 1903 that an old village woman entered the house in which the rebels were sleeping and informed them that the village was surrounded by hundreds of Turkish soldiers. Dimitar Gushtanov proposed that they take shelter in one of the stone houses in the village and try to hold out until evening, when they might try to escape.

The rebels held off a much larger force of Turkish soldiers for many hours and did eventually manage their escape as darkness fell. Some say that Gotse, in his usual disregard for his own safety, urged the group to take shelter on the edge of the village in order to spare the village from destruction as the soldiers closed in on the rebels. It was while the rebels moved out over open ground, seeking cover in a dry creek bed and behind low stonewalls that several of their number, including Delchev and rebel leader Gushtanov, were hit by Turkish bullets. Gotse had stood up in order to fire his gun and was struck in the chest by a bullet. As he fell he was heard to shout one last time: "Strike out at the oppressors, shoot the dogs down!" He was only the first of many who would lay down their lives for their people in that war of liberation in the months and years to come.

Everyone, however, immediately recognized the terrible loss they had suffered with Gotse's passing. Few had inspired as he had, and few had argued as persuasively for Macedonian self-sacrifice for self-determination. As he often said to the groups he met with: *"The liberation of Macedonia must come from an internal revolt. Whoever tells you otherwise, deceives you and himself."* And he also would emphasize that: *"No one has the right to play politics with Macedonia. Our struggle is a life and death struggle. We can't let others decide whether we should live or die, and when... We shouldn't leave it to others to give us orders... We don't need guardians, and even less so, rulers..."*

While some leaders of the revolt, such as the Vlah Macedonian rebel leader Pitu Guli, from the central mountain town of Krushevo, would die in the initial battles of the campaign, most of the IMRO leadership would survive the first days and months of the August 2nd Ilinden Uprising. Few, however, would live much beyond that. Gotse's close friend and comrade from his student days in Salonica, and a major figure in the organization as well, Damyan Gruev, would be killed in a skirmish with Turkish troops two years after Gotse's death. Other prominent leaders such as Pere Toshev, Nikola Karev and Georgi Sugarev would also die in battles with Ottoman troops in the year 1905. Only a few major figures would live much beyond that period. The "mountain tsar" Yane Sandanski, survived until 1915, when he was assassinated while living at the Rozhen Monastery in the heart of his Pirin Mountains. Gjorche Petrov, another major figure of the movement, was among the longest-lived, meeting death in 1921.

Of the thousands of rebels who stood up on the 2nd of August, 1903, some 700 fell in those first weeks and months of the revolt. Perhaps one reason that few would survive the years that followed was a strong sense of duty to the civilian population that the rebels had exposed to such suffering as a result of their actions. Because the Ottoman troops could not easily capture or kill the rebels themselves, who had mountain refuges to retreat to, Turkish troops retaliated against the defenseless civilian population. According to fairly reliable sources, in the immediate aftermath of the Ilinden Uprising, 4,694 civilians were murdered, 3,122 women were raped, 12,440 houses were burned down, 201 villages destroyed, 75,835 people were left homeless and some 30,000 people went in to permanent exile in neighboring countries or across the oceans.

But the network of rebel bands that had been organized throughout the land as part of the committee organizing of the IMRO remained. Besides the leading chetas of Gotse Delchev and Pitu Guli and those of the prominent revolutionary voivodas who had survived the uprising, such as Yane Sandanski, Gjorche Petrov, Jordan Piperkata and Birincheto, there were major chetas that continued to operate in the various regions. In Debar there was the band of the rebel chieftain Naki Janev. The cheta of the voivoda Smile remained active in Kichevo. Bands led by Atanas Krshakov and Mitre Vlaot remained active in the Kostur region. Elsewhere there were also bands led by the voivodas Andrea Dimov, Atanas Babata, Petar Chaulev, Pesho Samardzhiev and Djakon Evstatij and there were many other lesser known bands that remained active as well.

Nearly every village and town of Macedonia has its history of organized resistance to the Ottoman regime during that period. While the movement's members were sworn to secrecy, there is a history of battles, bravery and fallen warriors told in folk songs and recited in old stories throughout the land.

There is, for example, the story of Done Stoyanov, an IMRO courier from the town of Shtip. He was searched one day on the outskirts of the town of Bitola and three hundred rifle bullets, ten hand grenades and a package of dynamite were discovered inside the sacks of rice on the pack mule that he was leading. He was beaten and tortured by the Turkish authorities for many days but he refused to reveal anything about the organization and its plans. He and his story live on in songs and in the memory of the people. They will always honor this extremely courageous man who fought and suffered for their freedom. And his story is only one of many that come down to us from that time when the "whole fair land was a red, red hell."

It is, however, the faith, courage and self-sacrifice of so many of the leaders of the movement that is most prominently paid its due. For example, the Macedonian national hymn, which begins with the words: "Today over Macedonia is born a new sun of freedom…" ends with the names of four of the leaders of the Ilinden period: "Gotse Delchev, Pitu Guli, Damyan Gruev, Sandanski!"

In addition to their brave deeds, such men also emboldened their coutrymen with wise words:

I do not expect the swift liberation of Macedonia. That may not even come during my lifetime, but I wish to protect the people and to organize them, and if that is accomplished, it will end in their liberation.

(Yane Sandanski)

We should not expect our liberation to come by way of the Greeks, nor the Bulgarians, but only we Macedonians can wage successful war for the liberation of our Macedonia.

(Nikola Karev)

Don't give in, brothers, in the struggle for our precious freedom! Strike with courage and bring freedom to the suffering Macedonian people!

(Georgi Sugarev)

A free Macedonia will only be realized through our own efforts and means...

(Gjorche Petrov:)

Freedom will come even without us, because the whole people want it; from the smallest child to the oldest among us, as much as we want water and bread.

(Pere Toshev)

There were also many courageous women who joined the struggle for freedom before and during the period of the Ilinden Uprising. Hundreds of women risked their lives as couriers, delivering messages, munitions and guns throughout the land. Thousands of others prepared food and clothing, and provided shelter and medical care to the rebels fighting for freedom. A significant few stood as equals with the men in the struggle for freedom. Some were women schoolteachers who took leadership roles in the secret system of committees. A select few particularly brave, strong women even joined the rebels as armed insurgents. We even know the names of certain of these brave women fighters. These included Kostadinka the voivoda from Izvor, Rumena the voivoda known as the "Mountain Czarina," who formed her own rebel cheta at the St. Joakim Osogovski Monastery in the Kriva Palanka region, and Srebra Apostolova from the Lerin region.

Some of these women fought alongside their husbands on the

field of battle. Ana Maleshevska married and then fought alongside her husband, the voivoda Atanas Babata in the Kratovo region. Kata Hristova of Vevchani also married and then joined her husband the voivoda Stavre Gogov in the fight for freedom. During the period leading up to the uprising there is not a single documented case of betrayal of the movement by the women who participated. They proved to be among the movement's most loyal members.

Gotse Delchev- "Apostle of Freedom" of the IMRO

Chapter Nine

The Young Turk Revolt and the Balkan Wars of 1912-13

A memorandum on the independence of Macedonia submitted by the Macedonian colony in St. Petersburg to the Conference of the Representatives of the Great Powers in London., 1st March 1913:

Macedonia, which was liberated by the Russians 35 years ago was returned to its former Turkish rule with the Treaty of Berlin. This event proved for Europe to be a source of constant worries and strong disturbances and for Turkey a motive for the postponement of the internal revival and the settling of its relations with its neighbours, while in Macedonia itself it caused new streams of blood and unparalled sufferings of the people. All the diplomatic conferences, all the projects, all the statements of foreign monarchs and the intercession of European supervision did not help.

Now Macedonia is again liberated. But Europe is prone to make the same mistake which was made in 1878. Instead of proclaiming

Macedonia an autonomous state, its new liberators have decided to divide it among themselves; we are convinced and deeply believe that the aware and democratic sections of the Bulgarian, Greek and Serbian people have not participated in this fratricidal partition of the Macedonian people. Yet Macedonia has all the natural and historical rights to self-determination. Over the centuries it has been an autonomous political unit or included in the structure of other states. This has resulted from its geographical location and individuality. The borders of Macedonia are clearly marked by the mountain chains that surround it and by the coast. This geographical whole and the whole system of fertile valleys and fields arrayed like a fan also determine the economic wholeness and indivisibility of the country.

Also the population of the country is homogeneous. According to the data of various authoritative researchers, 2/3 of the population of Macedonia belong to a particular Slav group. In order to avoid any friction among the peoples adjacent to Macedonia in future, in order to give the less significant groups of other nationalities mixed in the Slav majority - Albanians, Greeks, Wallachians, Turks and Jews - the chance of having a free and unobstructed national life, the only way is to establish a free independent Macedonia. Thus, it is more suitable for all the neighbours of Macedonia that this country remain undivided, since by any division, sections of our living compatriots will remain under foreign authority and will perish.

The Macedonians have won their right to self-determination over their whole recent history, as well. They fought for centuries in the name of independence and freedom, and particularly after the Treaty of Berlin, they organized innumerable insurrections and distinguished themselves by determination and courage. During the past war the Internal Macedonian Organization and the 27 emigrant brotherhoods formed a large number of Macedonian units, which had a great influence upon the course of the war and captured through their bravery Ynver Pasha's army of 12,000 men.

At the critical moment for the Serbian army near Kumanovo, when it started withdrawing, 6,000 Macedonian fighters appeared and with bombs in their hands attacked the rear of the Turkish army. The Turks fled in panic, leaving everything to the victors. The Serbs and Bulgarians deliberately say nothing about these huge Macedonian victories and permit nobody to write about them. In addition, the Macedonians have more than once shed their own blood for Greek, Serbian and Bulgarian freedom and have thus won their rights as a fighting force. The Macedonian army is at the moment fighting along with the allies and numbers some 70,000 fighters and soldiers. Horrible terror now reigns in Macedonia, the 'freedom' of the allies has no limits, none of the Macedonians has the right to travel outside Macedonia in order to protest before the European states. Whoever attempts to do this is either murdered or put in prison. The armies of the allies have surrounded the whole of Macedonia with an iron band.

As a result of all this, the Macedonian Colony in St. Petersburg, fulfilling its sacred duty towards its fatherland and conscientiously applying the slogan "Macedonia to the Macedonians", protest and cannot remain indifferent when the allied Balkan states (Bulgaria, Serbia and Greece) - our brothers in blood and faith - aim to dismember our fatherland, which stands on the same cultural level as them, and which is also by the number of its population (three and a half million inhabitants) greater than Serbia or Greece separately. The Colony cannot look without pain at the disintegration of its unfortunate fatherland, at the burial and destruction of the political and spiritual life of the whole nation. The partition of Macedonia by its brothers is the most unjust act in the history of peoples, a violation of the rights of Man, a disgrace to the whole Slav race.

The Turkish subjugation has been replaced by Christian subjugation, but that ill-omened hour is not far away (it is approaching - the Macedonian fighters have already come out against the enemies of their fatherland), when the Macedonians shall openly declare to the whole world:

We had rather die in the struggle for our liberation than live in slavery again".

Here is what is needed for the Macedonian people:

1. Macedonia should remain a single, indivisible and independent Balkan state within its geographical, ethnographical, historical, economic and political borders.

2. A Macedonian national assembly should be established on the basis of general elections in Salonika in the soonest possible time, which would work out in detail the internal structure of the state and determine its relations with the neighbouring states.

Authorized representatives of the Macedonian colony (The Memorandum was signed by the representatives of the Macedonian colony - Dr. G. Konstantinovich, N. Dimov, D. Chupovski and A. Vezenkov.)

The Murszteg Reform Program was the last hope for the Great Powers of Europe to salvage the Ottoman Empire in Macedonia. While the Murszteg Reform Program proved fruitless for the Macedonians, it raised hopes for Greece, Bulgaria and Serbia.

Item 3 of the Murszteg Reform Program, which stated: "as soon as the rebellion is put down, the Great Powers would demand an administrative reorganization of the Macedonian territory based on nationalities," caught the eye of the Greek, Bulgarian and Serbian advocates.

It was well known by the end of the 19th century that there was a separate and distinct Macedonian identity, whether or not many Macedonians still found it convenient to call their language Bulgarian in the absence of a standardized national language based solely on Macedonian dialects. Krste P. Misirkov had already in 1903 published his treatise *On Macedonian Matters* that laid out the principles upon which a Macedonian literary language could be based. That treatise, however, was almost immediately seized and destroyed by the Bulgarian authorities and did not receive the wide public attention it deserved until much later.

Despite Misirkov's work and a growing consciousness of a separate and distinct Macedonian identity, the new Balkan states rushed to invent Greek, Bulgarian or Serbian nationalities within Macedonia in order to further their expansionist ambitions. The foreign agitators found one convenient avenue for this invention by cleverly substituting "nationality" for "religious affiliation". By the end of the 19th century, the Christian millet of Ottoman Macedonia was already divided into two millets, the Greek Patriarchist millet and the Bulgarian Exarchist millet. First, since there was no Macedonian millet there was no "governing body" to represent a Macedonian religious denomination. Second, since all Christians in Macedonia already belonged to one millet or another, it was easy to make "nationality" claims on behalf of "religious affiliation". All Macedonians who belonged to the Patriarchist fold were considered to be Greek by nationality. Similarly, all those Macedonians who belonged to the Exarchist fold were considered to be Bulgarian by nationality. By introducing Serbian churches and schools, Serbia later used similar tactics to claim the existence of a Serbian nationality inside Macedonia.

All Macedonians who belonged to the Patriarchist church were given Greek or "Hellenized" names. Similarly, all Macedonians that belonged to the Exarchist church were given Bulgarian names. In many instances brothers born from the same mother and father were given different last names because they happened to go to different churches. Their choice of church had nothing to do with loyalty to one faction or the other, but rather with the church's location relative to home. Each brother attended the church nearest to his house as he had always done for many years. The sad part was that now with every spoonful of religion came a dose of venomous propaganda. Brother was pitted against brother, one fighting for "Hellenism" and the other for "Bulgarism".

At the beginning of the Ilinden rebellion most Macedonian villages belonged to the Bulgarian Exarchate Church. With increased Greek activities through Karavangelis and others like him, however, the tide was turning. Greek success was mainly due to Turkish-Greek collaboration and the Turkish military's assistance. The Macedonian people were bullied and pressured to such an extent that they were willing to do almost anything to escape further punishment.

This collaboration that was advancing the Greek cause did not go unnoticed by the Bulgarians. British fears of a Turkish-Bulgarian war were allayed when Bulgaria on April 8th, 1904 signed a peace agreement with Turkey. Bulgaria promised to put an end to rebel operations in

Macedonia from bases in Bulgaria in exchange for Turkish promises to implement the Murzsteg Reform Program and to extend it to the Edirne region. Russia was not pleased by the agreement, especially since Bulgaria herself was beginning to make moves towards annexing the Edrene region. Being of strategic importance, Russia was hoping to eventually annex the Dardanelles for herself.

The prospect of declining Bulgarian incursions inside Macedonia was welcome news for the Greeks. They could now import fighters from Crete to fight the Macedonian cheti without Bulgarian interference. However, while they reduced military incursions, the Bulgarians stepped up Exarchist activities, creating stiff competition for the Greek church. The clergy on both sides were going after the same flock. Both sides had appointed themselves religious guardians of the people. In the eyes of the world, they became missionaries of the Christian faith in Macedonia. This competition to attract parishioners created friction between the opposing factions. Friction turned to violence in villages where both groups existed and fought for control over the village church. The Turks were indifferent to this dispute between Christian groups and remained neutral in the dispute. When fights erupted, the Turks would often padlock the church so that neither group could use it. As competition for control of the village churches intensified, so did vigilantism.

Disputes over a particular village church drew the attention of both Patriarchists and Exarchists, who sent their hatchet men to eliminate the so-called "troublemakers". Many priests, teachers, notables and community leaders lost their lives this way.

The Western Powers had little use for the Ottoman Turks and their Islamic state, but they generally preferred the status quo in Macedonia. There were two factors that hindered the Powers from taking any action. The first was the lucrative Ottoman import-export markets. The Ottoman consumer was dependent upon western capitalist production for a variety of goods, and the Western capitalists did not want to lose this lucrative market. The second was the power struggle between the Great Powers themselves over the Balkans. The Powers were locked in a diplomatic dance in which no one could freely maneuver without upsetting the others. Each of the Great Powers knew that a sudden or massive shift in any one's policies would result in a dispute that would involve them all. No one wanted a "world war."

Britain at one point, however, had contemplated the creation of an autonomous Macedonian state, but knew that Russia and Austria would be against it. The Balkan historian Dakin, in his work, *The Greek Struggle in Macedonia 1897-1913,* (1966, 152) makes this point clear when he states that:

It was fortunate for Greece at this juncture that Lansdowne's plans foundered in a sea of European politics and that both Russia and Austria opposed Macedonian autonomy.

This is an important fact for all to know which runs contrary to Greek propaganda that no Macedonians existed before 1945. This is one more piece of documented evidence that a Macedonian nation did exist and that many Europeans knew this as far back as the 19th century. Few, it seems, realize how close that nation came to achieving independence.

The Ilinden rebellion was all about Macedonia for the Macedonians, their right to live as equals with other peoples in the world. The Great Powers must still own up to their historic role in denying the Macedonian people their rightful place in the world. It is time to put an end to blatant Greek propaganda. Macedonians are certainly not a threat to anyone. Those who committed crimes against the Macedonian people and continue to deny their existence obviously have a problem. But why continue to punish the victims?

The Western powers were not happy with the way Turkey had been implementing reforms in Macedonia, but at the same time they could not agree among themselves as to how to affect that process. The Ilinden Uprising created a new sense of urgency. However, a reform movement was brewing within the Ottoman Turkish state itself. As Australian-Macedonian historian Michael Radin (1993, 125) explains in his book *IMRO and the Macedonian Question:*

During the later part of the 19th century new social forces had emerged within Turkey. Given the conditions of absolutism within the Empire, the emergence of liberalism seemed inevitable. This new creed took the form of political agitation, calling for a broad spectrum of reforms. It was headed by an embryonic Turkish bourgeoisie, and supported by a European-educated intelligentsia.

The Young Turk movement had been active for at least thirty years, ever since Turkish students were allowed to attend European schools in significant numbers. Among other things, the Young Turks were in favour of granting self-government to Macedonia, Thrace and Albania and believed that the Ottoman Empire could be salvaged through reforms. When the 1903 Ilinden rebellion started many of these European educated students had already joined the ranks of the Turkish military as junior officers. The atrocities committed and the methods used to deal with the rebels during the Ilinden aftermath, however, went against these young men's principles and many deserted the Turkish army. Some joined up with Albanian paramilitary bands in order to enlist them in a campaign to depose the Ottoman Sultan. Some attempted to establish contacts with IMRO in hopes that IMRO too would join them in their movement against the Sultan.

By 1905 the Young Turks organized under the banner of "Union and Progress" and established themselves in Salonica away from the control of the Sultan in Istanbul (Constantinople). It was not too long before they gained some measure of command over the local Turkish army, especially in Macedonia. It was not too difficult to convince many of the soldiers serving in Macedonia that there was no honor or sense to the attacks on and murder of women and children, in the absence of the guerilla fighters, who were beyond their reach.

After observing the actions of the Young Turks, the IMRO leadership was convinced that it would be better to work with them than against them. The Young Turks were offering self-government and significant agrarian reforms if they gained power, which was attractive to most IMRO leaders. Gotse Delchev, Damyan Gruev and Nikola Karev were already dead, which left the IMRO leadership in the hands of only a few others. Some, such as Gjorche Petrov, favoured a policy of urban insurrection. Others, such as the legendary "tsar of Pirin," the voivoda Yane Sandanski, however, favoured support of the Young Turk regime for their prospective agrarian reform programs.

The actions of the Young Turks did not go unnoticed by the Sultan, who complained to the Great Powers but did not receive an immediate response. The coup d'etat did not materialize until regional commander Enver Beg from Albania was summoned to Istanbul to receive a military promotion from the Sultan. Fearing it was an assassination attempt, Enver Beg and his supporters fled to the mountains and called for the revolution to begin.

The rebellion first materialized in the larger cities in the form of demonstrations. On June 22nd, 1908, Salonica alone drew over 20,000 protesters. By July 3rd, the Young Turk officers took control of most of the Sultan's forces and by July 22nd Macedonia was free of Ottoman military occupation.

True to their word, the Young Turks released all political prisoners and began work on reforms. Their first act was to send the Sultan an ultimatum, demanding reinstatement of the 1876 Constitution. Being in no position to resist, Sultan Abdul Hamid II reluctantly agreed. As soon as the constitution was reinstated, amnesty was proclaimed for all those under arms, including the local Macedonian cheti and all foreign bands. Macedonians, Serbians and Bulgarians all took advantage of the amnesty and came down from the mountains and laid down their arms. The Greeks, who had the most to lose, were at first hesitant, but warmed to the idea. They had their own ambitions that they might reclaim the former glory of the Phanar in Constantinople, the Turkish Istanbul.

As it turned out, however, the Young Turks were very suspicious of the Greek intentions and watched their every move carefully. The Greek dream to rule from the Phanar in Constantinople did not materialize. In time, by deactivating and expelling armed bands, the Young Turk regime brought some stability to Macedonia.

The Young Turk regime, headquartered in Salonica, worked unimpeded for over six months. Then, with support from Yane Sandanki's cheta, the Young Turks attacked and successfully took Istanbul. Unfortunately, by now it was becoming evident that the Young Turk regime was too dependent on the Turkish establishment and bureaucracy for its continued survival. As a result, it had to abandon much of its reform program to safeguard its own power. In actual fact, after all this time in power, the Young Turk regime did very little to alleviate the social and economic suffering in the Macedonian villages.

To get the Young Turks to deliver on their promises, Sandanski had a plan of his own. He proposed that in exchange for IMRO's help, the Young Turks would redistribute much needed land to the poor landless Macedonian peasants. Additionally, to ensure the land reforms were put in place according to the agreement, Sandanski requested that he personally be allowed to oversee the creation of a peasant militia to supervise the implementation. Unfortunately, while Sandaski's proposals were widely accepted by the Macedonian peasants, they attracted negative attention abroad. The first to complain were the Greeks. Radin documents on page 127 of *IMRO and the Macedonian Question* how Greek leaders worried that:

The consequences of Sandanski's plan, as unfortunately confirmed by events, would be terrible [for Greeks]. Unless something else, like a war, or an agreement between the European Powers, settles the Macedonian question in our favour, it is my opinion that there can be no doubt that settlement of the agrarian question would create possibilities for the final settlement of the Macedonian question...

Sandanski's approach to the Young Turks was a radical departure from IMRO's previous strategy (seizure of power by revolutionary means). To take advantage of the new situation and stay on course, IMRO created an offshoot dubbed the "National or Peoples' Federative Party"(NFP). The NFP was officially launched in early 1909 and worked with and pressured the Young Turk regime to develop a quasi-parliamentary system and to preserve the national and territorial integrity of Macedonia within an Ottoman Federation.

By the time the NFP was organized and ready to deal with the issues at hand, the Young Turk regime was losing momentum and beginning to stagnate. By now it was obvious to IMRO that without support from the broad base of Turkish society, the new regime was fighting a losing battle. Its rise to power had resulted from a coup and the regime itself was no more than a dictatorship.

The Young Turk regime was a Western backed idea, an alternate approach to a problem with no easy solution. The majority of the IMRO's leaders could no longer agree to support the regime and were contemplating breaking off relations with the Young Turks. To complicate matters, class struggle, based on growing interest in socialism, was on the rise in Europe, causing conflict between the rich and the poor and dividing people along class lines. The so-called "religious war" between the Patriarchists and Exarchists was also having its effect, further dividing IMRO and the Macedonian people. By 1910 armed propaganda in Macedonia was replaced by Greek, Bulgarian and Serbian "political clubs" which worked against the aims of the NFP agenda and leaders.

While Russia was having mixed feelings about the Young Turk regime, the European powers, and especially Britain, which had helped create the new regime, were relieved to be rid of the old reform programs. Britain approved of the cooperation between the NFP and the Young Turks. This, however, only fueled tension between the NFP, that wanted to create an autonomous Macedonia inside an Ottoman Federation, and that faction of the IMRO that still wanted independence through armed rebellion. Unfortunately, the Young Turk regime, despite all its promises, did not meet expectations and reverted to the old Turkish manner of rule. To prevent further coup attempts by more extreme factions, the Young Turk regime reverted to dictatorial rule instead of promoting more liberal programs of governmental reform. This was expressed in a number of repressive laws in Macedonia, including laws on strikes, political association and the right to self-defense. This policy reversal again destabilized Macedonian society by bringing back the old oppressive political climate. The NFP and all other political, cultural and professional organizations were effectively banned, forcing the IMRO to again resort to clandestine activities. Macedonian society once again endured growing anarchy.

The Young Turk regime resettled almost a quarter of a million Turks in Macedonia between 1910 and 1911 in hopes of maintaining control of Macedonia if the regime lost control of Istanbul. Faced with struggles on several fronts, however, including the Albanian revolution of 1909-1912, the Italian-Turkish war in Libya in 1911, growing domestic opposition, the resurgence of armed insurgent bands, and finally the emergence of a new army that was loyal to the Sultan, the Young Turk regime could no longer maintain a grip on power and on July 13, 1912 it capitulated to the Sultan.

In the meantime the Great Powers were locked in a struggle of their own in which no one could maneuver without upsetting the delicate balance of the status quo. While the Great Powers were held in check by their own political machinations, the new Balkan nations were not remaining idle. Alliances such as the Serbian-Bulgarian pact against Greek-Turkish collusion or the Greek-Rumanian pact against Bulgarian aims in Macedonia came and went.

As Russian-Austrian relations deteriorated new alliances emerged. Dividing lines grew clearer as Russia began to warm to Britain and France while Austria began to draw closer to Germany. Italy remained neutral for a time and took certain pre-emptive actions against Turkey, but it was prohibited by the other powers from attacking the centers of Turkish power. It was through these campaigns, however, that Italy occupied the Dodecanese Islands.

Even though Italy was restrained from further campaigns, it weakened Turkey enough for the three new Balkan states to consider campaigns of their own. Italy's actions were seen as a sign of things to come and created an atmosphere of urgency for the new states to expedite their own plans for territorial expansion.

Each wanted a part of Macedonia, but no one alone dared reach for it. The three new wolves of the Balkans, with Russian help, came to realize that each alone could not accomplish what the three could do together. They swallowed their pride, put their differences aside, and by the end of 1911 they negotiated joint action.

As a way of denying Austrian aspirations in the Balkans, Russia encouraged the idea of a Serbian-Bulgarian pact. Russia hoped that jointly, Serbia and Bulgaria would be able to withstand Austrian advances in Macedonia without her involvement. After getting them to agree to talk, Serbia and Bulgaria listed their terms, but could not reach an agreement. Autonomy for Macedonia was one major issue of contention that they could not agree upon. While Sofia supported the idea of autonomy, Belgrade opposed it. Finally, for the sake of expediting the negotiations, all parties agreed that the "autonomy question" would be left for later, to be dealt with after the "liberation" of Macedonia.

Russia made it clear to both parties that they could not invade Macedonia without Russia's permission and only if Turkey became a threat to the Christian population. In the meantime, Serbia was encouraged to take steps to annex Albania and Kosovo.

A draft Serbian-Bulgarian agreement was reached and signed on March 13th, 1912. Included in the agreement was a crude delineation of prospective boundaries, but there were ominous suggestions that the final boundaries might have to be settled by force of arms. The Russians, however, insisted that Tsar Nikolas II would arbitrate any disputes regarding the exact territorial boundaries.

Even before the Serbian-Bulgarian agreement was finalized, Greece was already starting negotiations with Bulgaria. The Greek-Bulgarian negotiations, like the Serbian-Bulgarian, were conducted in secret, known only to the Greek King, Prime Minister Venizelos and their negotiator, The Times of London correspondent J. D. Bourchier, who was an old friend of Venizelos. Like the Serbs, the Greeks had always opposed the idea of Macedonian autonomy, but the Bulgarians were unwilling to proceed until Greece agreed to the autonomy. The Greek-Bulgarian treaty was signed on May 30th 1912, with both parties promising not to attack the other and to come to each other's defense should Turkey attack them.

The "Balkan League of Nations" was created in June of 1912, and shortly thereafter, Turkey was given a signed ultimatum bearing the League's signature, which in short, read: "deliver the promised reforms in Macedonia or prepare to be invaded".

There was much intrigue, agreements, counter agreements and secret deals among the member states of the League of Balkan Nations. Greece, Bulgaria and Serbia, each, from the outset, was determined to exploit any situation that developed, purely for its own gain. Dakin (1966, 440) explains why the League held together in his work, *The Greek Struggle in Macedonia 1897-1913:*

The League of Balkan Nations in fact was simply a device for synchronizing a military effort upon the part of the four powers (Greece, Bulgaria, Serbia and Montenegro) who had come to realize that the simplest way to settle the Turkish question, before it was too late, and while circumstances were favourable, was to attack Turkey simultaneously and present the European powers with a fait accompli.

All that remained now was to provoke Turkey into committing an offence against the Christian population and the invasion could begin. Using proven terrorist tactics to prepare the way, Vrhovists, masquerading as IMRO agents, conducted raids inside Macedonia in hopes that the Macedonian bands would be blamed. When the Turks investigated the disturbances, both Patriarchist and Exarchist authorities corroborated their stories and pinned these acts on the Macedonians.

As expected, the Turks responded swiftly and dealt with the situation in the usual manner. Unfortunately for the Turks, their actions were welcome news to the League's spies who dispatched them to the European press. The Turks, in the eyes of the world, had once again committed atrocities against the Christians in Macedonia and something had to be done. It was now up to the Great Powers to decide the course of action.

Along with documentation of Turkish atrocities, the foreign press also received convincing League propaganda. The League had launched a propaganda campaigns against the Turks, detailing every Turkish act for European consumption. A war was imminent, but according to the League's propaganda, it was a necessary war to "liberate" the enslaved Christians from Turkish oppression. The League, through extensive media campaigns, called on all Christians in Macedonia to join the League in their effort to oust the oppressive Turk.

Here is what Yane Sandanski, however, had to say:

We ought to work on the awakening of the consciousness of the Macedonian masses that they are an independent nation...because those who seek to 'liberate them'... will actually be coming to enslave them...

As mentioned earlier, the Western Powers had not exhausted the full potential of the Ottoman markets, and so they were unwilling to let the Ottoman regime in Macedonia collapse. At the same time Britain, France, Italy and Russia were greatly concerned about the aggressive attitudes of Germany outside the Balkans. More importantly, they were concerned with the Turkish regime's possible negotiation of a Turkish-German alliance.

When Russia proposed the idea of a "Balkan League of Nations" it was welcome news to Britain, France and Italy. The League was viewed as an anti-German front, a way of ejecting the Ottoman regime from Europe and at the same time, safeguarding British, French and Italian interests and expansionary ambitions. The not so obvious Russian motive for sponsoring the League, was to guarantee its own influence in the Balkans, perhaps through Serbia, or Bulgaria, or both.

On October 18th, 1912 Montenegro declared war on Turkey with the League quickly following suit. The battles that ensued were fought almost entirely on Macedonian soil, once again causing Macedonian suffering.

Russia, the architect of the Balkan League was against a war in 1912, and so were France and Britain. A war at this point might throw off the delicate diplomatic balance and escalate into a "world war." Russia feared that the half-millennium old Ottoman Empire might not be so easy a target as the League had estimated. Britain and France feared a backlash from Germany and Austria now that Turkey was warming up to them as a prospective ally. To stop the League's aggressive actions, both Britain and France threatened them with economic sanctions but that was not enough to suppress the appetites of the three hungry Balkan wolves.

The League's plan was to surround the Turkish army in Macedonia and force it out to Istanbul. To everyone's surprise, however, the League won an unexpected decisive victory in just six weeks. Five Ottoman divisions were surrounded and defeated in two battles in Bitola and Kumanovo. With the exception of Sandanski and a force of 400 Macedonians who fought and liberated Melnik and Nevrokop, the League received no opposition from the Macedonians. In fact, the enthusiasm of the local people created by the arrival of the "liberators" not only helped the League fight harder, but it also encouraged thousands of Macedonians to enlist in the League's armies. Radin documents this in his, IMRO and the Macedonian Question, on page 143, where he writes:

A Macedonian Militia force of 14,000 fought under the Bulgarian command in the East. The 'Volunteer regiment', directed by IMRO veterans, consisted of a thousand Macedonians, Turks and Albanians. In the Serbian and Greek armies, Macedonian detachments such as the 'National Guard' and the 'Holy Band', were given the task of encircling the Turks to fight their retreat.

Macedonian chieftains such as Vasil Chakalarov, the protector of the Lerin and Kostur regions, joined the fight to help the League get rid of the Turks. The League's victories and their propaganda were so convincing that the entire Macedonian nation welcomed the "liberators" with open arms.

The moment the three wolves evicted the Turkish army from Macedonia, however, they quickly worked out a partitioning plan along the following lines: Serbia was to receive the northwestern portion of Macedonia, which included Skopje and Bitola to the south, and to the west of Lerin, east to Gevgelija and west to the Albanian Mountains. Bulgaria was to receive all of Thrace, west to Gevgelija, south to the Aegean Sea and east from Solun. Greece was to receive north to Lerin, west to the Albanian Mountains, all of Epirus and east to Salonica. Michael Radin (1993, 143) describes the establishment of the new order:

To ensure their hegemony and quell any dissent, the occupying forces set up the apparatus of government and, by legislative decrees, extended their own constitutions to these new bodies, from which Macedonians were absent. Indeed, in many provincial centres, such as Gevgelija, a double or triple condominium was established, much to the detriment of the Macedonian citizens.

In view of the Macedonian contribution to the League's success in evicting the Turks, on December 12th, 1912, Sandanski called for Macedonian autonomy. The League's occupying armies, however, refused to budge and initiated a violent assimilation program. The

Macedonian fighters that fought side by side with the League's armies found themselves policed by a joint League command ensuring that no resistance would arise. The League also pursued Sandanski and his men, but Sandanski evaded them and found refuge in his native Pirin region until his assassination in 1915 by Bulgarian agents.

The changing conditions inside Macedonia forced the IMRO leadership to seek refuge in foreign cities away from home. Some of the more prominent leaders moved to St. Petersburg and joined the Macedonian community living there. This small group of Macedonians consistently lobbied for Macedonian statehood and in the war's aftermath, acted as a government in exile. The most outspoken advocate among the Macedonian leaders was Dimitar Chupovski who published the "Macedonian Voice" and continuously protested to the Great Powers against Macedonia's partition. In June 1913 he wrote:

The division of Macedonia among the brother nations is the most unjust act in the history of these nations – it is trampling on the rights of man, and a disgrace for the entire Slav race.

In total, eleven issues of "Macedonian Voice" were published and distributed throughout Europe, spreading messages such as the following:

A great terror reigns in Macedonia now. The 'freedom' of the allies has no frontiers, no one from Macedonia has the right to travel outside, to protest or complain before the European states. Whoever disturbs this order is either killed or imprisoned. The allies surround Macedonia with a Chinese Wall...

The Macedonian people must not stand idly by and accept the unworthy fate of being divided so that others may profit from it. "In the name of the Macedonian people, we demand that Macedonia remain a single, indivisible, independent Balkan state within its geographical, ethnographic, historical, economic and cultural frontiers...Macedonia represents a unified body both from the historical and natural viewpoints, and cannot voluntarily end its many centuries of existence by agreeing to be broken up...Can we allow a people to be, at one and the same time, Bulgarian, Serb and Greek? Is it not simpler to assume that the nationality attributed to us is dictated by the big power politics of the interested parties who wish to take over Macedonia?

By November it was becoming apparent that Turkey was running out of options and on November 12th, 1912, called on the Great Powers to bring about an armistice. To deal with the situations, a peace conference was scheduled for December 16th, 1912, to take place in London. Having some time to adjust to the new situation, the Great Powers, for the first time, diverged from the usual "status quo" recommendations and considered making concessions to the victors. Austria, however, was not very happy at the prospect of a "large Serbia" let alone allowing Serbia access to the Adriatic Sea. Austria was eyeing the Adriatic region as a prospective sphere of influence for herself. Being unable to make concessions by herself, however, Austria did the next best thing and agreed with Britain to the idea of "creating" a new state (Albania). Another reason why Austria did not want Serbia to have access to the Adriatic Sea was because a "Serbian port might become a Russian port."

This attempt to deny Serbia access to the Adriatic not only left Serbia landlocked but upset Russia, causing her to break relations with Austria. Italy too was affected by this diplomatic power play, which pushed her to improve her relations with Austria. This, as it turned out was the critical historic moment that gave birth to the "Triple Alliance" (Germany, Austria-Hungary and Italy) and the "Triple Entente" (Britain, France and Russia), a division that would have future consequences.

As a result of this sudden change of events, Austria began to amass troops along the Serbian border. At the same time, fearing German intervention, Russia ordered a halt to Bulgarian and Serbian advances towards Istanbul. To fully curb Serbian and Russian expansionism, France, Britain and Italy voted to grant the newly created Albanian state full independence. This not only saved Albania from partition by the Greeks and Serbians, it also made her a Great Power protectorate, which Albanians enjoy to this day.

By 1912 it was well known that a Macedonian nation with a Macedonian consciousness existed and had made known its desire for independence. The actions of its leaders were well documented and familiar to the Great Powers. Yet, despite all their pleas for a place at the table, Macedonians were not allowed to attend the London Peace Conference of December 16th, 1912. Numerous petitions were made by IMRO affiliates in St. Petersburg, all were ignored. Also, Chupovski's memo to the British delegation, was not aired. Here is what Chupovski (in part) had to say:

In the name of natural law, of history, of practical expediency, for the Macedonian people, we ask that Macedonia's right to self-determination be admitted, and that Macedonia be constituted within its ethnic, geographical and cultural borders as a self-governing state with a government responsible to a national assembly. (Radin, 1993, 147)

The London Conference adjourned on August 11, 1913 officially declaring an end to the First Balkan War. Despite all of the wheeling and dealing that went on during the conference, the resolutions left all parties dissatisfied. Serbia was dissatisfied with losing the Albanian territory. Serbia appealed to Bulgaria to grant her access to the Aegean Sea via Salonica and the Vardar valley. Greece also was not happy with Bulgaria's invasion and annexation of Adrianople region. So to balance her share, Greece wanted Serres, Drama and Kavala as compensation. That too was rejected by Bulgaria.

Bulgaria expressed frustration at not achieving her "San Stefano Dream" of an enlarged Bulgaria according to the 1878 treaty. She was bitter about Russian failure to back her in that demand during the London Conference negotiations.

Seeing that Bulgaria was not going to budge, and the fact that neither Greece nor Serbia alone could take on Bulgaria, should a conflict arise, Greece and Serbia concluded a secret pact of their own to jointly act against Bulgaria. In short, the objective was to take territory from Bulgaria west of the Vardar River, divide it and create a common frontier.

After stumbling upon this Greek-Serbian pact, despite Russian attempts to appease her by offering her Salonica, Bulgaria, in a moment of weakness, was lured into league with Austria. By going over to Austria, Bulgaria in effect broke off all relations with the Balkan League. The Bulgarian shift in loyalties displeased Russia, who then made it clear to Bulgaria that they could no longer expect any help from the Russians.

In what was to be known as the Second Balkan War, the Bulgarian army, unprovoked, attacked its former allies on June 30th, 1913, again on Macedonian soil. Preferring the element of surprise, Bulgaria turned on her former allies and renewed the conflict, officially turning the Macedonian mission from "liberation" to "occupation". There were two things, however, that Bulgaria didn't count on, Romanian involvement and Austrian treachery. The bloody fight was short-lived as Rumania, Montenegro and Turkey joined Greece and Serbia and dealt Bulgaria a catastrophic blow. The promised Austrian support did not materialize as the risks of Austrian involvement outweighed any benefits. The real surprise, however, was Rumania's involvement. Up til then Rumania had remained neutral and had refused to get involved. No one, not even Bulgaria, anticipated this attack from the north. On the other hand, this was a once in a lifetime opportunity for Rumania to regain lost territory.

Even Turkey was able to regain some of what she had recently lost to Bulgaria. Engaged on too many fronts at the same time, Bulgaria was unable to repel Turkey and prevent her from taking back the Adrianople region.

The biggest winners were Greece and Serbia, both of whom received exactly what they had wanted, virtually unchallenged. Macedonians, of course, suffered most in the conflict, due to their collaboration with one side or another. As frontlines shifted, Macedonian citizens were exposed to the retaliation of one or another of these opposing sides in the conflict. As Michael Radin (1993, 149) described the result:

Those Macedonians who assisted one faction were butchered by another faction for showing sympathy to the enemy. The Carnegie Relief Commission, dispatched to the Balkans in late 1913, reported the incredible story of human suffering. In Macedonia alone, 160 villages were razed, leaving 16,000 homeless, several thousand civilians murdered, and over 100,000 forced to emigrate as refugees.

This devastation was committed in a relatively short time and by those who marched in and were welcomed as "liberators". Worst and most unexpected was that Christians were responsible for this slaughter of fellow Christians, reminiscent of the 1204 Balkan incursions of the Western Crusaders.

After a great deal of jockeying for position, deliberating and negotiating, the warring factions agreed to an armistice and peace among Rumania, Bulgaria, Greece and Serbia. It was negotiated in August of 1913 in Bucharest. The map of Macedonia was again redrawn without Macedonian participation. The new boundaries ignored previously agreed upon considerations such as distribution of "nationalities" (not that any truly accurate lines of demarcation existed), the Macedonian people's democratic desires, etc. The Bucharest delegates instead imposed their artificial sovereignty upon the Macedonian people. With the exception of one minor change in 1920 in Albania's favour, these dividing lines have remained in place to this day. 51% of the total Macedonian territory went to Greece, 39% to Serbia and 10% to Bulgaria. August 10th, 1913 will always be remembered as one of the darkest days in Macedonian history.

Not since Roman times had Macedonia been partitioned in such a way. Now it was possible for three brothers to be forced to assume three different (imposed) identities, forced to speak three different foreign languages in their own homes and treated as foreigners in their own land. The future will show that where half a millennium of Turkish oppression and a century of forced Hellenization/ Bulgarization couldn't erode Macedonian consciousness, Greek, Bulgarian and Serbian military aggression, in less than a decade, would have substantial success.

The once proud Macedonian nation that long ago had conquered the world, bridged East and West, introduced Christianity to Europe, safeguarded ancient knowledge and protected the West from Eastern invaders had now been broken and reduced to a mere shadow of its former self. The force of this latest intrusion transformed the Macedonian nation into a passive people seeking homes in foreign lands and hiding in the twilight. Even the dead knew no peace. Macedonian graves were even vandalized to further erase all evidence of the people's past on the land.

In order to fully possess the Macedonian land, these depraved creatures consumed by greed, not only took as their own all Macedonian treasures, including history, culture, religion, literature, folklore, and ancient knowledge from the Holy Mountain (Mt. Athos), they lied to the world, and to their own people about " true identities" and blamed all ills in the land on the innocent victims. Their propaganda would turn "lies to truths" and "truths to lies" until all people were poisoned with hatred, an artificially created hatred, which would curse Macedonians until it eventually rendered them mute. Silence was obligatory and children would not even dare to cry, for if they uttered anything Macedonian, a terrible curse would befall them, which could only be partially lifted if they would leave their lands or submit to the will of their new masters. The proud name "Macedonia" which echoed through the centuries and outlasted many kingdoms and empires, would become a "dirty word," never to be spoken. The Macedonian language, the mother of all Slav languages, the "Voice of Eastern Christianity" would be "muted," to be spoken only in the shadows, in fear that "enemy ears" might be lurking. In time it would become known as "our language" spoken by "our people" a mute language spoken by a nameless nation. Over time the Macedonian nation, the Macedonian people and the Macedonian language would become "an anachronism" in its ancestral land.

This was the fate that befell the Macedonian people in the first half of the 20th century, all with the blessings of the Great Powers (Britain, France, Russia, Germany, Austria-Hungary and Italy).

the Macedonian rebel chieftain Apostol

Chapter Ten

Macedonia During World War One and Its Aftermath, 1912 to 1939

"So you're from Breznitsa," he said. "From Breznitsa...from Breznitsa..., he kept repeating as he turned the pages. He slid his index finger from the top to the bottom of every page and then turned the page. Finally he said, "From Breznitsa. Here. Village of Breznitsa," he repeated in Greek. "The priest there is Hristos Hristomanos, Elenikos. That means that you're Greek. It all depends on the nationality of your village priest."

The cousins looked at each other. They remembered that nobody in the village could understand the language the priest spoke in church; he sang in a funny language the villagers used to say. The priest was from Breznitsa, but he had been educated in Greece, in Greek. On the cousins' faces there was a look of amazement, but of enlightenment as well, since they'd finally discovered why the priest was so important.

"That's right," said Srbin.

"That's right," Shishman repeated.

"Do you see now?" asked the mayor, exulting.

"So we're Greek," said Shishman. "That's that."

(from the novel *Cousins* by Meto Jovanovski. Holt and Jovanovski transl., 1987, 104)

The joy of liberation quickly died down as the fires of burning villages lit the night skies. Macedonia was in flames again. Liberators turned to occupiers and rained death and destruction down on the Macedonian populace. The political, economic and ethnic unity of Macedonia was no more. Greek soldiers who came to liberate their Christian brothers from the oppressive Turks and terrible Bulgarians were now burning, torturing, and murdering people. In the words of Sir Edmond Grey:

The Balkan war began as a war of liberation, became rapidly a war of annexation, and has ended as a war of extermination.

(Bogov, 1998, *Macedonian Revelation, Historical Documents Rock and Shatter Modern Political Ideology).*

The extent of Greek atrocities was revealed to the world when a lost mailbag was discovered that contained letters from Greek soldiers in Macedonia to their families in Greece. The mailbag was turned in to the Carnegie Relief Commission and the contents of the letters were made public. Expecting to fight for the glory of the fatherland, the soldiers instead found themselves torturing, murdering, burning houses and evicting women and children from their homes in a most vile campaign of conquest. The letters revealed that the soldiers were acting on direct orders from the Greek authorities and the Greek king himself. According to the authors of these letters Macedonian families of known Exarchists (Macedonians belonging to the Bulgarian Church) were ordered by force to: "take with them what they could carry and get out. This is Greece now, and there is no place for Bulgarians here." Those that remained were forced to swear loyalty to the Greek state. Anyone who refused to take the loyalty oath was either executed as an example of what would happen to those who resisted, or they were deported from the country. To explain the mass deportations, Greek officials were claiming that the inhabitants of Macedonia were leaving by choice or becoming Greek by choice. The truth is, no one was given any choice at all. John Shea in his book *Macedonia and Greece, The Struggle to define a new Balkan Nation*, (1997, 104) explained that:

A thousand Greek and Serbian publicists began to fill the world with their shouting about the essentially Greek or Serbian character of the populations of their different spheres. The Serbs gave the unhappy Macedonians twenty four hours to renounce their nationality and proclaim themselves Serbs, and the Greeks did the same. Refusal meant murder or expulsion. Greek and Serbian colonists were poured into the occupied country... The Greek newspapers began to talk about a Macedonia peopled entirely with Greeks-and they explained the fact that no one spoke Greek by calling the people 'Bulgaro-phone Greeks' ... the Greek army entered villages where no one spoke their language. "What do you mean by speaking Bulgarian?" cried the officers. "This is Greece and you must speak Greek."

In 1913 professor R.A. Reiss reports to the Greek government: "*Those whom you would call Bulgarian speakers I would simply call Macedonians...Macedonian is not the language they speak in Sofia... I repeat the mass of inhabitants there (Macedonia) remain simply Macedonians.*"

Michael Radin (1993, 149) describes the extent of the tragedy documented:

The Carnegie Relief Commission, dispatched to the Balkans in late 1913, reported the incredible story of human suffering. In Macedonia alone, 160 villages were razed leaving 16,000 homeless, several thousand civilians murdered, and over 100,000 forced to emigrate as refugees.

History again turned its eyes away from the Greek, Bulgarian and Serbian atrocities in Macedonia to focus on new events that were about to unfold and engulf the entire world. After losing Bosnia and Herzegovina to Austria in 1908 and the Albanian territories in 1912 (again because of Austria), Serbians grew bitter and resentful.

To the nationalist Serbs the Habsburg monarchy (Austria-Hungary) was an old and evil monster which prevented their nation from becoming a great and powerful state.. On June 28, 1914, a young Serbian nationalist, Gavrilo Princip, assassinated the heir of the Habsburg monarchy, the Archduke Francis Ferdinand, and his wife at Sarajevo. (Gilbert, 1970, 104)

Within two weeks of the assassination the First World War broke out, engulfing all of Europe in war. It was inevitable and only a matter of time before such a war involving the Great Powers would erupt in the Balkans. The Great Powers were incapable of exercising diplomacy either among themselves or with the new Balkan states they had helped create. Macedonia was sacrificed in order to appease the new Balkan states, but that did little to satisfy their appetites.

While World War I raged on, consuming the lives of millions of young men and women, Greece, Bulgaria and Serbia were each practicing their own brand of chauvinism in Macedonia. For the next five years, with the world busy with its own problems there was no one to hear the anguished cries of the Macedonian people at the hands of the new tyrants. If the gravestones of the dead Macedonians could speak, they would tell tales of torture and executions, deception and lies. They would say: "Our Christian brothers came to liberate us but instead they killed us because we were in their way of achieving greatness. We were labeled 'criminals' because we would not yield to their demands. I ask you, is it a crime to want to live as free men? Is it a crime to want to be Macedonian? Is it a crime to want to exercise free will? It is they who are the criminals for befouling everything that is Christian, for their lies and deception, and for murdering us to possess our lands. History will record August 10th, 1913 as one of the darkest day in Macedonia's long history, the day our future died".

The triple occupation worsened living conditions in Macedonia, but the fighting spirit of the Macedonian people continued to live underground and abroad. Three generations had fought for freedom and independence. Their struggles culminated in the mass uprising of the Ilinden generation, organized by the brave and idealistic leadership of the IMRO. They were defeated, not by the Turks, not by Muslim oppression, but by Christian cruelty and deception.

Soon after the occupation, underground societies sprang up everywhere, urging the Macedonian people to refuse their new fate and oppose the partition. As a result, many Macedonians refused to collaborate with the new officialdom by not participating in the new institutions. This, however, did not deter the military regimes occupying Macedonia from their campaign of systematic denationalization and violent assimilation.

The world struggle for domination by the Great Powers inevitably returned to Macedonia. As the Entente Powers (Britain, France, Russia and Italy) fought the Central Powers (Germany and Austro-Hungary), Bulgaria, smarting from her losses at Bucharest, remained neutral. In a turn of events that surprised the Greeks, the Entente Powers approached Bulgaria with an offer of a substantial portion of Macedonian territory in exchange for her alliance. Bulgaria, however, seemed to prefer the company of the Central Powers. Perhaps they offered her a bigger portion, because by late 1915, her armies marched in and invaded Macedonia. To quote the Bulgarian War Minister General Nikolaev:

We care little about the British, Germans, French, Russians, Italians, Austrians or Hungarians; our only thought is Macedonia. Whichever of the two groups of Powers will enable us to conquer it will have our alliance! (Radin, 1993, 154).

While the Serbs were engaged in combat on their northern border, the Greeks were debating which side to take. Their hesitation or "National Schism", as it was later called, lay in the differences that emerged between the Greek Prime Minister Venizelos and the Greek King Constantine I, over which side to join. Venizelos was a strong supporter of the Entente and within days of the outbreak of hostilities, was ready to offer Greek troops to fight alongside the Entente forces. King Constantine, on the other hand, did not share Venizelo's enthusiasm for the war and believed that Greek policies would be served best by staying neutral. Being married to Sofia, the sister of Kaiser Wilhelm II, however, predisposed Constantine to favor the Central Powers. The tug of war between Prime Minister and king divided the people of Greece into two camps and the country slid towards civil war. Having the authority to do so, Constantine replaced Venizelos with a pro-German prime minister and to end the impasse, called for an election. Unfortunately for the King, Venizelos once again emerged victorious with a clear majority of the votes. Bulgaria's invasion of Serbian territory, due to a Greek-Serbian treaty, obliged Greece to come to Serbia's aid, but the king's camp refused to comply. They argued that Bulgaria was not the only aggressor in the war and insisted on remaining neutral. Venizelos, on the other hand, called on parliament to support his position and to send Greek troops to fight alongside the Serbs and to allow landings of Entente troops in the Salonica region. Venizelos was again forced to resign on October 5, 1915. It signaled a total breakdown in relations between the king and the prime minister. Britain and France, however, approached Venizelo's successor, Alexander Zaimis, and offered him the return of Cyprus to Greece in exchange for aid to Serbia, which was in dire need of assistance.

Soon after that Zaimis too was forced to resign. New elections were held in December, but the Venizelos camp refused to participate. Events came to a head when the Royalists refused to allow evacuated Serbian troops to travel from Corfu to join the Entente forces on the Salonica front. Backed by the Entente, a group of pro-Venizelos officers took over the government offices in Salonica. They created a provisional pro-Entente government there with its own army. Once again many Macedonians, deceived by the propaganda of the warring sides, joined in the war effort in hopes of liberation, only to end up as "cannon fodder" for both sides at the front. Month after month Macedonian casualties mounted and towns and villages only recently reconstructed were again reduced to rubble.

The Salonica Front facilitated the occupation of Greece. France had dispatched 60,000 troops to the Balkans in hopes of safeguarding the Skopje to Salonica rail line. By late 1917 Entente troops were achieving supremacy over the Bulgarians and Germans in Macedonia. No sooner was the battle over than a problem developed between British and French commands in Macedonia. While the British General Milne supported Venizelos and his attempts to constitute a pro-British provisional government in Greece, the pro-Macedonian French General Sarrail opposed Venizelos and sought to drive the Greek army out of

Macedonia. Michael Radin has pointed out, however, that:

The ambitious plan for Macedonian autonomy drafted by the French command in 1915 and 1916 were but mere progressive steps to ensure France a strategic outpost for capital expansion. (Radin, 1993, 155).

Once again Macedonians were caught in the middle of someone else's war. To salvage what it could from the situation, France recalled Sarrail and replaced him with a pro-Greek commander, thus avoiding a diplomatic crisis. After he established a government in Athens and consolidated his power in Greece, Venizelos was then able to commit a total of nine divisions to Macedonia to assist the Entente forces on the Salonica Front. To further prove his devotion to the cause of the Entente, Venizelos committed two more divisions to fight the Bolsheviks in Russia.

When the war ended on November 11, 1918, a general armistice was signed and a Peace Conference was convened in Versailles, France. Venizelos arrived in Paris as the principle negotiator for Greece, determined to reap his reward for his solid support for his victorious allies. One of Venizelos's ambitions was to resurrect the "Megaly Idea" by annexing parts of Asia Minor, Smyrna (Ismir) in particular. He convinced the world that the Christians living in Asia Minor were Greek and should be part of Greece. Unfortunately for Venizelos, Italy had prior claims in Asia Minor (Anatolia), creating a problem for the peacemakers. Greek ambitions were viewed with great suspicion by Italy. Therefore, in order to strengthen her claims, in March 1919, Italy began to build up troops in the region. The Greeks viewed this as a threat to their own claims, so, before a final territorial solution was reached, they demanded concessions. The reasons given were that the Greek people in Asia Minor were endangered by Turkish aggression and needed protection. After much protest on the Greek side, Britain, France and the Americans finally gave them permission to send a small defense force. Under the protection of allied warships, on May 15, 1919, Greek troops began their landing in Smyrna. Instead of staying put, however, as per prior agreements, they began to occupy western Asia Minor.

No sooner were the Central Powers driven out of Greek territories than the Greek Government, by passing Law 1051, created a new administrative jurisdiction for governing the newly acquired lands in Macedonia. When it started to become clear that the Entente Powers were winning the war, encouraged by Woodrow Wilson's principles of nationality, Macedonian lobby groups sought to participate in the Peace Conference in Versailles. They were encouraged to do so by Wilson's fourteen principles of nationality, which implicitly asserted the right of all nations to self-determination.

In his address to the Pan Slavic Assembly in Odessa in August 1914, Krste Misirkov called for Macedonian autonomy to be achieved by diplomatic means. A letterwas composed and circulated in May of 1915, specifically supporting this latest call for autonomy.

The student organization "Independent Society", in Geneva Switzerland under the slogan of "Macedonia for the Macedonians," demanded the application of Wilson's principles in order to create an autonomous Macedonia based on the principles of the Swiss Federative model. Remnants of the IMRO also participated in the call for an autonomous Macedonia. After the Bulgarians murdered Yane Sandanski, his supporters fled the Pirin region to save their own lives and later regrouped in Serres to form the Serres Revolutionary Council. Responding to a plan for Southern Slav unification, the Council issued a "Declaration of Autonomy" in October 1918, in which it appealed for Macedonian membership in a Balkan Federation on the basis of Macedonia's territorial integrity. The Serbian rulers of what would become the Yugoslavian Kingdom of the Serbs, Croats and Slovenes rejected this proposal. Thus, failing to learn the lesson contained in the declaration that explained that:

By striving for political and economic hegemony over the Balkans, Balkan nationalism has thrown the Balkan peoples and states into deep contradictions and conflicts which must be begun by war, and finished by war and always war.. (Radin, 1993, 158-159).

Once again the Macedonian people tried to plead their case and once again they were shut out of negotiations concerning their fate. How many more wars must be fought and how much more blood must be spilled before the world's leaders realize that the Macedonian people must be included in any attempt to resolve the Macedonian question?

The Peace Conference, which was supposedly "the tribunal of international conscience", had no place for "Wilsonian Justice" or for the self-determination he had envisioned. The so-called "peace makers of Versailles" in the end only rewarded aggression and served their own narrow self-interest.

With the stroke of a pen, in 1919 at the Treaty of Versailles (Paris), England and France sealed Macedonia's fate by ratifying the principles of the Bucharest Treaty and officially endorsing the partition of Macedonia. This gave Greece the license she needed to pursue forced expulsion and denationalization of Macedonians and to begin a mass colonization of transplanted Greeks into the annexed territories of Macedonia. The Neuilly Convention allowed for forced exchanges of populations. About 70,000 Macedonians were expelled from the Greek occupied part of Macedonia and sent to Bulgaria and 25,000 people with an affinity for Greece were transferred from Bulgaria to Greek occupied Macedonia.

Michael Radin in his *IMRO and the Macedonian Question* (1993, 160) expresses the Macedonian view of this injustice, when he writes:

Macedonia's fate has been the subject of every kind of political combination, negotiation and treaty since 1912, each more immoral than the last, each ignoring completely the local interests and desires of a population which, with the stroke of the statesman's pen, can be condemned to national dissolution, and denied the right to a free national life while Armenians, Albanians and Jews receive political freedom.

The prevailing European powers, no doubt, believed that the strategic importance and untapped wealth of Macedonia must only be entrusted to their allies in the Balkans. What was surprising, however, especially to the Balkan delegation, was the raising of the Macedonian Question by Italy. On July 10, 1919, Italy along with the USA made a proposal to the "Committee for the Formation of New States" for Macedonian autonomy. France openly opposed the motion, while Britain proposed establishing a five-year Macedonian Commissary, under the sponsorship of the League of Nations. Greece and Serbia, by absolutely refusing to acknowledge the existence of a Macedonian Question, assured the motion's failure.

Another item that came out of Versailles was Article 51, the League of Nations' code to "protect national minorities". Article 51 of the Treaty of Versailles espouses equality of civil rights, education, language, and religion for all national minorities. Unfortunately, article 51 was never implemented by the Balkan states nor enforced by the League of Nations. Greece and Bulgaria violate and ignore this provison of the UN charter to this day. Why is this? Because, to this day, Greece and Bulgaria claim that the Macedonian ethnic identity does not exist and has never existed. Therefore, what minority requires protection? The Greeks must someday answer the following questions honestly;

1. To what minorities were they referring when on September 29, 1924 their Minister of Foreign Affairs Nikolaos Mihalakopoulou signed an agreement with the Bulgarian Foreign Minister Kalkoff?

2. To what minorities were they referring when on August 17, 1926 they made an agreement with Yugoslavia regarding the nationality of the "Slavophones in Greece?

(Pages 159-161 G.A.L. I Kata Tis Makedonias Epivouli, (Ekdosis Deftera Sympepliromeni), Athinai 1966).

On September 29, 1924, Greece signed an agreement with Bulgaria declaring that the Macedonians in Greece were Bulgarians. Not to disappoint the Serbians, when they found out about the Greek-Bulgarian agreement, the Greeks changed their mind and on August 17, 1926, declared that the Macedonians in Greece were, in reality, Serbs.

As it turned out, the loudly proclaimed "Wilson principles" at the Paris Conference were only for show. The real winners by the end of the conference were those who needed to be rewarded for their services to the Entente's war effort, which included Venizelos of Greece. Again, Macedonian activist in Australia, Michael Radin sums up the results of the conference:

The entire forum was a farce, and its offspring the Versailles Treaty, the ultimate insult to the dignity and self-esteem (what remained of it after continuous war and bloodshed) of the long-tormented Macedonian people. Those Macedonians prodded by conscience, by the mistrust gained after generations of suffering, and by the desire for freedom, thereafter treated the Versailles Treaty, and all political treaties, with the contempt they deserve. (Radin, 1993, 166).

At the conclusion of the Treaty, not only did Greece get back what she had previously annexed, but she additionally received a large portion of Epirus, Western Thrace, Crete and the Aegean Islands. It is important to mention here that when Albania's affirmation of independence was signed at the London Conference in February 1920, additional Macedonian territory was partitioned. A narrow strip of land running through Lake Ohrid and southward along Macedonia's western boundary was awarded to Albania.

Soon after arriving back to Greece victorious, Venizelos, in a speech in Salonica, announced his plans for a "Greater Greece" (the Megaly Idea) and for the bringing of all "Greek peoples" together under a single Greater Greek state.

Old men in the Macedonian villages, sitting on the porch telling tales of bygone wars, described how, as young soldiers they chased the Turks to Ankara, yelling "two Turks to a bayonet!" They also told stories of how it took them sixty days to gain sixty miles and how they lost them in one day of retreat. What they were talking about were the Greek exploits in Asia Minor. After building up a large military presence in Asia Minor, a major offensive was launched in March 1921, and by the end of the summer, the Greek armies reached the Sakarya River about forty miles from Ankara. The assault on Asia Minor was an "exclusively Greek initiative" without the blessing of the Entente Powers and as a result they found themselves alone and running out of ammunition. They knew they couldn't count on Italy or France for help but the realization of their predicament sunk in when Britain too refused to help them. By early autumn the Greeks were pushed back beyond the halfway point between Smyrna and Ankara, reaching an uneasy military stalemate.

Realizing that they couldn't possibly win militarily or politically, the Greeks turned to the Paris Conference of March 1922 looking for a compromise solution more to their benefit. The proposed compromise called for the withdrawal of the Greek armies and placing the Christian population under the protection of the League of Nations. Sensing a victory, Mustafa Kemal of Turkey insisted on an unconditional evacuation of the Greek forces, a demand unacceptable to the Greeks. Still counting on British kindness, in July 1922 the Greeks unsuccessfully attempted to get permission from their allies to enter Istanbul.

Turkey launched a full-scale offensive on August 26, 1922 (a dark day for Greece and her Megaly Idea) near Afyonkarahisar and forced the Greeks into a hasty retreat back to Smyrna. On September 8 the Greek army was evacuated, and the next day the Turkish army invaded Smyrna. The worst came on the evening of the 9th when outbreaks of killing and looting were followed by a massacre of the Christian population. Some 30,000 Christians, mostly Armenians, perished. As a result of the violence as many as 250,000 people fled to the waterfront to escape the slaughter.

The Asia Minor campaign was over, along with the "Megaly Idea" of a Greater Greece. Worse yet, as a result of this catastrophic Greek military adventure, over one million Turkish Christians were displaced, most of them into Macedonia. Their settlement affected the demography of the Macedonian landscape, as well as the morale of the Macedonian people.

An entire generation of Macedonian young men, who were drafted into the Greek military, were sent to the Asia Minor campaigns, and many lost their lives there. The Greek authorities never acknowledged their services, nor was any compensation ever paid to the families of those who lost their lives. The reason often given for the omission by the Greek authorities, "they were Bulgarian". In other words, the Greeks repaid those who died for Greece by letting their widows and children live in poverty.

By the Treaty of Lausanne in July 1923, the Greco-Turkish war came to an end. Greece and Turkey signed a population exchange agreement using "religion as the basic criterion for nationality". The November 1925 issue of *National Geographic Magazine* best illustrates the magnitude of the human flood, the audacity of the Greek and Turkish authorities and the total disregard for human life in that exchange:

History's Greatest Trek, Tragedy Stalks the Near East as Greece and Turkey Exchange Two Million of their People. ...1922 began what may fairly be called history's greatest, most spectacular trek- the compulsory intermigration of two million Christians and Muslims across the Aegean Sea." " ...the initial episodes of the exchange drama were enacted to the accompaniment of the boom of cannon and the rattle of machine gun and with the settings pointed by the flames of the Smyrna holocaust."

(Melville Chater, 1925, 533).

Melvin Chater goes on to write for *National Geographic* in that same article that:

Stroke of the Pen Exiles 3,000,000 People. It is safe to say that history does not contain a more extraordinary document. Never before in the world's long pageant of folk-wanderings have 2,000,000 people- and certainly no less than 3,000,000 if the retroactive clause is possible of complete application-been exiled and re-adopted by the stroke of the pen. (page 569). ... Even if regarded as a voluntary trek instead of a compulsory exchange, the movement would be without parallel in the history of emigration. ... One might just add that history has never produced a document more difficult of execution. It was to lessen these difficulties that exchangeability was based in religion and not race. Due to five centuries of Turkish domination in Greece, the complexities in determining an individual's racial status are often such as would make a census taker weep. (page 570). Greece with one-fifth Turkey's area has 1,5000,000 more people. Turkey with a population of 5,000,000 and naturally rich territory contains only 15 people to the square mile...Greece, with less than one fifth of Turkey's area, emerges with a population exceeding the latter's for the first time by 1,500,000 people averaging 123 to the square mile. (page 584).

However, there was a human cost that Chater exposes:

History's Greatest Trek has cost 300,000 lives. Conservative estimates place it at 300,000 lives lost by disease and exposure. (page 584)

Richard Clogg in his *A Short History of Modern Greece*, (1986,

121) describes the demographic change this brought to Macedonia:

The actual exchange was weighted very heavily in Turkey's favour, for some 380,000 Muslims were exchanged for something like 1,100,000 Christians." "The total population in Greece rose between 1907 and 1928 from 2,600,000 to 6,200,000." "After the Greek advances of 1912, for instance, the Greek elements in Greek Macedonia had constituted 43 percent of the population. By 1926, with the resettlement of the refugees, the Greek element has risen to 89 percent.

After all this, surprisingly, Greece still claims her population to be homogeneous and direct descendants of the peoples of the ancient City States. And as Antonios Kandiotis, Metropolite of Florina states:

If Greece exists today as a homogeneous ethnos, she owes this to [the Asia Minor Catastrophe]. If the hundreds of thousands of refugees had not come to Greece, Greek Macedonia would not exist today. The refugees created the national homogeneity of our country. (Karakasidou, 1997, 141).

According to Anastasia Karakasidou, almost half of the refugees were settled in urban centers and rural areas in Macedonia:

Searching for locations in which to settle this mass of humanity, the Greek government looked north to the newly incorporated land in Macedonia. ...by 1930, 90 percent of the 578,844 refugees settled in rural Greece were concentrated in the regions of Macedonia and western Thrace. Thus Macedonia, Greece's newly acquired second 'breadbasket' (after Thessaly), became the depository for East Thracian, Pontic, and Asia Minor refugees. (Karakasidou, 1997, 145).

While Greece was contemplating re-populating Macedonia with foreign refugees, other developments in Macedonia created contradictions in the Greek argument for the non-existence of a Macedonian ethnic identity:

A book of great importance to Macedonian linguistics and historiography was published in Athens; that was the primer entitled ABECEDAR (A B C), printed in the Latin alphabet, and intended for the children of the Macedonian ethnic minority in Greece - the 'Slav speaking minority' as Sir Austin Chamberlain, British diplomat and delegate to the League of Nations, and Sir James Erick Drumond, General Secretary to the League of Nations, referred to the Macedonians in Greece. (Kushevski, 1983, 184).

In 1920 Greece signed before the League of Nations a treaty obliging it to grant certain rights to the minorities of non-Greek origin in Greece. Four years later, in 1924, at the suggestion of the League of Nations, Greece and Bulgaria signed the well-known Kalfov-Politis Protocol under which Bulgaria was obliged to grant the Greek minority in Bulgaria their minority rights (language, schools and other rights), while Greece, recognizing the Macedonians from the Aegean part of Macedonia as a 'Bulgarian' minority, was to grant them their minority rights. This agreement was seemingly very much in favour of Bulgaria, but when in 1925 the Greek government undertook certain concrete steps towards the publication of the first primer made for the specific needs of that minority, it made it clear that there were no grounds on which Bulgaria could be officially interested in any 'Bulgarian minority' or expect the primer to be in Bulgarian, because that minority, although speaking a Slav language, was neither Bulgarian nor Serbian.

The very fact that official Greece did not, either de jure or do facto, see the Macedonians as a Bulgarian minority, but rather as a separate Slav group, a Slav speaking minority in Greece, is of particular significance. The primer, published in the Latin alphabet, was based on the Lerin - Bitola dialect. After Gianelli's Dictionary dating from the 16th Century, and the Daniloviot Chetirijazichnik written in the 19th century, this was yet another book written in the Macedonian vernacular. The primer was mailed to some regions in Western Aegean-Macedonia (Kostur, Lerin and Voden), and the school authorities prepared to give Macedonian children, from the first to the fourth grades of the elementary school, instruction in their own mother tongue. All of this is well-documented in Grigorios Dafnis, 'Greece between the two world wars', Elefteria newspaper, March 15, 1953, Dionisios Romas in Elefteria newspaper of October 9 and 12, 1954 and Dimitrios Vazuglis in Racial and religious minorities in Greece and Bulgaria, 1954.

The Greek government, however, never made a sincere attempt to solve the question of the Macedonians and their ethnic rights in Greece.

While measures were being undertaken for the opening of Macedonian schools, a clash between the Greek and the Bulgarian armies at Petrich, followed by a massacre of the innocent Macedonian population in the village of Trlis near Serres, put an end to the school project. Whether contrived or not, this incident so frightened Macedonians, that they did not push for recognition of their minority rights, and many sought safety by moving to Bulgaria. The Greek government took advantage of the Yugoslav-Bulgarian disagreement over the question of the Macedonians in Greece to exert further pressure on the Macedonian population. They hoped to resolve the Macedonian ethnic question through forced resettlement of the Macedonian population outside of Greece.

The ABECEDAR, which actually never reached the Macedonian children, is in itself a powerful testimony not only to the existence of the large Macedonian ethnic minority in Greece, but also to the fact that Greece was under an obligation before the League of Nations to undertake certain measures in order to grant this particular minority their rights. (Hristo Andonovski).

Even before Greece had secured her grip on Macedonia, officials were sent to administer "the new lands". The first official Greek administrator arrived in Solun near the end of October 1912 accompanied by two judges, five customs officials, ten consulate clerks, a contingent of reporters and journalists and 168 Cretan soldiers. Among other things, the first order of business was to "Hellenize the New Lands". John Shea, in his book, Macedonia and Greece, The Struggle to Define a New Balkan Nation, on page 109, describes the extent of the ethnic-cultural cleansing:

After the Greeks occupied Aegean Macedonia, they closed the Slavic language schools and churches and expelled the priests. The Macedonian language and names were forbidden, and the Macedonians were referred to as Bulgarians, Serbians or natives. A law of November 21, 1926, declared that all place names (toponyms) were to be Hellenized. All of the former names of cities, villages, rivers and mountains were discarded and Greek names put in their place. At the same time the Macedonians were forced to change their first and surnames; every Macedonian surname had to end in 'os', 'es', or 'poulos'. The news of these acts and the new, official Greek names were published in the Greek government daily Efimeris tis Kiverniseos, no. 322 and 324 of November 21 and 23, 1926. The requirement to use these Greek names is officially binding to this day. All evidence of the Macedonian language was removed from churches, monuments, archeological finds and cemeteries. Slavonic church or secular literature was seized and burned. The use of the Macedonian language was strictly forbidden also in personal communication between parents and children, among villagers, at weddings and work parties, and in burial rituals."

The act of forbidding the use of the Macedonian language in Greece is best illustrated by an example of how it was implemented in the Township of Assarios (Giuvezna). Here is a quote from Karakasidou's book *Fields of Wheat, Hills of Blood:*

[We] listened to the president articulate to the council that in accordance with the decision [#122770] of Mr. Minister, General Governor of Macedonia, all municipal and township councils would forbid, through [administrative] decisions, the speaking of other idioms of obsolete languages within the area of their jurisdiction for the reconstitution of a universal language and our national glory. [The president] suggested that [the] speaking of different idioms, foreign [languages] and our language in an impure or obsolete manner in the area of the township of Assirios would be forbidden.

Assirios Township Decision No. 134, 13 December 1936". (Karakasidou, 1997, 162).

By 1928, 1,497 Macedonian place-names in the Greek occupied Macedonia were Hellenized (LAW 4096) and all Cyrillic inscriptions found in churches, on tombstones, and on icons were destroyed (or overwritten) prompting English Journalist V. Hild to say: *The Greeks do not only persecute living Slavs (Macedonians)..., but they even persecute dead ones. They do not leave them in peace even in the graves. They erase the Slavonic inscriptions on the headstones, remove the bones and burn them.*

In the years following World War One the Macedonian people were subjected to harsh and systematic denationalization by all three of their occupying neighbors. The "denationalization schemes" were so extensive and so aggressively pursued that in the long term, they eroded the will of the Macedonian people to resist. According to a report by the Association of the Macedonians in Poland, *What Europe has Forgotten: The Struggle of the Aegean Macedonians*, page 8, describes some of these harsh measures in Greece:

In Greece, in 1929 during the rule of Elepterios Venizelos, a legal act was issued 'On the protection of public order'. In line with this Act each demand for nationality rights is regarded as high treason. This law is still in force.

On December 18, 1936, Metaxas' dictatorial government issued a legal Act 'On the activity against state security' on the strength of which thousands of Macedonians were arrested, imprisoned, expelled or exiled (EXORIA) on arid, inhospitable Greek islands, where many perished. Their crime? Being ethnic Macedonian by birth.

On September 7, 1938 legal Act No. 2366 was issued banning the use of the Macedonian language. All Macedonian localities were flooded with posters: 'Speak Greek'. Evening schools were opened in which adult Macedonians were taught Greek. Not a single Macedonian school functioned at the time."

Many Macedonians were fined, beaten and jailed for speaking Macedonian. Adults and school children alike were further humiliated by being forced to drink castor oil when caught speaking Macedonian.

In Vardar Macedonia, the Yugoslav government attacked the problem of denationalization and assimilation by enacting laws such as the September 24, 1920 "Resolution for the Settlement of the New Southern Regions" designed to effectively exclude Macedonians from owning any property. The Macedonian language was banned along with cultural institutions through a uniform code known as the "December 30th, 1920 Edict" which was aimed at persecuting all political and trade union associations.

The best of the arable Macedonian land was awarded to Serbian army officers who had survived the World War One Salonica Front. Land was also awarded to the Serbian administrators of Macedonia including government bureaucrats, judges and the police. The denationalization measures included aggressive re-education programs producing "little Serbs" out of the Macedonian children. As for the unwilling adults, they were given two options - "live as a Serb" or "die as a Macedonian"!

In Pirin Macedonia, the Bulgarian government enforced compulsory name changes and through repressive political and economic measures, stepped up the assimilation process. Initially, land reforms favored the poor, including the Macedonian peasants Later, however, that too changed and the Macedonians were exposed to a similar fate as the Macedonians in Aegea and Vardar.

The Macedonians in Albania, posing little threat to Albania's authority, fared relatively better than their kin in Greece, Bulgaria and Serbia. The village inhabitants were not persecuted or subjected to any comprehensive or systematic denationalization programs. As a result, the Macedonian culture flourished, original names remained and the people were not punished for speaking Macedonian.

As mentioned earlier, many of the IMRO regional leaders, fooled by the Balkan League's propaganda, voluntarily joined the League's armies in 1912 to help oust the Turks and liberate Macedonia. When it was over and the so-called "liberation" turned into an "occupation", they were subject to imprisonment by the League's soldiers. The ones fortunate enough to escape, fled to the Pirin region and joined up with Yane Sandanski's cheta, which was still active at the time. After Sandanski's assassination in 1915, however, many of his comrades went underground. Some later re-emerged in Serres to form the "Serres Revolutionary Council". The left wing of IMRO re-emerged prior to the 1919 Paris Peace Conference with high hopes of settling the Macedonian question by lobbying the delegates. After realizing that their efforts were in vain, they merged with the Provisional Mission of Western Macedonia to form IMRO (United). They declared "Macedonia is alive, united in spirit, if not in substance." Unfortunately, because of Macedonia's division and the impenetrable barriers erected, putting up a united national front was difficult, if not impossible. Even though there was much desire to achieve a united, autonomous Macedonia, mobilization of the populace was nearly impossible.

How was IMRO to achieve its goals under such conditions? Some leaders believed that by internationalizing the Macedonian question and by working with the supportive political elements of each Balkan state, the denationalization process could be slowed, even reversed, and a climate for reunification created. The leadership of the IMRO believed that new, revolutionary, non-nationalistic tactics were called for. By joining the "international class struggle against a common oppressor", IMRO believed self-determination could be achieved.

The only political elements that sympathized with the IMRO's objectives at the time were the communist parties of the respective Balkan states. The IMRO called on the Macedonian people to join the class struggle and support those sympathetic to the Macedonian cause. Many Macedonians did rise to the task, but they found that they did not have much in common with the exploited working class in their respective new countries. Macedonians felt that they were exploited first, because they were Macedonians, and second, because they were of the working class. To win them over, the Communist International (Comintern) was obliged to consider concessions such as offering Macedonians autonomy and the right to self-determination, or at least recognizing the Macedonian national identity with full rights and privileges. The Comintern saw the Macedonians as a potentially strong ally in their cause. Unfortunately, there were problems, many problems. First, there were disagreements between the various Balkan state communist parties concerning the concessions to be made. Then, there were fears of losing Macedonian territory, if autonomy was considered. Moscow, the leading Comintern member favored a Balkan Federation with the whole of Macedonia as one of its republics. Bulgaria, unfortunately, still dreaming the San Stefano dream, balked at the idea.

With no way of penetrating the barriers imposed by the partition of Macedonia by the Balkan states, IMRO was never again able to resurrect the organization that had once led to the Ilinden Uprising. As a consequence, its role slowly diminished and the organization disappeared after the German occupation of the Balkans in 1941.

After the World War One there was a peace of sorts in Europe. Unfortunately, Macedonians continued to endure denationalization, forced assimilation, forced emigration, and economic impoverishment at the hands of their new masters. As time would tell, Europe would not have lasting peace, a new menace was emerging that would soon engulf the entire world in a new war. Once again someone else's war would be fought on Macedonian soil, and once again it would prove even more devastating, almost fatal to the Macedonian people.

Second Brigade of Macedonian Partisans in World War Two

Chapter Eleven

Macedonia During World War Two and Its Aftermath, 1939-1949

Comrade Tatsko Nasteichin sat hunched on the small steps of the former headman's house; his face was turned to the red ball of the setting sun. He appeared to be dyed entirely red and the wound on the right side of his face had become a red flower that had just opened. With half-closed eyes, he gazed listlessly over the gardens that spread out just beyond the headman's house. He was overtired and much in need of sleep. He huddled in his greatcoat, wanting only to be alone, when old Lukanski's voice came to him.

"Eh, Tatskole, my child," the old man's voice called with restraint. "Eh, hero," gently the old one called to the commissar.

Tatsko recognized Old Lukanski's voice, jumped from his place, and like a proper soldier, quickly found himself at the father's side.

"Eh," the old one called again, but now nothing, nothing at all was said, as he held him firmly and tightly in a hug.

"Eh," for some reason as the old one loosened his grip the commissar returned the firm hug himself.

"Eh, Tatskole, is my son alive?" the old one whispered sharp and excited. "Thank God," the old man spoke again more calmly, "finally you're back."

"We were victorious," returned the commissar with a wide, glowing smile on his face, and now his head wound had reddened and truly resembled a blossoming flower.

"So," spoke old Lukanski, also smiling, "it means you finally were victorious."

"We've won, we're victorious," once more the commissar repeated it all, still smiling. "We've won, our glorious revolution is won," he repeated, blinking his eyes before the sun. "We've won," he repeated once more. "The road is open for us now, no one can stop us." Then, he moved his hand, pointing somewhere in the distance. "The revolution only advances, only forward, never back."

The old man was silent now, he seemed to listen with interest to the commissar's talk, but not a word of it had any connection to him. He made his way up the stairs to the place where Tatsko sat, and likewise blinking, peered out over the gardens growing dim in the setting sun. He lit his pipe and softly, through one corner of his mouth, as if to squeeze it out word for word, he asked:

"Where is my Damyanko? Where is my son?" the father asked. "Why hasn't he returned with the brigade?"

The commissar, as if he had been waiting for the old man's question, began to spin his tale, to talk about the brigade, about the path of the brigade, about the last march and about his comrades.

"That was our last victorious attack," explained the commissar. "The brigade plunged as one into the battle. The instant just before it began everyone could see that freedom was at hand, the dawn of freedom. It took his life. Nobody saw him alive afterward." Comrade Tatsko spoke, and the old one, as if he hadn't heard any of what passed through his head, repeated:

"What happened to my son, my Damyanko?"

Comrade Tatsko was silent now, and didn't know what to do. He stroked his clean, shiny beard. Then, he loosened the collar on his new shirt. It felt like someone was tightening a cord around his neck. And not hurrying, he very slowly sat down near the old one. With a quiet and determined voice he announced:

"Comrade Damyanko Lukanski will be proclaimed a people's hero. He fought bravely till the last hour. The people will erect a large monument to him. He was a warrior, a true comrade." The commissar spoke movingly, with simplicity and humanity, as if all of this flowed from his heart. There was no trace of falseness in his voice, nothing untrue in these words. He spoke about his comrade and companion in war, Damyanko Lukanski.

The old man listened to all of this impatiently, without a word, and in his eyes there had already formed a large tear, heavy as a stone, and just like a stone, it began to skid down the contoured slopes and crossed his face. Once the commissar was silent, the old man again spoke with the same thick voice:

"Damyanko, my son," the old man whispered as if he were calling to his son. "Damyanko, my dear child," said the old man, "God hasn't given me your return, not alive. You've left me, God hasn't given me a chance to see you again, you've gone from me..."

(excerpt from the short story "Father" by Zhivko Chingo)

After the conclusion of the Great War and the Soviet Bolshevik Revolution the Great Powers were in ruins and began their lengthy process of rebuilding. Russia's desires for imperialist ventures and her obsession with destroying the Ottoman Empire brought immense economic suffering to her people.

While the Macedonians in the Balkans were suffering from denationalization and oppression, the world around them was changing. Lenin's rise to power put an end to Russian imperialist ambitions in the Balkans, especially the Tsarist desires for annexing Istanbul (the old Constantinople), and Edirne, the Adrianople region. Germany on the other hand, bitter about her latest defeat, began to rebuild her economy.

Smarting from their latest bouts with Germany, France and Britain too began to rebuild their economies and military strength.

Germany as the vanquished party and instigator of the Great War was forced to pay restitution for damages to the victorious nations. In spite of all efforts made to recover from the Great War, the economic situation in Europe was worsening and came to a climax in October 1929 when the stock market crashed in the United States.

The economic collapse of the 1930's and the "Great Depression" polarized the world into "left and right" idealogical camps. On the left were the supporters of the working class and communism, while on the right were the supporters of industry and capitalism.

The struggle between left and right came to a climax when civil war broke out in Spain in July 1936. Germany was in support of the right and sent troops to fight on the side of the Spanish government. Germany at the time was only allowed to have a small army, so to compensate for her limited numerical capability she focused her efforts on producing a technologically superior force. Germany's small but capable army was field-tested and battle hardened in the Spanish conflict. This explains much of her early success in World War II.

The Balkan states were not spared the effects of Russian and German influence. To maintain control of his kingdom, and under the influence of the fascist model of government in several European states, King George II of Greece made his state a dictatorship and in 1936, after the Greek premier's death, he appointed General Metaxas to take charge of Greek affairs, who at the time was minister of war. While there were some prospects for basic human rights for the Macedonian people in the Greek state in the early 1920's, those prospects died as Greece tightened her grip on Macedonia by implementing more racist assimilation policies. If that was not enough, on December 18, 1936 the Greek government issued a legal act concerning, "Activities Against State Security". By this act thousands of Macedonians were arrested, imprisoned, and expelled from their homeland. Among other things Metaxas, on September 7, 1938 by legal act 2366, outlawed the Macedonian language and prohibited people from speaking it by imposing heavy fines and imprisonment.

In 1938 Australian author Bert Birtles in his book *Exiles in the Aegean* wrote:

In the name of 'Hellenization' these people (Macedonians) are being persecuted continually and arrested for the most fantastic reasons. Metaxa's way of inculcating the proper nationalist spirit among them has been to change all the native place-names into Greek and to forbid use of the native language. For displaying the slightest resistance to the edict-for this too is a danger to the security of the State-peasants and villagers have been exiled without trial. (Shea, 1997, 112).

Once in control of the Greek state Metaxas acted against the labor unions and their leaders and declared strikes illegal. He then turned to suppressing all political opposition, outlawed all political parties and imprisoned the leaders who would not pledge their loyalty. The communist party too was outlawed and driven underground. The press was also heavily censored.

Being a military man himself, Metaxas dedicated much of the state's finances to modernizing the Greek army in terms of manpower and military hardware. In the sphere of education, he re-wrote Greek history to support his own ideological bias, declaring that there were three great periods in history: the classical, the Byzantine and his own regime, which was then known as the "Regime of the Fourth of August". He created a National Youth Organization to bring together the children of the various social classes and provided military training for boys and domestic skills for girls.

There were, however, contradictions in Greece at the time. Although the Metaxas regime was ideologically similar to that of fascist Spain and Italy, the Greeks always remained loyal to Britain.

In Yugoslavia, events were progressing in a similar manner to those in Greece. After King Alexander declared himself dictator of Yugoslavia in 1929, he suspended the constitution and subdivided his kingdom in such a way that the Serbs would be a majority in all districts. He also abolished trade unions and removed personal liberties.

The Serbian occupied territory of Macedonia was referred to as "South Serbia" and the Macedonian language was forbidden from being spoken in public. The history of the Macedonian people and their surnames were changed as well, to give them a Serbian emphasis. Place names too were changed and replaced with historically Serbian names.

Unlike the Metaxas regime, after the 1930's the Yugoslav government began to relax its tight grip and allowed unofficial and limited use of the Macedonian dialects to be spoken in the streets of Macedonia and in plays and drama clubs.

In Bulgaria, events followed a somewhat similar course as in Yugoslavia and Greece. A military coup was imposed in May 1934, the 1879 constitution was abolished, and independent political organizations and trade unions were abolished. In 1935, King Boris III, in a bloodless coup, overthrew the old dictatorship and replaced it with his own Royal one.

Bulgarian governments since Bulgaria's inception in 1878 have officially and adamantly denied the existence of the Macedonian nationality, arguing that Macedonians are Bulgarians. Thousands of Macedonians who have over the years tried to express different views have been jailed or exiled. The attitude that Macedonians are Bulgarians was used to justify forced assimilation and to deny Macedonians their basic human rights. Ever since her modern creation in 1878, Bulgaria has been obsessed with possessing Macedonia and this has caused immense suffering for the Macedonian people.

The downfall of the Tsarist Russian Imperial Empire, the break-up of the Hapsburg Austro-Hungarian Empire and the demise of the Ottoman Empire, removed three of the Great Powers from internal Balkan influence. While Britain played a less active role, France and Italy attempted to form competing alliances in the Balkans but did not have the military might to enforce them. The Balkan governments, on the other hand, for the first time, had an opportunity to adjust their relations with each other and form alliances to protect their mutual interests. Unfortunately, their hatred for each other and fear of losing Macedonia always prevented such an alliance and allowed outsiders to again manipulate their internal affairs.

Germany's humiliating defeat in the Great War, coupled with her economic plight in the 1930's, gave rise to a new kind of German radicalism. Hitler exploited that and turned it to his own advantage. Hitler, in the short term, also gave the German people what they desired most, work and hope for a better future. Unfortunately, in the long term, he delivered disaster not only to the German people but also to many other nations, including the Macedonians.

As a new-world order emerged, new alliances began to form. On one side stood the Axis partners, initially consisting of Germany, Italy and Japan, then as war broke out, Albania, Bulgaria, Romania, Hungary, Finland and Thailand joined in. On the other side were the Allies consisting of Britain, the Soviet Union, the USA, and China. As the war progressed, more and more nations joined the allies, totaling about fifty before the war was over.

In September 1940, Germany, Italy and Japan signed a mutual cooperation agreement, which basically identified their intentions with respect to each others spheres of influence, and defined their political, economic, and defense strategies as well as their obligations to each other. The agreement came to be known as the "tripartite pact".

After war broke out in the Balkans, the first to fall to fascist aggression was Albania. By an ultimatum delivered to Albanian King Zogu on March 23, 1939, Italian troops landed in Albania and occupied her territory on April 7, encountering little resistance.

Soon after consolidating control in Albania, on October 28th, 1940, Italy declared war on Greece. Greece however, turned out to be a tougher nut to crack and Metaxas's foresight in arming his state paid off. Official history praises Greece and the Greek soldiers for their bravery and fighting spirit but neglects to mention Macedonian contributions and sacrifices made to defend Greece against invasion. Macedonians were the first to be dispatched to the front lines in Albania and took the full brunt, not just of the offensive but of the winter cold as well. More Macedonian men suffered from gangrene than from Italian bullets and bombs. Unprepared for the frigid temperatures, many men lost their fingers, toes, limbs and even their lives to frostbite. Food too was in short supply and the brave Macedonian soldiers had to fight off starvation as well as the Italians. They did this to protect a country that refused and still refuses to recognize them.

All their sacrifices were in vain, in any case, because six months later, on April 6th, 1941, the German army marched into Greece. Again the Macedonians fought bravely, but they were no match for the well-trained, well-disciplined German army. (If you wish to learn more about World War II, specifically about events that involved Greece, Yugoslavia, Bulgaria and Albania, please read Volume 4 of The Marshal Cavendish Illustrated Encyclopedia of World War II, but don't expect to find anything about the Macedonian contribution).

There is a story told of a Macedonian soldier, a real old coot, who refused to surrender to the invading Germans and continued to fire at them in spite of orders to cease. He held his position until he ran out of ammunition and the Germans practically grabbed him by the neck. Expecting to meet his maker, he stood up and bravely faced his enemy. But instead of killing him, the German soldiers, one by one, shook his hand and praised him for his bravery, then let him go. (This, however, is only how they behaved in the very beginning, later, during the partisan guerilla war, their policy was to "kill ten innocent civilians for each German soldier killed").

When the Germans reached Athens, the Greek government capitulated, and the soldiers on the Albanian front were left on their own. Some were told to go to Epirus and regroup, expected to make the long trek on foot. Others were told nothing and were left to roam the countryside. Eventually they were all picked up by German patrols, disarmed and sent home.

At home, the returning soldiers were given a hero's welcome. Unfortunately, for those who were wounded and lost fingers, toes and limbs to frostbite, there was no compensation or solace for their suffering.

The German invasion was a welcome relief for the soldiers from the Italian front, but at the same time it posed an uneasy uncertainty as to what was going to happen next. No one was certain how the new invaders were going to react. The Macedonian people, having ample prior experience with occupiers were expecting the worst. As time would show, however, the new invaders were a mixed blessing for the Macedonian people.

After the war broke out in Europe, Bulgaria allied itself with the Axis powers and on March 1, 1941, joined the German-led pact. The entry of German troops into Bulgaria put Yugoslavia in a difficult position. To avoid German wrath, on March 25, 1941 the Regent, Prince Paul, also joined the German-led pact. This did not sit well with young King Peter, however, who with the help of the Yugoslav military, staged a coup and deposed the Regent. This meant that again Hitler had to negotiate with Yugoslavia. Hitler was counting on Yugoslavia to allow him passage to attack Greece. The new situation so angered Hitler that instead of negotiating, he signed directive number 25 declaring Yugoslavia an enemy of Germany and ordered her destruction. Hitler wanted a swift strike against Yugoslavia, so he withdrew troops from the Russian campaign.

It took Hitler's army twelve days to occupy Yugoslavia, a small diversion in his destructive career, but there are those who believe that this little diversion changed the course of history. To begin with, it gave the Soviet Union just enough time to adequately prepare for an offensive, which ultimately led to Germany's defeat. Secondly, the violent nature of the attack created the right conditions for a partisan uprising, which ultimately helped to establish the Republic of Macedonia.

The battle for Yugoslavia and Greece was swift and effective. When it was over the Germans, as an ally to the Axis powers, allowed Bulgaria to occupy Vardar (Yugoslav occupied) Macedonia and the eastern region of Aegean (Greek occupied) Macedonia. Later, after the Italians left, Germany allowed Bulgaria to occupy western Macedonia as well.

Many Macedonians from the Vardar region, who had suffered under the Yugoslav regime, welcomed the Bulgarians as saviors and liberators. Their euphoria was, unfortunately, short-lived as the Bulgarians quickly began to oppress and forcibly "Bulgarize" the Macedonian population. If there had been any pro-Bulgarian sentiment before, it quickly disappeared after the occupation. Germany's use of force against Yugoslavia, coupled with the Bulgarian occupiers' oppression of the Macedonian people, gave birth to an underground Macedonian resistance movement.

In Aegean Macedonia, after the Germans settled in, life for the Macedonian people took on an uneasy normalcy. The Greek police, which had supported the Metaxas' regime before the occupation, now cooperated with the German military and again became active in Macedonia. To counter this oppression, the old *komiti* (committee organization organized by the IMRO during the Ilinden period) rearmed and went back to active duty. The "old timers" were angered by Greece's oppressive laws and were spurred back into action by Bulgarian propaganda condemning the Greek oppression. The Bulgarians were well aware of the unfavorable conditions the Greek government had created in Macedonia and tried to take advantage of the opportunity that the German occupation presented. Komiti actions were limited, at best, and were restricted to the Italian zones of control, because the Germans would not tolerate any armed actions in their zones.

The Partisan movement in Yugoslavia was more organized and progressive than that in Greece. Led by Tito, the communist Partisans in Yugoslavia organized a war of national liberation in which the Macedonians, led by commander Tempo, fought on an equal footing. Macedonians had formed their own units for resistance even before they were recognized and accepted by Tito. The first anti-fascist war of national liberation began in the Republic of Macedonia on October 11, 1941. October 11th is the "Second Ilinden" for the Macedonian people. Since 1941 they have celebrated it as "the Macedonian Day of Revolution". The Macedonian people, by their actions, have earned their place in the world. By their endurance of terrible hardship and suffering, and the ultimate sacrifice of the blood of their young fighters for freedom, the Macedonian people demonstrated their determination to have freedom. The Great Powers in 1829 (by the London Protocol) satisfied the Greeks by making Greece a country. Similarly, in 1878 (by the Congress of Berlin) Russia liberated the Bulgarians, making Bulgaria a country. Unlike the Greeks and Bulgarians, however, the people of Vardar Macedonia had to fight for themselves and, thus, to earn their place in the world among the free nations.

In just over a year of occupation the Macedonians of the Vardar region had endured enough Bulgarian oppression to last them a lifetime. In April of 1942 they demonstrated their discontent. Macedonian

Partisans took action against the Bulgarian army and were massacred in a bloody battle. Unarmed Macedonians took to the streets to protest the massacre, and they too were cut down.

To escape retaliation, units of the Macedonian Partisan force fled into Aegean Macedonia. Some entered the Italian zone near the village of Besfina and the rest entered the German zone in the vicinity of the village of Sveta Petka and quickly went underground. The Besfina force, before it had a chance to make contact with the local population, was spotted by the *komiti,* who quickly sprang into action. Seeing uniformed men on the Besfina hillside startled the old *komiti*. Thinking that it was a Greek police (*andari*) force, the komiti appealed to the local Italian garrison and were given arms and permission to attack them. When the *komiti* began their offensive action, the partisans backed off and sent representatives to negotiate. They went from village to village and spoke with the local chiefs. The strangers wore handsome uniforms and conducted themselves seriously, with charm and charisma. They spoke long and well about freedom, liberty and the treachery of the Bulgarian fascists.

When the *komiti* found out that the uniformed men were Macedonians, they accepted them with open arms, gave them their weapons and many voluntarily joined their cause. The Partisans of Sveta Petka, because of the German presence, had to work under cover and they too succeeded in recruiting volunteers from the local population. After the partisan penetration, the Macedonian people of Aegean Macedonia learned about Bulgarian atrocities and ceased to believe the Bulgarian propaganda. The old Ilinden guard was demobilized and replaced by a Partisan movement.

Partisan organizers took extraordinary measures to explain to the Macedonian people that they were fighting for freedom and for the liberation of the Macedonian people from the tyranny of the occupiers. The Macedonian involvement in this war and later in the Greek Civil War was not about "communist ideology" or about alliances or obligations to the new Super Powers. It was simply the next stage in the long struggle for liberation from oppression and to fulfill a longing for freedom, re-unification, and self-rule. The Macedonian contribution to the fight against fascism is not only under-emphasized, but historians also misinterpret it. The Macedonian people, during the Second Great War (WWII), fought on the democratic side and fought against fascism and for the liberation of the states in which they lived. The Macedonian people, like the other peoples in the Balkans, fought to liberate their homeland and thus earned their place in the world. This cannot be ignored and must be recognized and recorded in the annals of history.

Word of a Macedonian Partisan movement in Aegean Macedonia spread like wild fire. People soon came out onto the streets to freely speak their native Macedonian language, to sing songs and write Macedonian plays and poetry. The Partisans even set up Macedonian schools and taught children patriotic songs, poems and Macedonian history using the local Macedonian dialects. The younger generations, for the first time, saw written words in their own Macedonian language. Tis new-found freedom brought happiness to the lives of the oppressed Macedonian people, who welcomed the partisans into their villages as "our own boys and girls". The new-found confidence and strength projected by the Macedonians terrified the Greeks, especially the andari and their collaborators. For a while they were no longer a threat.

The Germans and Italians did not care one way or another about Macedonian affairs as long as there was no trouble for them. Macedonian interest in Partisan activities continued to grow, bringing new recruits and volunteers to the cause. Youth organizations were created with young men and women recruited to be the eyes and ears of the community and to help defend the villages. Many young volunteers of military age were recruited and trained to perform policing and civic duties in the newly formed organizations. The Macedonian organization known as NOF, *Naroden Osloboditen Front,* or People's Liberation Front was formed and recruited fighters from the Kostur, Lerin and Voden regions. NOF even cooperated with Greek organizations of similar ideology. Later, there was talk of re-uniting Macedonia, possibly through a Balkan confederation. Britain, unfortunately, was against the idea and discouraged Greece from taking part in such discussions. Bulgarians also could not agree and withdrew support. As usual, the Bulgarians wanted to become the rulers of Macedonia, which was, of course, unacceptable to the Macedonians.

There is a story told that about five hundred young Macedonian civilian men gathered at the village of D'mbeni eager to join the Partisan movement. Word of this reached the Greek Partisan leadership, who appeared to be frightened by the prospect of a strong all-Macedonian force. There was nothing the Greeks feared more than losing Macedonia. The Greeks by this time had formed their own Partisan movement (outside of Macedonia) and began to negotiate with the Macedonians about combining forces. For some time Greek Partisan representatives tempted the Macedonians to join them. When negotiations failed to achieve results, the Greeks tried ordering the Macedonians to surrender their arms. Macedonians were well aware of past Greek treachery and refused to join them or surrender their arms. Instead, they sealed the borders from Bigla to Korcha, rendering them inaccessible to Greek partisans. Although the Macedonians acted alone initially, they would later join a wing of the EAM, the Greek Popular Liberation Army.

The leadership of the Macedonian force in western Aegean Macedonia was shared between the *voivoda* Ilia Dimov code named "Goche" and the Oshchima *voivoda*, Mito Tupurkovski, code named "Titan". Both commanders were loved and respected by their men for their fighting abilities and their leadership.

In an ironic twist of fate, while Mito Tupurkovski engaged the Germans in fierce battles, his mother Sulta was accidentally killed by a stray German bullet. It was an ordinary summer day in 1944 and for some time now the local people had become accustomed to German patrols making their routine rounds, inspecting the road conditions and the communication lines between Zhelevo and Breznitsa. Early each morning two German soldiers left Zhelevo on foot for Breznitsa and a pair left Breznitsa for Zhelevo. When the patrols met they reversed direction and continued this routine all day.

On this particular day, ten Partisans came to Oshchima and decided to attack one of the patrols and take the soldiers hostage. They set a trap in a ditch near Ternaa and sat in wait. While they were waiting, two men from Oshchima, Paso Boglev and Giro Keleshov went to a nearby mill. Paso left his donkey to graze on the road above and stepped inside the mill. When the Germans passed by they borrowed the donkey and one of them rode it as they made their way. When they reached the Partisan trap, the only armed Partisan fired a rapid-fire volley in the air. Unfortunately, after the initial burst, his gun jammed. The Germans quickly took cover in the ravine and started to fire back. Discouraged by their failed attempt the Partisans quickly fled into the mountains. The loud gunfire alerted the German garrison in Zhelevo and reinforcements were quickly dispatched. Paso and Giro also heard the gunfire and came out of the mill to investigate. Seeing a rushing vehicle with armed soldiers headed towards them startled the two men and they fled in panic. Paso ran down to the river and hid out of sight. Giro, unfortunately, ran up the hill and was in full view of the German patrol. The Germans, thinking he was the culprit, gave chase. Giro was a fast runner and the Germans couldn't catch him. Before he could disappear into the woods, one of the soldiers fired a rapid-fire volley at him. Who would have expected that a bullet from that round would mortally wound Mito's mother Sulta, who was quietly sitting in her yard enjoying a beautiful summer's day? Giro escaped unharmed, but, unfortunately, Sulta died from her wound on August 20th, 1944.

In September 1944 German troops began to withdraw from the Balkans. Fearing reprisals, many Macedonians evacuated their villages and set up temporary homes in the mountains in seclusion. As it turned out the Germans were not a threat, so after a month or so villagers returned to their homes. The people who lived near main roads were afraid to return and took up residence with relatives in secluded villages and stayed there until all the Germans were gone.

There was at least one incident where the Germans did do damage. This was in the village of Ternaa where returning Germans found their "host village" empty, became enraged and stoned two old people to death.

To protect soldiers from being attacked out in the open at night, the Germans assigned them residences inside the villages among the locals. Each house was identified with a marker and returning soldiers used it for shelter. In Oshchima, as in other villages, identification numbers were stamped on the outside door of each house. Time and time again the same soldiers came back to the same house. According to stories that the Stefou family told, several German soldiers used to spend the night at their house. When someone was missing the grandfather would motion "what happened" and point in the direction where the man had last sat. The Germans would then motion back "sleep", meaning that he was killed or would say "mama" for gone home on leave to visit his family.

After all the German and Bulgarian occupying forces withdrew from Yugoslavia, the Partisans numbering about 800,000 men were in full control. There were no outside invasion forces (Allied or Russian) inside Yugoslavia, so foreign interference was not a problem. At that time the Macedonian Partisans possessed a sizeable force and wielded considerable influence in the ranks of the Tito regime. The Macedonian people had done their share of fighting for the liberation of Yugoslavia from the fascists and earned their place as equals among the Yugoslav people.

On August 2nd 1944, Macedonia was officially proclaimed a republic within the Yugoslav Federation. A Bitola-Lerin dialect was chosen and adopted as the official language of the Republic and the city of Skopje was chosen as the new republic's capital.

No sooner had the Germans withdrawn from Greece than the British military arrived in Athens. Athens was evacuated on October 12, 1944 and a British occupation force entered the city a few days later. While Britain entered Greece with only four thousand troops, most unfit for combat, ELAS (the Greek Partisan force) had seventy thousand men armed and ready for combat. Even the British admit that if the Greek partisans had wanted to, they could have seized power. The conditions were certainly right. The question is why didn't they, and what was the Civil War all about? Official history provides no answers, only more questions.

It took the British a couple of months to get organized and by mid December 1944 they had fifty thousand soldiers of their own and some loyal Greek troops to back them. The local Greek troops came from the ranks of the *andari* (National Republican Greek League), the same men who had fought alongside the Germans. They exchanged their German gear for British uniforms, and they were back on the streets again attacking the partisans.

As Greece started to collapse, before Germany invaded in 1941, King George II fled and formed a government in exile in London, which was recognized by the Allies as the official government of Greece. Also, the British, in advance of the German departure, established a center of Greek activity in Cairo where a Greek army, navy and air force operated under British command.

After the British consolidated power in Greece, they were able to support the British appointed Greek government and ordered the Partisans to demobilize. What is interesting here is that before the British were able to militarily enforce a disarmament, they ordered the Partisan forces to disband. What is more interesting and noteworthy is that EAM (the Greek Popular Liberation Army) agreed to demobilize its own forces with hardly any conditions. The only condition worthy of mention is the request for Britain to disarm the "government support units" EAM's main opposition. Knowing full well that Britain would never allow communist rule in Greece and also knowing that the Soviet Union signed an agreement with Britain not to interfere in Greece, EAM still believed it could come to power with no outside help.

When the British went ahead with the original plan, ignoring EAM's request to disarm the Government Support Units, EAM withdrew from the government. EAM then protested against British actions by organizing demonstrations and general strikes. When the Athens square began to flood with thousands of demonstrators, the police were ordered to fire on the crowds, killing fifteen people. To make matters worse, Churchill approved a plan for Britain to occupy Athens by any means necessary, if required. ELAS still held more than three-quarters of Greece, but because it could no longer count on outside (Soviet) support, it had to re-evaluate its own position.

Under these conditions, EAM on January 1945 accepted an armistice, trading guns for votes. The Varkita agreement was signed on February 12, 1945 requiring all units to demobilize and surrender their weapons. The British, once again affirmed their allegiance to the Greek government by giving Athens full political and military support, expressing their willingness to fight to prevent a Partisan victory. The biggest losers of the Varkita agreement were the Macedonians. As soon as EAM signed the agreement, all anti-Macedonian laws were back in force and the Macedonian people lost all that they had gained during the German occupation. EAM/KKE (Greek Communist Party) made absolutely no effort to safeguard Macedonian rights in the agreements with Britain and, as a result, began to lose favor with the Macedonian leadership. When the Macedonian Partisan forces were ordered to demobilize as part of the Vartika agreement, the Macedonian leadership refused. Goche and Titan refused to disarm and disband without guarantees that no harm would come to their men or to the Macedonian people.

The question of "what will happen to Aegean Macedonia under Greek communist rule," was still unclear. Greece, unfortunately, was determined to rid itself of the Macedonians one way or another and outlawed the Macedonian forces. A strike force was assembled by ELAS (the Greek Partisans) and sent north to intervene and arrest the Macedonian outlaws. Instead of putting up a fight, however, the Macedonian brigades crossed over the Yugoslav border and entered Vardar Macedonia where they were a welcome addition to existing Macedonian forces fighting the Albanian *balisti* (German allies) in Tetovo and Gostivar. The Macedonian leadership could have stayed and fought the ELAS, but it would have made no sense to bring the war home to Macedonia. They knew very well that British troops would soon follow and they would be fighting a senseless, bloody war in their own backyard.

With the Macedonian forces out of the way, the Greek police were back and up to their old tricks. This time it wasn't only the Macedonians who were their victims. They hated the Greek partisans nearly as much. With practically no one to stop them, the Greek police escalated their terror activities arresting, torturing and murdering people indiscriminately. This included the EAM, ELAS and KKE (Communist Party of Greece) leadership. By the time elections were held, most of the Partisan leadership had disappeared. They were either in jail serving hard time on fabricated and trumped up charges or they were dead.

The elections were scheduled for March 31st, 1946, but instead of voting, the Greek Partisans re-armed themselves and rebelled against the Greek government. The rebellion first manifested itself as an attack in Greece on the village of "Lithohorion," situated east of Mount Olympus, directly south of Katerini in Thessaly. Other attacks soon followed, and in no time the conflict escalated into a full-scale civil war, engulfing not only Greece but Macedonia, as well.

In a bizarre turn of events the same ELAS, who less than a year before had turned their guns on the Macedonian fighters, now extended their hands in friendship. All was forgiven and forgotten when the ELAS leadership asked the Macedonians for their help. This time they came with offers of "equal rights", "recognition" and even possibilities of "re-unification with Vardar".

Many Aegean Partisan fighters who had crossed over to Vardar Macedonia only the year before came back. On their return they organized themselves under NOF, the Macedonian National Liberation Front and fought side by side with the ELAS. Many were well aware of the saying "beware of Greeks bearing gifts", and knew that the Greek offer was too good to be true, but there was always that small ray of hope that, perhaps, this time the outcome for Macedonia might be different. Besides, their families, homes and lives were in Aegean Macedonia, so what other choice did they really have? They returned because they were lonely, because they loved their families and because they had to live with the guilt of leaving their loved ones in dire straits. Every Macedonian born in Macedonia, even in the most desolate places, knows the feeling of homesickness and yearns to return.

The new alliance between ELAS and NOF opened many opportunities for the Greek Partisans beyond the Greek borders. While the Greek government controlled the big cities and towns, the Partisan strength was in the villages and mountains. Most of the Partisan recruits came from the peasant population and showed themselves to be idealistic, hopeful and determined to fight. Camps were set up in mountainous seclusion where new recruits were given combat training. There were also training camps and supply depots set up outside Greece, in Albania and Yugoslavia. One such camp was the town of Bulkes located in northern Yugoslavia. Bulkes was a beautiful town with neat

174   This Land We Do Not Give

rows of lovely houses and fertile lands that could feed an army. The Germans built Bulkes to house German families but after the German armies retreated, some residents of Bulkes were kicked out while others left voluntarily. The empty town was loaned to the Greek Partisans to use as a supply depot for warehousing food, uniforms and weapons. Bulkes was also a training centre for officers, and an administrative centre for propaganda. During the partisan days the town of Bulkes was administered in the true spirit of socialism.

By early 1947 the Partisan force was showing real strength in military capability and real promise of delivering on other commitments to the Macedonian people. About 87 Macedonian schools were opened in the Lerin and Kostur regions. A record number of students (10,000) were reported attending school. Macedonian language, literature and culture were flourishing. The Greeks, unfortunately, were never at ease with the Macedonian gains and there was visible resentment and mistrust between the two peoples. Greek chauvinism seemed to rear its ugly head even at the best of times. Macedonians, on the other hand, were never at ease about revealing their real names or identities, particularly to the Greek Partisans. One Macedonian explained it to me this way, "If they knew that you were Macedonian, then you had to watch both your front and back, because you never knew where the next bullet was going to come from".

In Macedonia the ranks of the Partisans were swelling mostly with volunteers from the Macedonian villages. Some who had combat experience were promoted to the rank of officer. The Greeks were hesitant and careful not to promote Macedonians to high ranks. Those they reserved for Greeks only. In addition to enlisting men, the Partisans also drafted women as nurses, field medics, tailors, menders, launderers, cooks, supply organizers and even armed combatants. For a while the Partisans grew their own food in donated and abandoned fields. The workforce managing the harvests and delivering food to the Partisan camps was made up mostly of women volunteers.

Britain was not happy with the new developments and pressed the Greek government to expand its military capability and to arm itself with heavy arms.

Up to 1947 the British Government appointed and dismissed Greek Prime Ministers with little attention to constitutional formalities. British experts dictated economic and financial policy, defense and foreign policy, security and legal policy, trade union and unemployment policy. (Jelavich, 1983, 306).

For her interference inside a sovereign state's affairs and for allowing heavy-handed tactics, Britain received criticism from the United States, whose dollars were used to rebuild Greece. Both the Greek government and the Partisans were recruiting fighters from the same population. While young men were drafted to fight for the Greek government, their wives, sisters, brothers, mothers and fathers were drafted to fight for the Partisans. There were heavy propaganda campaigns conducted on both sides, poisoning the minds of the young and impressionable, dividing and tearing the community apart and pitting brother against brother.

This was the Greek legacy to the Macedonian people who offered their help. This was the "Greek curse" that many Macedonians must bear for partnering with the Greeks. To this day many Macedonians harbour hard feelings and struggle to make amends. To this day the Macedonian community remains divided on this issue.

Ever since the day the British set foot in Greece they were determined to get rid of the Partisans by any means necessary, including acts of violence and terror. From mid-1945 to May 20th, 1947 the Partisans in western Macedonia alone suffered terrible losses. John Shea (1997, 116) in his *Macedonia and Greece, The Struggle to Define a New Balkan Nation,* lists some of the information and statistics on those losses claimed by the Partisans:

13,529 Macedonians were tortured, 3,215 were imprisoned, and 268 were executed without trial. In addition, 1,891 houses were burnt down and 1,553 were looted, and 13,808 Macedonians were resettled by force. During the war, Greek-run prison camps where Macedonians were imprisoned, tortured, and killed included the island of Ikaria near Turkey, the island of Makronis near Athens, the jail Averov near Athens, the jail at Larisa near the Volos Peninsula, and the jail in Thessaloniki. Aegean Macedonian expatriates claim that there were mass killings on Vicho, Gramos, Kaymakchalan, and at Mala Prespa in Albania.

In 1946 the Greek police attacked a band of musicians from Oshchima and Ternaa at Popli while they were on their way to play at a wedding in Rudari. The musicians were severely beaten and their musical instruments were destroyed. For one young man his trumpet was his only means of support.

In 1946 a Greek policeman shot and killed Sofia Ianovska from Zhelevo for fun. The woman, whose husband was in Canada at the time, was standing on her front porch waiting for her children to arrive from work. The crazed policeman fired at the woman because she was looking in his direction, instantly killing her. According to local accounts, no inquiry was made regarding the shooting, nor was the policeman ever questioned about his actions.

In 1945-46, in retaliation for one of their own being killed, the *prosfigi* (people that Greece imported from Asia Minor during the 1920's) of Popli killed Nikola Cholakov, a man from Orovnik. The only connection Nikola had with the dead man was that he was a supporter of the opposite side in the conflict.

The *prosfigi* in Macedonia committed a number of atrocities against Macedonians during that period, but they were never punished for their crimes. The Macedonian Partisans had the strength and opportunity to round up all the *prosfigi* in north-western Macedonia and massacre them to the last one, but instead they used sound judgement and left them alone. The Macedonians understood that the *prosfigi* were also victims of Hellenism.

The Greek government in Macedonia worked closely with local collaborators and enlisted a certain number of reliable informants from the Macedonian population. The collaborators worked hard to identify all those who were sympathetic to the Partisans and reported on their activities on a regular basis. Anyone reported aiding the Partisans was severely punished and sometimes executed.

In the spring of 1947, all those who were on the "bad guys" lists were rounded up, arrested and locked up in the Lerin jails. Those accused of aiding the Partisans were taken out and executed. The rest, after spending one hundred days in jail, without a trial, were sent to various concentration camps in the most desolate Greek Islands.

There is reason to suspect that the Greek government, even before the Greek Civil War, had plans "to deal with the Macedonians in Greece". As John Shea (1997, 116-117) describes it:

In 1947, during the Greek Civil War, the legal act L-2 was issued. This meant that all those who left Greece without the consent of the Greek government were stripped of Greek citizenship and banned from returning to the country. The law applied to Greeks and Macedonians, but in its modernized version the act is binding only on Macedonians. It prevents Macedonians, but not former communist Greeks who fought against the winning side from returning to Greece and reclaiming property. On January 20, 1948, the legal act M was issued. This allowed the Greek government to confiscate the property of those who were stripped of their citizenship. The law was updated in 1985 to exclude Greeks, but still binding on Macedonians.

Clearly acts L-2 and M were designed to work against the interest of the Macedonian people. Even innocent Macedonians who left before the Civil War were not allowed to return. The question is, what was Greece planning to do with the Macedonians? The way acts L-2 and M were enforced over the years raises other questions. If there were no Macedonians living in Greece, as the Greeks claim, then what ethnicity were these people that the Greek government refused to allow back? Why is it that Greek law makes the distinction between Macedonians and Greeks when it suits Greece but not when it benefits the Macedonians?

By the end of 1947 battles were raging everywhere and the war was slowly moving north into Macedonia. Clearly this was a "Greek war," but once again the Macedonian population was being drawn into it. The Greek air force and mechanized artillery units gained control of most cities and main roads. The Partisans were literally trapped and continued their strictly defensive campaigns mainly from the mountains of Vicho and Gramos.

As the situation became critical, both sides stepped up their recruitment campaigns and again were drawing from the same population. The Partisans could no longer count on volunteers alone and began to enlist fighters by force. They drafted anyone they could get their hands on, male or female. In addition to support roles, women were now armed and given combat duties to fight alongside the men against the well trained, well disciplined and heavily armed Greek army. Such was the fate of Macedonian daughters, sisters, and mothers, most of whom were taken by force to fight in someone else's war.

As the war intensified, the Greek air force regularly bombed Macedonian villages, putting the civilian population, including the children, in danger. To save the children, in the spring of 1948 a temporary evacuation program was introduced and implemented on a voluntary basis. It is estimated that about 28,000 children between the ages of 2 and 14 were rounded up and taken across the border into Yugoslavia. (See the next chapter). From there they were sent to various Eastern Block countries.

Again, it should be pointed out that the evacuation program was sponsored and organized by the Greek Partisan leadership, which was fully versed in "Greek Law" (act L-2), yet they carried out the children's evacuation program and lied to the trusting mothers that the evacuation was only a temporary measure. Almost all of the Macedonian children who were evacuated in 1948 are still not allowed entry into Greece.

By the spring of 1949, the Greek Civil War became a "killing field" consuming the Macedonian population. Some of the children who were previously evacuated were brought back to fight against the battle hardened Greek army. Children that were strong enough to carry a rifle, regardless of age, were snatched from the child refugee camps in Romania and brought back to Greece. Two of three groups that were brought back were instantly massacred upon engaging the Greek Army. They were all under the age of fifteen and had no combat training and no idea of what to expect.

The third group was spared only because mothers protested against such barbaric acts. The Partisans demobilized the third group before it reached the battlefields and sent the children home.

By the twisted hand of fate, Zachariadis the supreme commander of the partisan forces and his cronies, in their wisdom, decided to make a final stand against Greece that would make or break the partisan movement. Their rationale was that the partisans needed to occupy a large town or city to serve as their base. This would make them worthy of consideration and perhaps gain the attention of the Super Powers, especially the Soviet Union. There are many who share the belief that the partisan attack on Lerin on February 12, 1949 was nothing more than an attempt to exterminate the Macedonian fighting force and terrorize the rest of the Macedonian population into leaving Greece, because that is exactly what happened.

In one last-ditch attempt to regain the initiative, the Partisans attacked the city of Lerin. They hoped to create a base of operation and show the world that they were a force worthy of recognition. Their effort, however, was not rewarded. They did not capture Lerin and lost most of the force in the attempt. Seven hundred young Macedonian men and women died on that fateful day, their bodies buried in a mass grave. The Partisan leadership waited until dawn before ordering the attack. Wave after wave of innocent young men and women were slaughtered, cut down in their prime by Greek machine-gun fire. The horror of the slaughter became visible at dawn, when the first light revealed the red blood-stained terrain. The fresh white snow was red with the blood of the fallen.

To this day opinions are divided on the rationale of attacking Lerin so late in the war. The war was almost over and the Greek army, supported by Britain, was unstoppable. In retrospect, some believe that gaining control of Lerin would have given the Partisan leadership a bargaining chip for surrender. Looking at the facts, however, reveals a more sinister plan. By that time it was known that Britain would not allow a communist presence in Greece. Britain's position had been accepted by the Soviet Union and by Stalin himself. The partisan leadership understood that it could no longer depend on support from the Communist Block countries under Soviet control. Yugoslavia had by then split from the Eastern Block and the Greek-Yugoslav border had been closed. The Communist Party that promised Macedonians human rights and freedoms slowly began to distance itself from its commitments. Most of the Partisans who fought in the battle for Lerin were new recruits and inexperienced fighters. Most of the force was made up of Macedonian men and women under Greek leadership. The Partisan command hesitated when it was time to launch the offensive, thus giving the enemy extra time to prepare its defenses. The hesitation demoralized the partisan combatants, who were not prepared for the prolonged outdoor winter cold.

A cursory analysis of developments prior to the Lerin assault and a post-mortem of the aftermath led to one inescapable conclusion. As mentioned earlier, the assault on Lerin was designed to destroy the Macedonian Partisan force. By offering the Lerin offensive instead of surrendering, the Partisan leadership "sacrificed its own force". By accident or by design the assault on Lerin contributed to the deaths of many Macedonian fighters and to the mass exodus of the Macedonian population. Many believe that the Greek Civil War succeeded in "ethnically cleansing" the Macedonian people where many years of assimilation had failed.

Fearing reprisal from the advancing Greek army, in August of 1949 waves of refugees left their homes and crossed over into Albania to save themselves. When the war was over, Greece did not want them back. As a result, they were sent to Eastern Block countries that were willing to take them.

Years later some tried to return, but Greece (act L-2) would not allow it. Even innocent Macedonians, who did not participate in the conflict, including the evacuated refugee children, were refused entry (again act L-2). Years passed and still they were refused entry over and over again. They were not even allowed to visit ailing relatives. Finally, in 1985, as mentioned earlier, a repatriation policy was introduced and amnesty was given, but only to those of "Greek origin". This again excluded the Macedonians.

As bombs and artillery shells rained down on the Macedonian countryside, the frightened Macedonian people, mostly made up of old men and women, and mothers with young children, took with them whatever they could carry and left their homes for the safety of the mountains. From there they were told to go to Albania and meet up with their relatives.

There is one story told by a Greek general's assistant who wishes to remain anonymous:

One such group left the village of Kolomnati and was headed down the mountain towards Rula when it was spotted by a young Greek officer. The young man immediately telephoned his general and informed him of the situation. 'Should we intercept?' inquired the young officer. 'No, let the troublemakers go, we don't want them here,' replied the old general.

When the Greek army broke the Lerin front the Partisan force that survived the onslaught fled for Albania. The fighters closest to the city were captured and imprisoned. Those who confessed to having voluntarily joined the Partisans were all executed. The others were either exiled in the Greek Islands or released after serving their sentences in local jails.

In its pursuit of the fleeing Partisans, the Greek army managed to cut off the escape route of a group of Partisans who were manning the cannons and artillery fire at Bigla (the cannons after the war were put on display in the city of Lerin). Being unable to flee for Albania, the Bigla group attempted to cross into Yugoslavia near Prespa Lake. At the Yugoslav border they were stopped by the Yugoslav army, which agreed to allow them passage only if they voluntarily disarmed. Expecting to continue the war from Albania, the Partisans were reluctant to disarm and chose a different escape route. Unfortunately, they attempted their escape during the daytime and were spotted by the Greek air force. Many were killed by machine gun fire from above and some drowned attempting to swim across Lake Prespa. Only a small group made it to Albania.

When they arrived in Albania, to cover for their own blunders, the leaders of the Bigla group concocted stories claiming that Tito's forces attacked them and would not allow them entry into Yugoslavia. Later the same men changed their stories and told the truth about what happened. Unfortunately, by then Greek Partisan and Yugoslav relations had deteriorated. Even though Yugoslavia was one of EAM's strongest supporters, the Greek Partisans used this story in their propaganda campaigns to discredit Tito in the eyes of the Soviet Union.

When the Greek Civil War was over, the Partisan leadership assembled in the abandoned Italian camp of Bureli in Albania to assess what went wrong and why they lost the war. After some deliberation, they came to the conclusion that it was Tito and the Macedonian collaboration that sabotaged the war effort. The failure was blamed on the Macedonian Partisan leadership for co-operating with Tito's Partisans. Seven of the most loyal Macedonian leaders were accused of sabotage and sentenced to death. Fortunately, Enver Hodzha (Albania's highest state leader) did not want atrocities committed in his country and would not allow the executions to take place. The men were then taken to the Soviet Union, tried for treason and sentenced to life imprisonment to be served in the prison camps of Siberia. After Stalin's death, Krushchev re-opened their case and found the men innocent of all charges and released them.

After the Greek Civil War was over, life in Aegean Macedonia was no longer the same. The smaller villages were evacuated (some permanently) and the people were relocated to the larger towns under the watchful eye of the Greek police. The familiar joy and laughter was gone and the streets were empty of children. The Macedonian people, who only a few years before had reveled in life, were once again joyless.

A new-world order emerged from the Second World War. Two industrial giants, the Soviet Union and the Unites States, rose above the rest, and with their opposing ideologies, they would dominate the future world for half a century. One often gains insight into a conflict through the stories of individuals caught in the great historical cataclysms. Here is the story of Ristana and Nikola during the Greek Civil War and in the post-war period of the Cold War, collected by author Chris Stefou:

Ristana, daughter of Krsto and Petra was born in Oshchima on December 18th, 1930. As a child, Ristana lived with relatives and worked on their farm helping them with chores and learning to knit and crochet. Ristana was in grade three when the Greek-Italian war broke and the schools closed so she hardly received much of an education. With her grandfather's help, however, she learned how to read, write and to do arithmetic.

Even though Ristana had little training she did have a talent for writing and enjoyed writing letters for practice. She was sixteen years old when her enthusiasm for writing almost got her into real trouble.

One night Ristana's feet were aching badly from walking barefoot so she asked her grandmother to make up the usual concoction which helped but only gave temporary relief. This particular night Ristana's feet were aching badly causing her to moan with pain. Every time she moaned her grandmother ran to her aid, re-applying the homemade potion. This went on well into the late hours of the night. As it turned out, the same night, Greek police patrols (burandari) were in the area looking for partisans. As they witnessed a light (kandilo) move from room to room several times in the dark of night, they were sure something was going on. Convinced that there were partisans inside they surrounded the house and crashed through the door. The first person they ran into was Ristana's grandmother from whom they demanded to know where she was hiding the partisans. When the grandmother explained that there were no Partisans in the house they demanded to know why there was a light moving from room to room in the dark of night? Ristana's grandmother explained that she was nursing Ristana's feet because she was in pain, but they didn't believe her. Even after she took them to see Ristana with bandages on her feet, they still had doubts and began to search the house. Unfortunately, they found Ristana's letters, especially the one addressed to her uncle Stojan who was living in Bitola, Yugoslavia, a foreign country, which at the time, was not in good relations with Greece. It was explained to the police that this was not a real letter but something that young Ristana was doing for practice. Still unconvinced the police dragged the entire family out from their home in the middle of the night to the house of one of their informants. There the police consulted with an individual behind closed doors and released the family unharmed.

As the Greek Civil War gained momentum in Macedonia, both sides of the conflict drew able bodies from the same Macedonian community. By 1946 the partisans had drafted most of Ristana's family. At the same time Greek presence in the area intensified as Greek Monarchist patrols frequently prowled the village looking for Partisans. With family members as partisans, Ristana's family was considered traitorous by the Greek Monarchists and in breach of the law. One day as the Greek police approached Oshchima, fearing for her life (aided by her uncle Paso), Ristana left for the safety of Mount Moro. There she joined the partisan youth core and, along with others her age, was given responsibility for guarding Oshchima and couriering messages between Partisan command posts.

Ristana could have left with the refugee children during the 1948 mass exodus but her concern for her grandmother kept her at home. Unfortunately that was not to last as Ristana was drafted by the partisans. Initially she was sent to the village of Papli to work in the fields. Then about a year later, in July 1948, she was transferred to a military support unit where she transported supplies and worked in the fields. A group of several women were put together and placed in charge of transporting grain between villages in partisan held territories. The group was also responsible for harvesting crops as required. This lasted for several months until the winter of 1948 when Ristana was transferred to the military training camp in Rudari where she spent December and January in combat training and in the use of weapons. When her training was completed in Rudari she was dispatched to Trnaa for further training and assignment in preparation for the Lerin assault.

In February 1949 after all training was completed, troops, in good spirits, dressed in white capes, were transported near the battlefield and readied to fight. This was Ristana's first battle. She was anxious and thought about freeing the captives in the Lerin prison camp, where some of her family members were kept. If only this battle had taken place a couple of years earlier she could have freed her father and uncles. Now they were in prison in the Greek islands suffering humiliation, hunger and constant beatings.

After arriving in Psoderi near the battleground the Partisans were ordered to hold their position. Ristana remembers waiting for three days. They were unprepared for a long delay and many endured the cold sleeping in the snow in makeshift tents. After the third day Ristana's unit was ordered to take a defensive position at Trsianski Kalivi and block the Greek Army from mounting a rear attack.

Finally the order came down and the offensive on Lerin began but did not unfold as planned. The Greek Army anticipated every move and countered it with stiff resistance. The young partisans force was no match for the well-trained and battle-hardened army. The battle lasted all night. As dawn broke it revealed the horrors of war. The snow-white terrain was painted red with the blood of the dead and wounded. It was a terrifying sight especially for the inexperienced fighters like Ristana. She could not comprehend the loss of so many lives and why so many young and beautiful men and women had to be slaughtered.

Ristana's unit started out with four hundred but when the battle was over only forty were left standing, the rest were either dead or wounded. The survivors were re-grouped and re-assigned. Ristana was assigned to the field medics where she met up with her aunt Rina and Rina's friend Sevda from Oshchima. Running a gauntlet of machinegun fire, mortar fire and aerial attacks, Ristana carried the dead and wounded from the battlefield to the field hospitals.

The battle for Lerin consumed many fighters. Some were instantly killed while other,s wounded, froze to death from the cold.

With all the planning, organizing, training and preparing that went on, how could this have happened? Many questions were raised but few answers were given. Ristana believes the Partisan leadership was responsible for the catastrophe. Many blunders were made. Some may have been intentional. For example, before the assault a partisan surrendered to the Greeks and it was rumoured that he had revealed their plans. Then, there was the three-day delay between the planned and actual assault. Was the delay intentional? It was well known that the Greek army was waiting for reinforcements. Some claim that the attack was held back to give the Greek reinforcements time to arrive. Were these events a coincidence, a conspiracy to destroy the partisan force, or was the Partisan leadership simply incompetent? No rational explanation was given.

Due to the dead and dying foaming at the mouth, symptoms of nerve gas poisoning, it was alleged that the Greeks were using nerve gas during the battle of Lerin.

After the field medic assignment, Ristana, cold, frightened and hungry was re-issued her old machinegun and ordered to report to Kolomnati. Her new assignment took her to Bigla, Psodery, Trsie, Statitsa and finally Kolomnati. There, after some re-training she was assigned to a guard patrol responsible for guarding strategic points in the local mountains. This lasted for about three weeks before she was sent to Trnaa to prepare for an assault on the village Surovitch.

It was April 1949 and Ristana hoped to go home for Easter but her unit was shipped out earlier than expected. But before leaving she and her old friend, Leftera from Oshchima, were visited by Leftera's mother and youngest brother Alexander. They brought them zelnik and other goodies for Easter as well as news from home. For the rest of the partisans, Easter was celebrated with a small piece of zelnik and half an egg each. This was all the partisans could afford to give their fighters. Ristana celebrated Easter at Mount Malimadi and shared her egg with her friend Leftera.

As soon as the forces arrived at their destination, orders were given to carry out the assault on Sourovitch. Ristana's unit was left behind to guard the rear. It was well known that the neighbouring village, Exisou, harboured Greek patrols (Burandari) so it was Ristana's responsibility to make sure they weren't ambushed from the rear.

Ristana recalls it was cold that night and all she was wearing was a black cape. She had to lie flat on her stomach in the snow to support her machinegun pointing towards Exisou. Then the mortar shells began to fall, raining down on them as the Greek forces (Burandari) began to hit back hard from everywhere. Within minutes the partisan unit was decimated. Ristana was lucky to have escaped with her life. A mortar killed two people next to her, including a nurse. This was yet another sad episode in Ristana's life. Having to recall the experience, Ristana was reminded of another sad episode in her life. This one took place before she became a partisan. It was at a different battle in a different place and time. She recalls having to take a young woman, who was badly wounded, to the hospital. Ristana had a mule and because the woman was unconscious, she had to mount, her belly down, hanging over the back of the mule. Unfortunately the hospital was far and the poor woman died on the way. She died on top of the mule, slumped over with her long hair hanging down, bathed in blood. It was a sad sight, which haunts Ristana to this day.

After the unsuccessful attempt to capture Sourovitch, orders were given to report to the command centre in Trnaa. Once again Ristana came close to home but could not visit her family. Soon she was shipped out on guard duty guarding various strategic positions in the partisan held territories.

Like most women in the partisan force, Ristana was guard by night and housekeeper by day. Women with sewing skills, which included almost every woman, were responsible for washing and mending uniforms. Ristana recalls making shirt collars from shirttails to keep the necks of those wearing them warm. Women also took turns washing the camp's clothes in nearby rivers. One time Ristana recalls being promised time off from guard duty if she helped out with the laundry. She was so disappointed when she never received it because her unit was ordered to ship out. What was worse was she had to go on guard duty without a uniform. Her uniform was wet from being washed, so Ristana had to wear unsuitable regular garments, some of which were still wet from the wash. On top of the cold, as luck would have it, Ristana's camp was ambushed that night and she lost everything, her clothing, uniform, camping gear and her parka. The next night she was on guard duty again and she nearly froze to death. She recalls being helped up because her legs were frozen and she had lost all feeling in them. To return back to camp Ristana grabbed the tail of a pack mule and dragged herself behind it for what seemed like an eternity before she got some feeling back in her legs. Her frozen journey took her from Bel Kamen to Vitcho. Unprepared for the mountain climate, Ristana, like many others, experienced hardship and illness from the cold. Those who lost their gear and supplies during the ambush remained cold and hungry for a long time. When they passed through Kolomnati, Ristana was given some plain bread to chew on to ease her hunger, but after chewing and chewing she was unable to swallow any due to the pain from her sore throat. Ristana was sick, weak and in very bad shape. Her feet were sore, swollen and cold. The next day during exercise, she collapsed from exhaustion.

The winter was difficult, but it was finally over. After her recovery, Ristana was sent to Malimadi on various work details that included food gathering and bunker digging. She remembers this one particular day when joy turned to tragedy. It was a beautiful summer's day in early July and Ristana, along with a crew, was sent to pick cherries. Weather wise it was a perfect day and the crew had already picked six bushels of cherries before deciding it was time to return. On their way back they spotted a beautiful cherry tree loaded with cherries. The weather was perfect and picking cherries was a joyous chore for all so they couldn't resist picking a few more. Ristana for some reason became uneasy and tried to warn the others but one particular man, determined to get more cherries, paid her no attention. Unaware of the minefield he stumbled onto a mine and his leg was blown off. Unable to walk on his own the crew had to carry him on their shoulders while he bled profusely.

As the Greek Civil War intensified Ristana was assigned to various combat duties including manning anti-aircraft guns and guarding various partisan strategic positions. She was put back on the old routine doing guard duty by night and domestic chores by day.

All was going well for Ristana until the Greeks decided to attack her outpost. She remembers the day well because on the same day food rations were issued which included two kilos of canned beef, a rare treat for the partisans.

On this particular day Ristana was paired up with Leftera and sent on a routine assignment. They were issued a machine gun, two grenades and one hundred and fifty rounds of ammunition each. Being already overloaded by their combat gear, the women felt it would be unnecessary to carry all the food as well. After all, it was a short assignment and they were expecting to return to camp no later than the next morning.

The weather was clear and it was a beautiful warm August night when the women were interrupted by a fast approaching patrol. It was their relief who had arrived unexpectedly early. But instead of being relieved the women were dismissed from duty. Word came that the Greek forces were fast approaching. They had already taken Roula and were coming for their camp. The women were told to leave quickly and head for Albania. They were also strongly advised against returning to camp.

As the women left they could hear the engines of the Greek tanks approaching. Then came the artillery fire pounding the terrain to dust.

Their journey took the women to Vambel where they found Stojan, another Oshchimian, who also advised them to head for Albania. Stojan was wounded in the leg and he could not walk, so he remained behind.

Scared, tired and hungry Ristana and Leftera walked for several days, dodging Greek patrols, before they arrived in Albania. Upon crossing the border they surrendered their weapons and joined the others that had arrived in the camps.

After three days of rest Ristana's unit regrouped, rearmed and was loaded on trucks and taken back to the battlefields in Mount Gramos. In Albania, Ristana was issued food rations of bread and raw meat. Each individual was responsible for finding the means to cook the meat or eat it raw. In addition to food each combatant was issued a new Italian-made rifle, just uncrated and still coated with grease. The new rifles had no shoulder straps so Ristana fashioned one from her waist belt. She also ripped parts of her shirt and used it to clean the grease off the riffle before inspection.

At Gramos, Ristana resumed her old duties of guarding by night and doing laundry and mending by day. It was late August with frequent rainstorms and cold nights. The Greek forces were closing in and skirmishes were becoming unavoidable. Ristana recalls one time while on guard duty lying flat on her stomach, when she noticed Sofia, her partner, approaching very slowly, whispering to her that the burandari were in sight. But instead of firing at them, the pair grabbed their rifles and ran for their lives. The rest of the unit had already retreated.

It was raining that evening and the roads were wet and muddy. It was hard to run in the sticky and slippery mud. As the women hopped away to escape, bullets rained down on them, rifles crackled in rhythm with each step they took. Were they poor shots, or were they mocking the women? They didn't know for sure nor did they care. They were simply happy to be alive.

Upon their return the women were informed that their camp had been captured and they had been ordered to retreat to Albania. Ristana had problems with her feet and could not make the trip without rest so she hid in a secluded place behind some rocks and spent the night there. Later, on her way to Albania, Ristana met up with Leftera. Tired and hungry the women decided to skip camp and went to a nearby village looking for food. There they met a young Albanian mother who gave them some bread to eat to ease their hunger pains. Ristana was so grateful for the woman's hospitality that she gave her the only prized possession she had, her sewing needle.

At camp Ristana found family members who had earlier arrived with the refugees. It was a great comfort for Ristana to once again visit with family and receive news from home. Her relatives also gave her some of their spare clothing and socks.

Ristana was ill from her ordeal and had to be admitted to the hospital in Albasan where she spent two weeks recovering. Before she was released she was ordered to re-join her unit, which at the time was preparing to leave. The Albanians in the Albasan hospital, however, were refusing to let her go because, through some misunderstanding, she had been promised to marry a local boy. Ristana could not get out of the situation on her own so she sought help from Mihail another Oshchimian who at the time was also at Albasan. Mihail agreed to take her case to headquarters. Mihail also informed Ristana that her unit was leaving soon and that it was imperative that she be there. Finally after much wrangling she was released and was able to report for duty on time.

After the doctors examined her and found her fit, Ristana was issued new clothes and boots and was shipped out, not to combat, but to the Soviet Union. The Greek Civil War was over and the Partisan combatants were discharged from duty and joined the ranks of the refugees.

The Greek Government did not want any of them back so they became permanent refugees and were shipped out to the Eastern Block countries willing to take them. Ristana, and others from the fighting force, were taken by trucks to the port of Durresi, loaded on a cargo ship and sent to the Soviet Union. The Soviets then sent them to Tashkent, Uzbekistan for permanent relocation. Ristana remembers the trip well.

The cargo ship was a dump but the train and the liner inside the Soviet Union were luxurious. The Soviets did their best to make the refugees feel welcome. Unfortunately, the seas were too rough for Ristana, who suffered from motion sickness, and she could not enjoy the hospitality to its fullest.

In late fall of 1949 Ristana arrived at her final destination in Tashkent. After spending a month in quarantine she, along with other refugees, was issued permanent quarters in a converted camp formerly occupied by Japanese prisoners of war. The compound was divided into rooms, each with sleeping quarters for thirty-two people in sixteen bunk beds. There, Ristana met Nikola her future husband.

Nikola, son of Dimitar and Lena was born on October 15th, 1929 in the village Tresino in the Voden region. Nikola completed grade two in school before he was sent to work at the family farm full-time. Among other jobs, Nikola served as a shepherd and cow herder.

At age nine Nikola had an experience that changed his life forever. On his way home from work one day a policeman overheard him speaking to his cousin in Macedonian. Speaking Macedonian was forbidden in Greece. The policeman became furious with him, grabbed him by the neck and gave him the beating of his life. From then on Nikola developed a deep fear of uniforms and stayed clear of them. Unfortunately, as much as he tried he could not always avoid them. Years later he had an accidental and abrupt encounter with man in a uniform. The man was very old and was wearing a padar's (vineyard guard's) uniform, no threat to Nikola but his fear of uniforms sent him running. Nikola ran instinctively for safety before realizing that this man was not a policeman and his life was not in danger.

As the Greek Civil War escalated in Macedonia, Nikola's village experienced frequent visits from Greek patrols. Some elements in the Monarchist police force were unsavoury and regularly sexually assaulted women. Having no recourse to fight back, much of the population was frustrated and had no choice but to voluntarily join the partisans.

Harassment alone was not motivation enough to make Nikola leave his home, but he made his decision after witnessing the execution of an innocent twenty-three year old man. For no reason at all, the Greek police pushed the young man into the funnel of a running water mill to be crushed by the force of the water. The entire village was angered by the incident and on February 11, 1947, when the opportunity presented its self, many young men, including Nikola, took up arms and left Tresino to join the Partisans in Gramos. There, Nikola was issued an automatic weapon and sent into combat at the various fronts. By the time the conflict ended his unit of one hundred and twenty strong was reduced to eleven. When orders came to retreat, Nikola's unit was combined with another with specific orders to enter Albania. Unfortunately, there was a misunderstanding between the Albanian border patrol and his command and after twelve grueling, hunger filled and exhausting days they finally reached their destination. When they arrived, the active Macedonian leaders were arrested by the Greek Partisan authorities but were later released by special request of the Soviet Government. Nikola left with the refugees and was taken to Tashkent.

Nikola met Ristana for the first time in November 1949 at the refugee camp in Tashkent. On December 4th of the same year they married. Nikola joined a local construction company building houses for the refugees while Ristana took a job painting houses and delivering bricks to the bricklayers. Ristana found the winter very cold, especially since she had to travel in open transport trucks. About four months after her first job Ristana found a new job at the aviation factory. She started the job as a lathe operator making airplane parts, then moved on and joined a riveting crew assembling airplane bodies. Nikola also changed jobs, joining Ristana at the aviation factory making shipping boxes. A year and a half after settling down Ristana and Nikola's first child, Dimitar was born on June 1st, 1951. Three years later a second child, Lena, was born on April 15th, 1954. Sadly, however, Lena fell ill and died fourteen months later from severe diarrhea. Seven years had passed since Ristana and Nikola arrived in Tashkent but they still had hopes of returning home. Knowing that they had no chance of going back to Tresino or Oshchima, Nikola and Ristana decided to go and live in the Republic of Macedonia. Their third child, Sofia, was born on August 1st, 1957 and with their application accepted, Nikola and his family left Tashkent September 14th, 1957 for Bitola.

Bitola was home, but life was still difficult. Nikola found a job in construction while Ristana stayed home to look after the children. With the birth of their fourth child Violeta, born on April 12th, 1962, the family started looking towards Canada as a prospect for a better life. Members of Ristana's family lived there, including her mother and father who were willing to sponsor them. The family arrived in Toronto on July 8th, 1966 where they reside to this day.

a group of Macedonian refugee children

Chapter Twelve

The Plight of the Macedonian Refugee Children

Now if I can just get my mother to lift me up in her arms, so that I'm even with her head. This time I'm sure that I'll grab it - so I'm always begging her to pick me up.

But I always have to watch out that there aren't any other kids around, or they'll laugh at me and call me a little baby, which isn't fair, since I'm not little! I'm especially afraid to when Grandma Dala is there, since she told me that I was a little donkey who didn't need to be carried by his mother anymore. As if I didn't already know that I'm a big boy, since I'm going to be five years old soon, and don't I have my own dog and a lamb, I can ride on a donkey, and Uncle even made me a staff, with a handle and told me it was mine.

But every time I reach my hands up to try and grab the sky - even when I'm in my mother's arms - they come back empty. It doesn't make sense when I can see that the sky starts at her head, that I can't grab it. It appears to be a little higher. Maybe if my older cousin Itso picked me up, he's really tall, when his head hits the sky, I can grab it. I've got to finish this business, because I've got so much else to do. So

I've got to tell Itso the next time I see him. But he's always sleeping whenever he comes home. He sets down his rifle, a really big gun, we call it a blaster, he washes up, eats and then sleeps so that nobody can wake him. Cousin Itso eats a lot, he eats as much as everybody else together. When we make a pot of stew, he'll eat a whole pot all by himself, what everybody else eats combined. His mother, Grandma Dimana, and his wife, Auntie Ordana, gather up his clothes, as soon as he undresses and they boil them, as if we were going to eat them.

"That's the only way to kill the lice and their eggs. That's what Grandma Dimana says, and then she repeats it every time when he comes. But, why is he so tired, when his work is to make war, while how many hours do I play at war and I never get tired?

They say that he is fighting against the monarcho-fascists. I don't know them, and I've never seen them. Maybe they're from other villages. It seems that they're different than us, but definitely bad and that is why they fight against them. But when they get so tired too, why doesn't he just kill them with his blaster, which is the real thing. Is he too tired from fighting to pull the trigger? I'll have to remember to ask him when he comes. But I'll beg him to help me, since his gun is heavy, it's not possible to move it, even my brother Kolche can barely lift it. But if I really try and put my weight into it, maybe I can do it. When he comes another time, I'll try that. ...

(excerpt from the book by Petros G. Vocis, *Makedoncheto*, 1999)

It was a dreary spring day on March 25th, 1948 when it all began. It was a day filled with high emotions, tears and heartbreak for the mothers and children of western Aegean Macedonia. It was the day the Detsa Begaltsi (Refugee Children) left, and for most it was the last time that they would ever see their beloved family and home.

The idea of evacuating the children was proposed by a sympathetic group of young men and women at a Youth Conference in 1947 in Belgrade, Yugoslavia. The escalating conflict in the Greek Civil War posed a threat to the civilian population, which was a concern for the "progressive youth". Although they couldn't do anything for the civilian adults who were needed to support the war effort, there was a way to help the children. They proposed a temporary evacuation whereby the children would be sent out of the country to pursue their education in safety with the intent of being returned once the conflict ended. Although it was a good idea, the Greek Communist Party (KKE) saw no immediate need for such a plan and as a result it didn't give it much support. Partisan General Markos Vafiadis however, saw merit in the proposal because he believed that the conflict would escalate and concentrate in western Aegean Macedonia. He was, at the time, responsible for the defense of parts of western Macedonia that included the territories of the Lerin region and parts of Kostur and Voden regions. In 1947 the Partisans were at their peak strength and with the exception of the large cities were in control of all territories in western Aegean Macedonia.

When the Greek government began to use heavy artillery and aerial bombardment, the idea quickly gained KKE support and the "save the children" program was born. Before the program was put into action it gained approval from the Macedonian Liberation Front, the Women's Antifascist Front and the Red Cross. The host countries, willing to look after the children, were contacted to gain their approval and information campaigns were begun to inform the people about the program. The district and village organizations were also asked to participate and were eventually given the responsibility of organizing and implementing the actual evacuations. When the authorities in the Greek Government heard of this program they began the so-called "pedomazoma" (collect the children) campaign. The Greek army, upon capturing Macedonian villages, was ordered to evacuate the children, by force if necessary. After being gathered at various camps, the children were eventually sent to the Greek Island of Leros. There, they were enrolled in schools to study religion and became wards of the Greek Queen, Fredericka. After the conclusion of the Greek Civil War (1951-52) some children were returned to their homes in Macedonia while most, especially those whose parents were killed or fled the country as refugees, became wards of the Greek State and remained in dormitories until adulthood. All the children that remained at Leros were completely Hellenized and were never heard from again.

Pressure from the community prompted organizers of the "save the children" program to expedite the evacuation process to stop the "burandari" (nickname for Greek government soldiers and policemen) from taking more children.

The evacuations carried out by the partisans were done strictly on a voluntary basis. It was up to the child's parents or guardians to decide whether the child was to be evacuated or not. No child was ever evacuated by force or without consent. The evacuation zones were selected based on the severity of the conflict and the degree of danger it posed to the children. Central command organizers decided on the selection criteria and qualifications of which children were to be evacuated. The lists included all children between the ages of two and fourteen as well as all orphans, disabled, and special children. Before the evacuation was put into effect, women over the age of eighteen were enlisted from the local population and from the partisan ranks to be trained to handle young children. Widows of fallen partisans were also recruited as "surrogate mothers" to accompany and assist the children through the evacuation process and during their stay in the host countries.

The evacuation program began to gain momentum in early March of 1948 starting with the recruitment and training of the special teachers. The actual evacuations were carried out on mass, starting on March 25th through to March 30th, 1948 until all the designated villages were evacuated. Most children were transported through Yugoslavia and were sent to Hungary, Romania, Czechoslovakia and Poland. Some were evacuated through Albania and Bulgaria. As the numbers of the evacuated rose, children were also sent to East Germany and to the USSR. It is estimated that about 28,000 children in all were evacuated, most of them from northwestern Aegean Macedonia. Although smaller in number some orphans, children of partisans, and children of families that were in trouble with the Greek Government authorities were also evacuated. When their turn came the children from each village were summoned and escorted by partisan guides to the closest designated border crossing. For their safety, the children traveled under the cover of darkness and away from the main roads. In some cases, due to heavy aerial attacks and falling bombs, some villages evacuated their children in haste without escorts and they became stranded in the snow-covered mountains without shelter.

Mothers prepared luggage, a change of clothing, food and eating utensils before escorting their little ones to the designated meeting places. With eyes tearing mothers said goodbye to their loved ones before sending them into the hands of destiny. Their cries could be heard for a long time as they disappeared into the distance. It didn't take too long before the emptiness was felt and many mothers could not stop crying and contemplating the fate of their little ones.

The children walked in single file behind their surrogate mothers holding hands. The older children comforted the young as they moved into seclusion. Under the cover of darkness they silently slipped over the terrain, avoiding roads and open spaces being constantly reminded by their partisan guides to keep quiet. They crossed over high mountains and steep slopes ever mindful and vigilant of the flying Greek menace above as they made their way to the borders. The lucky ones spent the nights indoors in designated villages. The others however slept outdoors in the open spaces of the frigid mountains questioning the wisdom of their elders and wondering which was more dangerous the falling bombs or the freezing cold.

During their trek, one group came across a dangerously steep slope laden with loose rocks leading directly into the rushing waters of a river. Being too dangerous for the children to cross alone each mother had to make several trips carrying children on their shoulders one at a time. Expediency was in order as the slope was exposed to aerial view. One child was lucky that day as a tragedy was narrowly averted. In her haste to get across one mother tripped over a thorn bush, losing her balance. As she stumbled she managed to take the child off her shoulders and toss her up the slope. Luckily, the girl didn't panic and was able to brace herself. The mother then grabbed the child's feet and regained her own balance. It was a frightening experience for everyone in the group.

Another group, frightened by the heavy aerial bombardments, left their village under the cover of darkness at one thirty in the morning. It was cloudy and raining that night, ideal for escaping the bombers but a disaster for the morale of the children. It rained all night and through to the next day as the group hid in the mountains. They couldn't risk lighting a fire and being seen so they stayed wet and cold through the day, enduring nature's punishment. When night came they inched their way through darkness over snow covered, thorn infested terrain to the next village. The children were in shock and hardly felt the bleeding cuts on their feet. Some had no shoes and their mud soaked socks offered no protection against the sharp rocks and stinging thorns.

As one group made their way towards their destination one of the surrogate mothers couldn't stop crying. The person in charge of the group explained that there was no reason for her to be upset since all of the children were accounted for, fed, and looked after. But the mother was still upset and kept crying. When asked what was the problem, she explained that she couldn't properly take care of a six-month-old orphan baby that was left in her care. She only had one spare diaper and after washing it she had no means of drying it. The best she could do was put the diaper against her own chest. It never dried and she felt so sorry for the poor child who had to wear a cold, wet diaper out in the freezing cold.

The borders could only be crossed at night so the children had to wait in seclusion until it was dark. To prepare them for the journey the children had to leave the villages and head for the mountains before dawn. As they left they were told to leave their belongings behind, promised that they would be delivered to them later by wagon. As the children made their way past the border crossing, the wagon never materialized and they were left without food, utensils, blankets or a change of clothing. To this day many believe that the Greek partisans stole their belongings.

After crossing the Yugoslav border the children were taken to the village of Dupeni and from there to Ljuboino to wait for more arrivals. In the care of their surrogate mothers the children were placed in designated homes where they spent up to a week sleeping on straw covered floors, fifteen children to a room. Food was in short supply so each child was only given a slice of cornbread for supper before being put to bed still hungry. After a few days of hunger some resorted to stealing food from the village homes. After spending a week in Luboino, the children were transported by military trucks to Bitola where they boarded a train for Brailovo. In Brailovo each group was assigned to a home where they slept together with their surrogate mother in a room lined with hay for bedding. Morale was low and the children constantly cried from the enduring hunger and homesickness. Food was scarce so to preserve rations the children were fed one meal every other day. Those who lost their belongings had no bowls or spoons to eat with and resorted to using discarded sardine cans and whatever else they could find. Some found discarded toothpaste tubes and fashioned them into spoons. One surrogate mother found a rusty bucket and after cleaning it, used it as a soup bowl. The warm soup took on a red colour as the rust dissolved and came to the surface. The children were too hungry to waste it so she skimmed the rust off the surface and spooned it into all the children. An old woman seeing this felt so sorry for the bunch that she offered them her portion, preferring to stay hungry rather than having to watch the children starve. At this point most of the older boys were contemplating escape but their concern for the younger ones kept them from doing so. Some were so hungry they scoured the countryside looking for food, eating kernels of grain and corn and even resorting to killing wildlife to satisfy their hunger. After spending a little over a week in Brailovo, the various groups were transported to the nearest train station where each child was pinned with a name and destination tag and prepared for travel to the various host countries. Separating the children was not an easy task as the young clung to the older children and refused to be separated. Siblings clung to each other with all their might, fighting back with tears and cries. It took a lot of convincing and reassurances before they could be separated.

The first groups to leave were the younger children aged five to ten. Most of them were sent to Bela Tsrkva in northern Yugoslavia. These children were the most vulnerable and had to be quickly rescued before they died of starvation. In Bela Tsrkva, after spending some time in quarantine, the children were placed in dormitories with proper facilities and plenty of nutritious food. The rest, after spending a week or so at the train station were sent to Skopje. Life at the train station was harsh as most children were nearly starving and had no energy to move. Their hunger was so overpowering that the children had no energy to even complain about the tormenting lice. Many spent their time resting in the stable cars nestled in the warmth and comfort of the hay. The cars, left from WW II were used by the Germans to transport horses.

When they arrived in Skopje the children were given milk and food, which seemed like a gift from heaven after starving for so long. Without much delay, the train wagons were again divided and a group was sent to Romania while the rest continued on their way to Bulkes. Considering the episodes from the last separation, this time the authorities decided not to inform the children or the surrogate mothers. As a result, some children were visiting friends in neighbouring cars and ended up going to the wrong destination. Many mothers didn't know what had happened and worried endlessly about the fate of the missing children. When they arrived in Bulkes (Vojvodina) the groups were supplied with food donated by the United Nations and the children were bathed and given new clothes. From there they were taken by wagons to a nearby hospital for physical examinations. Bulkes was a town built by the Germans and occupied by the Greek partisans. It was teeming with activities geared towards supporting the war effort. Food was plentiful and the children spent most of their days living in empty schools and warehouses. Besides the Macedonians, there were also children from Epirus and Thessaly. As soon as they became comfortable however, the children were again on the move. After spending about a month in Bulkes, they were again loaded onto train cars, given some food and sent off to various destinations. Unbeknownst to them, they had been separated again and sent to Hungary, Poland or Czechoslovakia.

When the group destined for Czechoslovakia arrived, the Czech authorities stripped the children naked from their lice infested clothing, cut their hair and gave them a bath on mass. It was a new experience for the Macedonian children to be bathed naked in front of so many people. The local buildings and baths once belonged to the German soldiers, but since their expulsion, they became a haven for the refugee children. After spending time in quarantine, the children were taken to a new camp to join other refugee children that had arrived there earlier via a different route and were assigned quarters and schoolmasters. The children were re-grouped into pre-school ages 4 to 6, public school ages 7 to 12 and technical school ages 13 and over. The surrogate mothers were responsible for looking after the younger groups consisting of about twenty children each. Their duties included waking them up in the morning, helping them dress into their uniforms, supervising their morning exercises and making sure everyone ate a good breakfast. In the evening they supervised the children playing until they were put to bed. They also had to make sure shoes were polished and uniforms cleaned and properly hung for the night. Morning started with exercise and a good breakfast. The Czech teachers were professionals, trained in child psychology, who did their best to educate the children properly. In addition to the regular curriculum, the children were expected to learn various languages including Czech, Greek, Macedonian and Russian. On occasion, mothers and children were sent on work assignments to the farms to assist with gathering fruits, berries and mushrooms. With time mothers and children began to adjust to their new life with the exception of the usual fighting between Greek and Macedonian children, especially the boys. There was friction between the Greek and Macedonian children with frequent verbal insults sometimes resulting in fistfights. Eventually the Greek children were moved to a new camp, which put an end to the fighting.

When the group destined for Romania arrived, about one thousand five hundred children were off-loaded and sent straight to the baths and their flea-ridden clothes were washed in boiling water. After the bath, each child was issued under garments and pajamas and sent to a nearby compound formerly used by the Germans as a hospital during the war. The children stayed there from April until October 1948. Then on October 25th, 1948 many of the children were relocated to Poland. Most Macedonian children wore homemade woolen clothes that shrank during the hot wash. Fortunately, the good people of Romania donated replacement garments and the children were clothed before leaving for Poland. After spending six months in Romania in a quasi-supervised compound without any schooling, the children became wild and undisciplined. With one supervisor for the entire train, the trip to Poland was a joyride. Some children mischievously climbed through the windows of the railcars to the roof of the moving train and stood upright pretending to fly. When the train approached a tunnel they lay flat on their stomachs clinging hard to the roof of the rail car. As the billowing smoke from the steam engine enveloped them, their faces blackened beyond recognition. When they crossed into Poland the train was taken over by a Polish crew. A supervisor, trained to handle children was assigned to each car to deal with the rowdiness. For the rest of the trip, the children were well fed and rewarded with chocolates and apples for good behavior. When they arrived in Poland at the city of "Londek Zdrui", the children were placed under Greek supervision, grouped by age and assigned to various school dormitories. Children of unknown age were grouped by size and height. Initially the children refused to cooperate, mistrusting the administrators and fearing separation again. It took Red Cross intervention and much re-assurance to convince them to cooperate. Unlike the compound in Romania, the dorms in Poland were well staffed with one director and two or three assistants per dorm. Each dorm had eight to ten rooms with four children per room. There was no shortage of food, toys or games. The directors were responsible for supervising morning exercises, breakfast and getting the children to school on time. After school they made sure the children came back safely, were given supper and put to bed.

About 2,000 refugee children were sent to Hungary and assigned to quarters in a military barracks in Budapest. There each child was undressed, sprayed with pesticide, bathed, dressed in new clothing and given a package of toiletries that included soap and a tube of toothpaste. The children, not knowing what the toothpaste was, mistook it for food. The aroma of mint reminded them of candy and many wasted the toothpaste, attempting to eat it. Initially, Greek and Macedonian children were mixed together in a single group. But due to fights, the authorities were forced to split the children into smaller groups, segregated by village of origin. After spending three weeks in quarantine the groups were adopted by the Hungarian community. Each village community, supported by a factory complex, adopted a group. Some found themselves among the richest communities in the region and were privileged to live in quarters made of marble. Nearby there was a small lake teeming with exotic and colourful fish. Unfortunately, the children were all homesick missing their mothers and had little appreciation for luxury. Slowly however, routine began to take over as the children attended school and became involved in school and community activities. Besides the regular curriculum, the refugee children were expected to learn to read and write in their native language. Even though Greek officials administered the programs and scoffed at the idea, the Macedonian children were given the choice of learning Macedonian if they wanted to.

It should be mentioned here that the Macedonian programs were a direct translation (word for word) from the Greek programs. Even though the children were learning in their native Macedonian language, they were learning what the Greeks wanted them to learn. The Macedonian teachers were not allowed to diverge from the established programs. In other words, Hellenization and Greek propaganda continued to influence the Macedonian children even outside the Greek borders.

By 1949 casualties were mounting at home and reports were filtering through to the refugee camps where children received bad news about the fate of their parents and relatives. Morale was so low that the children became isolated, withdrawn and would not sing, talk, cry or even eat. To boost their morale the surrogate mothers, who wore black to mourn the deaths of their husbands, resorted to wearing white and colourful dresses. For the sake of the children, in spite of their own sorrow, mothers had to appear cheerful and put on happy faces.

As the Civil War in Greece intensified, the partisans were running out of recruits at home and began to look at the refugee children abroad as a possible source. Although draftees were recruited from all the camps abroad, most of the fighting force came from Romania. Initially, two new groups were formed and brought back for military training. The recruitment campaign and propaganda was so tempting that the youngsters couldn't resist it and were happy to volunteer. Any child strong enough to carry a rifle, regardless of age, was good enough for the draft. The first two groups recruited were instantly massacred upon engaging the battle hardened Greek army. They were all under the age of fifteen, had no combat experience and no idea of what to expect. The third group left Romania and went to Rudary, Prespa via Bulgaria and Yugoslavia. Upon arrival, the young soldiers were sent to Shterkovo, another village in Prespa, for about a month of military training and preparation for combat. The young men spent part of March and April 1949 performing military exercises, learning to operate weapons and set explosives. When word came that the first two groups of young fighters were decimated, there was a loud outcry by the community against such atrocities, "We did not save our children so you can slaughter them." The third group was only spared because many mothers demonstrated and voiced their anger against such a barbaric draft. The group was demobilized before reaching the battlefields and many of the children were sent back to the refugee camps. Some were allowed to go home only to end up as refugees again during the mass exodus in the fall of 1949.

As the Greek Civil War was coming to a close, western Aegean Macedonia was "bombed into dust" and Partisans and civilians alike fled to Albania to save themselves. When the war was over many wanted to return, but Greece did not want them back. Anyone who voluntarily fled was not allowed to return, regardless of whether they were guilty of any crimes or not. After spending some time in the camps in Albania, the people of Macedonia, again victims of someone else's war, became permanent war refugees and were sent to various Eastern Block countries. Before departure, the refugees were separated into two groups. One, made up mostly of Partisan fighters was sent to the USSR. The other consisting mostly of civilians and Partisan support staff was sent to Poland. After the groups were separated they were transported to the port of Durasi, loaded onto cargo ships and sent westward through Gibraltar to Poland and eastward via the Black Sea to the Soviet Union. The voyages were long and unpleasant. To avoid detection the refugees were literally hidden inside the cargo and at critical times ordered to remain immobile and quiet for long periods of time. When they landed at their destinations, the refugees were stripped and their flea-infested clothes were burned. After being powdered with pesticide and bathed in hot baths, they were then placed in quarantine where they spent about a month and a half resting idly before being relocated to permanent quarters.

After settling down and securing employment in their new countries, many parents who had refugee children began to look for them and with the help of the authorities were able to bring them home. As a result, many children left their host countries to join their parents in Poland, the Soviet Union, Yugoslavia, etc.

Refugees who had relatives in Canada, the USA and Australia through sponsorship made attempts to immigrate themselves and look for their children or have their relatives look for their children if immigration was not possible. Initially "the iron curtain" was shut tight and made it difficult to make inquiries, but as the Red Cross became involved it became easier. In 1953 during a Red Cross convention in Switzerland the question of the Refugee Children from the Greek Civil War came up and the various Red Cross agencies agreed to cooperate and exchange information with each other. After that, anyone requesting help to locate missing persons in Eastern Block Countries was not refused.

There are instances where Macedonians did experience problems with the Red Cross but these were due to Greek misinformation. When the Red Cross went looking for refugees in the Greek administered refugee camps they were told that the Macedonians were "migrant workers" and not refugees. Here is an actual account of what happened to one Macedonian woman in Poland.

The woman was well liked by her colleagues and in time became a model worker and qualified for a month's paid vacation. When her turn came, she was sent to a luxurious mountain resort. She was alone and felt uncomfortable going places but did agree to go and see the nativity in a local church. There she met two women who suspected that she was not Polish and were curious about how she had gotten there. After some discussion, it turned out the women were Red Cross workers and interested in finding people like her. When the women found out that she was a refugee interested in returning home, and that many others were in a similar situation, they urged her to seek help. She was given an address in Warsaw where she could meet with Red Cross officials and tell them her story. Upon returning from her vacation she and a friend went to Warsaw and after eleven days of appealing and pleading, their story was heard. Officials were curious as to why this hadn't come up at the refugee camps during the official Red Cross visits. As she recalls, unbeknownst to her, the Greek organizers made sure that the Macedonians were sent on day trips on the days of the Red Cross visits. Even after all this, the woman was still not allowed to leave. Greece would not accept her without a request from her husband. Her husband at the time was serving a prison sentence in the Greek concentration camps. It was not until 1954, three years later, that he was able to initiate the process for repatriation. The woman arrived home in May 1958 but could not stand the oppressive atmosphere and soon afterwards she and her family immigrated to Canada.

By 1950, Greece was taking extreme measures to close her borders with Albania, Yugoslavia and Bulgaria. Trusted Albanians from Epirus were brought into Macedonia and seeded throughout the border villages to act as eyes and ears for the Greeks. Greek authorities clamped down on the remaining population and no one was allowed to travel without permission. There were strict rules of conduct put into effect, including curfews. Anyone caught wandering outdoors past dusk was shot on sight. Many shepherds quit their jobs for fear of being killed and left their sheep wandering aimlessly. One little boy had an argument with his stepfather and ran away. The authorities were not at all sympathetic and wouldn't allow the family to go looking for him. The boy's mother and sister went looking for him anyway and brought him home safely at great risk to their own safety.

When the violence in Greece subsided, parents and relatives began to inquire about repatriating their children. Those who displayed some loyalty to the Greek cause were told that their children would be allowed to return if decreed by the Greek Queen Fredericka. Unfortunately, this process required connections with the local Greek authorities and a lot of money, money that most Macedonians did not have. Those considered for repatriation had to meet a number of conditions including the willingness to accept permanent Hellenization. Children from Partisan families were automatically disqualified. Those who weren't willing to change their names or weren't liked for some reason were also disqualified. As the years passed fewer children were allowed to return and requests for repatriation continued to be ignored. Parents and relatives died and still their children were not allowed to return, not even for a visit.

After travel restrictions to countries behind the iron curtain were lifted, parents in spite of the expense, old age and ill health made their way to visit their children.

One woman on her deathbed made her husband promise her that he would visit their daughter in Poland before he died. Feeling his own mortality the man, in poor health, made the long trek and after thirty years of separation saw his daughter for the first time. She will never forget her father's sacrifice.

Another woman who let all four of her children (two sons and two daughters) leave during the dreaded May 1948 evacuation, also made the trek to Poland to see them for the last time. The woman was crippled from a war wound and could hardly walk but knew that soon she would die and wanted to see her children one more time. She traveled by train and in spite of her condition made it to Poland in good spirits. When she arrived, two of her children, a son and a daughter came to greet her. The daughter recognized her mother and after a long and emotional hug asked her if she knew which daughter she was. Her mother would not answer because she didn't know and didn't want to make a mistake. That deeply troubled the adult daughter who began to weep uncontrollably. She did recognize her son and called out his name but would not answer her daughter's pleas. After a while she finally recognized her, wiped her tears and with a wide smile called out her name. It was an emotional but happy ending for that family. Unfortunately for every happy ending there are dozens of sad ones. One old couple did not have enough money or the strength to make the trip to visit their children. Since then, both have passed on heartbroken, with their desires to see their children unfulfilled.

Many of the people interviewed don't know why the Greek authorities wouldn't allow the children to return. In spite of pleas, even on humanitarian grounds, the Greek authorities decade after decade, government after government, maintain the same policy and will not allow the Macedonian refugee children to return home.

The aftermath of the war:

After all the remaining Partisans were captured or killed, people were slowly allowed to go home to their own villages. While many returned to their old homes, a few families decided to make their home in the new village. Some lost their farm equipment, tools, livestock and personal belongings to looters. For most, life had to start all over again. As tensions began to ease, those held in concentration camps were released and began to arrive home only to find their property gone. The Greek authorities, in addition to confiscating the properties of many of those who fled as refugees during the mass exodus of 1949, also confiscated the properties of those held in concentration camps. People were demoralized and constantly lived in fear of the authorities and retributions from their collaborators. There was a certain stigma attached to the relatives of partisans or their supporters that caused them to withdraw from society and keep to themselves. Those who served in the Greek concentration camps were constantly harassed with curfews, restricted mobility and suspicion of espionage. Many were followed by plainclothes policemen and pressured themselves become informants and spy on their neighbours. Strangers were viewed with suspicion and automatically assumed to be foreign spies.

As radios became affordable people began to purchase them and listen to various programs, including broadcasts from Eastern Europe and the Federal Republic of Macedonia. The Greek police became vigilant and on many occasions they were observed outside people's yards listening to hear what programs were playing. Those caught listening to foreign programs were accused of espionage. The Macedonian language was once again banned from use and the "M" word became a dirty word even if it was spoken on the radio. Ever since Greece invaded the Macedonian territory, successive Greek Governments refused to acknowledge the existence of the Macedonian language.

One by one, all those who came back from the Eastern European countries left for Canada, the USA and Australia because they could no longer stand the Greek oppression. They had tasted freedom and wanted more even if it meant abandoning their beloved ancestral homes. They remembered how life was before the latest Greeks clampdown and now it was not the same. The people too had changed, they were still courteous and kind but their spirits were broken. Everyone was afraid, careful not to say anything incriminating as if every word was going to be judged and punished. Children born during this time were brought up believing that this was how life was and it was supposedly the best life one could have. They were taught to understand that Greece was the cradle of democracy and no one in the world was freer than the Greeks. Those who knew better did not dare speak otherwise. There were certain things that could not be done or discussed, especially the Greek Civil War. Children were taught Greek chauvinist songs in school and sang them at home in front of their parents who didn't dare say anything. Even their children could unwittingly betray them. The Macedonian language became "our" language and could only be spoken in secrecy with relatives and trusted friends. The word "Macedonia" or "Macedonian" was banned from the peoples' vocabulary and could not be spoken, especially in public. Pre-school children who learned "our" language at home from their grandmothers spoke Greek with a heavy accent and were constantly teased and scolded for not knowing how to speak properly. If a child was caught speaking "our" language in class or in the yard, punishment ensued which varied from being publicly told not to speak "those filthy words" to being given a good dose of castor oil. Sometimes children sang Greek songs about the deeds of the Greek heroes and broke their parents' hearts. Their precious children were unknowingly idolizing the true criminals and murderers, Macedonia's worst enemies. Some parents, when their children were old enough to keep a secret, taught them that they were a different people, that they were Macedonian and not Greek. Other parents however, thinking that it was in the best interest of the children not to know their true identity, allowed them to believe that they were Greek. Their loyalties however were never rewarded since it was very rare for a Macedonian child to be accepted in Greek society. It was not because Macedonian children were incapable of being intellectual, as the Greeks would have us believe, but because the Greek Government systemically discriminated against Macedonians. Discrimination was common practice especially at the individual level. Macedonians were constantly put down and as a result kept to themselves. Sometimes, however, during heated discussions or unavoidable arguments Macedonians did show their discontent, but the arguments always ended with the lethal insult of being called a "Bulgar," the lowest form of life known to Greeks. The highest level of education a Macedonian child was permitted to achieve was grade six. Junior high was possible only for the children of those who had shown and continued to show loyalty to the Greek cause. One young man whose parents were killed during the Greek Civil War joined the Greek military and afterwards considered the army to be his only family. He was very loyal, studious and hard working but was constantly denied promotions. During a military exercise he saved a high-ranking officer from drowning and for saving his life the officer promised to help him if he ever needed it. After years of frustration, finally the young soldier went to the officer with his complaint. After some investigation, the officer advised him that his requests for a promotion were turned down because he was not Greek, more specifically because his parents were of Slav origin. This unfair treatment angered the young soldier enough to leave the Greek military, the only family he had ever known. Disheartened he left Greece altogether and joined his aunt in Toronto, Canada where he is currently learning to speak Macedonian. Even though he speaks no other language, he refuses to speak Greek.

After the fall of the dictatorship in Greece in the mid-sixties, many Macedonians were publicly encouraged by the Greek politicians to leave Greece because "there was no future for them there". Many of the empty villages in western Macedonia were filled with Albanians from west central Greece. Vlahs who originally lived in the highlands of Thessaly and spent summers in the Macedonian mountains took up permanent residence there. Many applied for and were granted the properties of post-Greek Civil War migrant families.

Macedonians that immigrated to Canada, the USA and Australia at the start of the 20th century organized village associations that assisted fellow immigrants in adjusting to their new countries. As post-Greek Civil War immigration accelerated, these village associations became a haven for new immigrants and their membership grew. Encouraged by their newfound freedoms, many of the new émigrés enjoyed their Macedonian culture and language in the diaspora. This was perceived as a threat to Greek influence both at home and abroad. As the associations grew in strength so did their threat to the Greek chokehold. To counter this, with help from the Greek Embassies and Consulates, pro-Greek factions began to infiltrate the Macedonian associations. The weaker associations were overpowered and rendered ineffective. Those that resisted managed to survive and preserve their unique Macedonian identity. For the ones that the Greeks could not subdue, parallel and competing pro-Greek associations were formed. The day a

Macedonian association held an event, the pro-Greek association held a similar event, to divide the people. Macedonians wishing to participate in events and prone to blackmail were discouraged from joining the Macedonian organizations and encouraged to join the pro-Greek ones. To this day many Macedonians will not go to any of the events fearing retribution from both the Greeks if they went to Macedonian events or fearing disappointment and disgust from the Macedonians if they went to a pro-Greek event. This is precisely why the Macedonian community in the diaspora has become a silent community. This suits the Greeks perfectly and leaves the Macedonians frustrated and disappointed.

The most anti-Macedonian organization to surface from all the Greek associations is the Pan Macedonian Association, which aims to not only divide the Macedonian Nation but also destroy everything that is Macedonian. To this day this organization preys on the weak, innocent, naïve and those that can be bought and continues to spread hatred and lies at every opportunity. The Pan Macedonian Association is a "false organization" fully financed by Greek taxpayers most of whom are unaware of its discriminatory practices and the friction it creates between fellow Greek citizens.

In addition to disseminating anti-Macedonian propaganda and lobbying for "the Greek cause", many of these so-called "Greek-Macedonian" organizations spy on Macedonian organizations and individuals, reporting their activities to the Greek authorities. Many activists and supporters of the Macedonian cause even though they are Greek citizens are barred from returning to Greece. Their cause is noble if they serve the Greeks at their own expense, but as soon as one attempts to serve his or her own cause, they suddenly become traitors.

Macedonians are refused entry into Greece at the border points without any explanation. Without consent, their passport is stamped "void" and thrown back at them. They do the same to individuals with foreign passports without respect for the foreign State's property.

After years of living in Australia, one man decided to visit the Republic of Macedonia. Upon entry his passport was stamped with a beautiful red symbol, a real treasure, which made him very proud and happy. His visit to Macedonia was so wonderful that he decided to cross over into Greece and visit the village Nered where he was born. Unfortunately, the Greek customs officials would not allow him entry. What was most unbelievable is the Greek officer took the man's Australian passport without his consent, and stamped it "void" all over. They literally destroyed the Macedonian symbol by repeatedly stamping "void" over and over until it was no longer visible. No explanation or apology was given.

The Macedonian Refugee Children wish to express their gratitude to the countries and people who opened their doors to them at a time of their greatest need. They treated them not as strangers or immigrants, but as equals. They also wish to express many thanks to the countries and people for giving them the opportunity of free education in their institutions. Only through their generosity away from Greek bias did the Macedonian children prove themselves equal to all the children in the world. Free from Greek oppression they excelled in education and talent becoming professors, doctors, engineers, poets, playwrights, composers, economists, etc.

Most of the refugee children today are living in the diaspora. A great number of them have immigrated to Canada, the USA, Australia and the Republic of Macedonia. Some remained in their host countries (Poland, Czechoslovakia, Hungary, Romania, Germany and Russia) and have made them their homes. They maintain contact with each other through associations and clubs and from time to time meet, attempting to gain entry to visit their homeland. Unfortunately, to this day they have had no success. Greece, after fifty-five years, still does not want them, not even to visit.

(Author Chris Stefou's note: I would like to thank all the people who participated in the interviews and made this record possible.)

the city of Skopje today

Chapter Thirteen

The Macedonian Republic 1946-2000

Angel

The stars of the dead give forth their light.

Such brightness from all sides

that ones eyes ache at the sight

and there is no shade for rest or sleep. Women,

mothers, children, old men, young boys and girls

with padlocks and keys hitched to their belts

climb up the mountain,

walk across the sky and call to their Angel,

and he responds and opens their eyes:

The star of our people rises

and from joy I feel I must clap with my hand

on stones, on my knees, and my heart

is full of tenderness, and the mountains tremble...

(excerpt from a poem from *Vigils* by Radovan Pavlovski)

The Ilinden Uprising, in particular, created a mythology among the Macedornan people of brave heroes who sacrificed themselves in the struggle for freedom. Songs and stories began to circulate among the people about the courage and self-sacrifice of a pantheon of martyred leaders - Yane Sandanski, Gotse Delchev, Damyan Gruev, and Pitu Guli, to name just a few. Their stature among the people soon rose to that of the martyred saints of the Orthodox Church and of the legendary outlaws known as haiduks, who had resisted the Turks from mountain refuges for centuries.

The stature of the fallen heroes of Ilinden rose in proportion to popular disdain for the villainy of a generation of rulers in the decades that followed. The Balkan Wars of 1911-12 and World War One and its aftermath, until the end of World War Two, was one of the bitterest, most unhappy periods in modern Macedonian history. The surrounding Balkan states had joined together in 1911 to drive the Turks out of Macedonia. Less than a year later, however, they fell to quarreling over how to divide the spoils of war in Macedonia. Then, again in World Wars One and Two and the Greek Civil War of 1945-49, Macedonia's neighbors continued their fight for control of Macedonian territory. Many conscipted Macedonians became casualties in these wars, in Greek, Serbian and Bulgarian armies.

Thus it was no wonder that Macedonia's partisan guerilla forces in World War Two looked back to 1903, when Macedonians had fought for their liberation under their own leaders, in organized local units called committees, for local autonomy and self-rule. Dealings with neighboring peoples throughout this period had been marked by treachery and deceit.

Native leaders were bullied or purchased or simply eliminated if they didn't cooperate in one of these neighbor's plans for Macedonia. Thus by the end of World War Two nearly all of Macedoria's people had rallied around the cause of "Macedonia for the Macedonians" promoted by the communist partisan leadership of the Balkans. The communist loss in the Greek Civil War and the Yugoslav break with the Soviet bloc in 1948, however, eventually led to the restriction of this movement to a small Macedornan republic that was one of the constituent republics of post-war Yugoslavia.

Contrary to so much Cold War rhetoric, life in communist-ruled Yugoslavia was better for most people there, including Macedonians, than it had ever been before. The split with Stalin in 1948 set the country on a middle course, somewhere between East and West, socialist and capitalist. Following the war there were instances of harsh retribution against those who were suspected of collaboration with the Nazis and against others who were perceived to be a threat to communist party rule of Yugoslavia. However, after the split with Stalin, many things began to change. Forced collectivization of agriculture ceased, and by the mid sixties the right of free movement of peoples was firmly established, as well as private ownership of businesses and property, on a limited scale. Health care and education became available on a scale never before imaginable and to all the people. And equally important to ethnic groups, such as the Macedonians, was the right to open expression of their native languages and cultures. Nation-states were established for the larger, compact ethnic populations such as the Macedonians, and autonomous provinces were established for the two large ethnic populations with a homeland across the Yugoslav borders in neighboring Hungary and Albania.

Despite continuing restrictions on the press and political and economic activity, the Macedonians of Yugoslavia had never had it so good. Before 1946 many people had been jailed or beaten for merely having the audacity to use their native language in public. Now there were books and newspapers and magazines and television programs in their language, and the children studied in school in their native tongue, and political and economic life, at least locally, were conducted in Macedonian.

It must have been a startling contrast after the bad old days of the thirties, when Serbian administrators had tacked the Serbian -ich ending on everyone's name. Serbian was the only language allowed in public life in pre -World War Two Yugoslav Macedonia, which had been renamed South Serbia. Then in the forties the Bulgarians allies of Nazi Germany imposed a similar regime based on Bulgarian language and cultural norms.

The communist Partisan movement had rallied people around a positive vision of a future with new justice for all and a new sense of purpose that is fully expressed in passages such as the following from a popular travel book from the Yugoslavia of the 1970's:

The Macedonian people seemed to find itself again as the peoples of Yugoslavia merged their determination and their action in answer to the appeal of the Communist Party of Yugoslavia and its leader Tito. Once again the Macedonian people was an entity without internal boundaries and without partition. Joining in the life-and-death struggle, it was united on the battlefield.

Fighting broke out at various points in Macedonia during the summer and fall of 1941. From the Aegean to Kozjak and from Pirin to Shara Mountain the Macedonians felt their strength, and the enemies felt the force of their blows. As the Partisans travelled back and forth over Macedonia, the struggles were constant and fierce. Instead of being annihilated by the punitive expeditions, the Partisan units increased in size. The first victims were slain, either in battle or in Bulgarian jails. This was the time of the national heroes Kuzman Josifovski-Pitu, Straso Pindzur, Cvetan Dimov, Mirce Acev, Stiv Naumov and many others, known and unknown.

These new fighters who set out against the enemy were to join the fighters from the 1903 Ilinden Uprising in writing glorious pages in modern Macedonian history. The free territory of Macedonia was created for the first time and increased in size. While the smell of gunpowder was still in the air, the Macedonians joined the other peoples and nationalities of Yugoslavia in proclaiming their hard-won right as a free and equal people: first at Jaice, on November 29, 1943 (at a meeting of the provisional wartime parliament), and then at

Prohor Pchinski Monastery on August 2, 1944, when the Macedonian people began to set up its sovereign state with the other nationalities in Macedonia. However, only in the Yugoslav portion did this people achieve its right to independence as a nation, with its own history, language and culture. This right was not acknowledged in Greece, while in Bulgaria it always depended on the political climate of the moment. At one point, that is, the national rights of Macedonians in Pirin Macedonia were recognized, and Macedonian schools, theatres, libraries and so on, were opened. Later all of these were closed and suppressed, so that recently the Macedonians in this part of Macedonia have been represented as Bulgarians, though, of course, this is exclusively the position of the Bulgarian authorities.

Within the Yugoslav Federation, the Republic of Macedonia has plotted the trajectory of its ascent and progress in the context of democratic and socialist relations. This right to statehood which the Macedonian people gained, and then later extended more broadly and deeply together with the other nationalities in Macedonia, constitutes the foundation for its unencumbered and complete social development.

(*Macedonian Vistas*, Boris Vishinski, Yugoslav Review, Belgrade, p. 60)

If it was not paradise, post-war communist Yugoslavia nurtured the new Republic of Macedonia. Josip Broz Tito, unassailable, long-lived leader of communist Yugoslavia, was the guarantor of peace and stability for four decades. However, after his death in 1980 the federal system of power sharing among the republics that his regime had established proved less durable. After limping along for nearly a decade, the system began to falter, and in 1989 the faulty seams of the Yugoslav ship of state began to burst.

Yugoslavia's two wealthiest republics, Germanic-influenced and Catholic Slovenia and Croatia, had been agitating for years for greater autonomy. For a while in the mid-eighties it looked as if the formation of new popular assemblies and talk of the revision of the federal constitution to create a more loosely-bound confederation of the republics might satisfy the demands of Slovenes and Croats. But then in 1989 the walls in Eastern Europe began to crumble. As the old Soviet

Empire collapsed, there was a new feeling among many Yugoslavs that the time had come to question the status quo in Yugoslavia.

Ironically, however, it was the Serbs, who would have seemed to have the most to lose by the break up of Yugoslavia, who hastened that break up by asserting their national aspirations most publicly and forcefully. They did so first in massive rallies in the capital Belgrade, then through their own "million man march" on Kosovo Polye. This was the site in their predominantly Albanian Moslem southern province of Kosovo where the Balkan Christian states, under the leadership of Serbian Prince Lazar, lost a decisive battle.

Serbs in 1989 rallied around a charismatic leader, a former communist team-player among the leadership, who had broken with the old communist line and had embraced Serbian nationalism. At the great rally in Kosovo in 1989 Slobodan Miloshevich declared that Serbs "would no longer remain on their knees" in Yugoslavia. In other words, Serbs would no longer let the other peoples in Yugoslavia continue to increase their power at the expense of the Serbs. They were particularly concerned about the danger of second class citizenship for the large Serb minorities in neighboring republics. And Kosovo, nominally a part of Serbia, was for all intents an Albanian Moslem state of nearly two million people. It had a slim ten percent population of Serbs and would have broken off from Serbia if marshal law had not been imposed by the Serb- run Yugoslav army.

If these rallies and the speeches of Serbian President Miloshevich were calculated to increase Serbian influence over affairs in Yugoslavia, they, in fact, had just the opposite effect. Slovenes and Croats began to agitate more openly than ever for full independence, and all of the republics moved ahead rapidly with multi-party elections of their own state assemblies.

The first republic to openly declare its independence was Slovenia in the spring of 1991. Slovenia's economy was the strongest in Yugoslavia. The Slovenes knew they could go it alone and prosper, especially if they could become integrated into the wealthier economic union of Western Europe, rather than continuing to be tied to the backward East.

Actual combat occurred when Yugoslav federal troops challenged

Slovenian republican guard efforts to take control of Yugoslav border posts on the Austrian - Slovenian border. Some 65 people died in a week of limited skirmishes before calculations by Yugoslav military planners led to a Yugoslav army withdrawal from Slovenia.

The Serb-dominated Yugoslav army command had concluded that Slovenia could wait. It was strategically less important, because it did not border Serbia and only about two percent of the population was Serbian. The real struggle would be with Croatia, which was poised to declare its independence at any moment. Croatia's rich agricultural and industrial zones that bordered Serbia, and the fact that nearly a fifth of the population was Serbian, fixed attention on that republic.

War with Croatia first broke out in the rich agricultural eastern border region of Croatia called Slavonia. The Yugoslav army initially presented itself as a third force, attempting to separate warring Serb and Croat factions. The outside world, for the most part, was inclined to favor some continuation of the Yugoslav state. American ambassador Eagleburger made a number of statements to that effect at the time. Macedonia's representative to the Yugoslav federal government, Vasil Tupurkovski, an able Western-educated politician, tried to play the role of arbiter in the conflict. He rushed from capital to capital in desperate pursuit of compromise accords that might head off the impending cataclysm.

But neither President Franjo Tudjman of Croatia nor Serbian President Miloshevich showed much interest in compromise. Did either or both of these proud, stubborn leaders imagine that instead of a limited border conflict, they were plunging their peoples into a vicious and enormously destructive war that would eventually cost hundreds of thousands of lives and untold suffering for millions of people?

In any event, it was not long before Yugoslav army neutrality began to break down, that is, if it ever really existed. The army increasingly became a tool of Serbian nationalist aspirations. The first majar battle of the war, far contro of the lovely Baroque-era Slavonian town of Vukovar, would set the tone for the war to come. Before it was over, thousands were killed or wounded. Many more were driven from their homes in the first wave of what has become known as "ethnic cleansing," and the former town of 50,000 was reduced to a pile of rubble.

And where did the Yugoslav Republic of Macedonia stand in all this? As I mentioned, Macedonian representative Tupurkovski vainly sought to plug the leaks in the rapidly sinking Yugoslav ship of state. But by August of 1991 things were very tense indeed in Macedonia itself. Someone set off a small bomb at the gate of a Yugoslav army station at Shtip, Macedonia. Macedonian recruits at a Yugoslav army base at Kriva Palanka staged a rebellion. They refused orders for deployment to the conflict zone to the north and issued a statement that they would not serve and kill and die for their country's leaders. "Let the sons of generals and governors go in our place," they declared. The Macedonian newspapers continually referred to the war to the north as 'brat-ubistvo" or brother-killing. Serbs and Croats are, in fact, so closely related that up until the outbreak of this war they had been willing to call their language Serbo-Croatian.

Nationalism was on the rise in Macedonia as well. A recently-formed nationalist party that had adopted the old revolutionary IMRO (Intemal Macedoruan Revolutionary Organization) title, after the revolutionary movement organized into local committees at the turn of the century, won more seats than any other party in the new state assembly. But a coalition of socialists and minority representatives denied them the most important leadership posts. IMRO's brash young leader, Ljupcho Georgievski, attained a post of second vice president, but he eventually resigned in protest.

The nationalists at that time called for a complete and total break with the Yugoslav government. Those in control, however, called for cautious resistance to Yugoslavia's government and continued dialogue. Their positions on an upcoming referendum on independence exemplified their differing approaches. The impulsive young nationalists called for an immediate declaration of independence by the state assemby. The more seasoned and cautious leadership of the state instead arranged for a national referendum in which voters would be asked to vote on the measured question - if no compromise can be agreed upon for a reconstituted Yugoslav state, do you favor the creation of an independent Macedonian state?

The older, seasoned leaders of the nation, men like President Kiro Gligorov, cared every bit as much about their Macedonian homeland as the opposition leadership. But as a former communist partisan and a participant in the Yugoslav government, he, perhaps, still had a lingering sense of loyalty to the Yugoslav state that had bestowed much that was good upon the Macedonian people. He too probably suspected that the good old days of former Yugolavia were now a thing of the past, but he was far less impulsive than the IMRO leadership.

There were all sorts of signs that August of the deteriorating relations between Macedonia and Serbian-dominated Yugoslavia. The month got off to a bad start when Serb authorities denied Macedonians access to the Prohor Pchinski Monastery situated right on their mutual border. Macedonian patriots liked to visit the monastery on August 2nd every year, because it was the date and site of the signing of the historic agreement at the conclusion of World War Two that had granted Macedonians their own nation state within Yugoslavia. That historic moment was often referred to as the Second Ilinden, since the First Ilinden marked the date of August 2nd, 1903, Saint Elijah's Day, when the first nation-wide uprising against foreign colonial rule had begun. The newspapers made much of the hostile reception that Macedonian visitors to the monastery received on August 2nd 1991. It was no surprise to anyone, however, because this antagonism on the part of the monastery's Serb proprietors on this holiday had been a source of public controversy for years.

It was perhaps this recent history of tension at the monastery on the Macedonian Serbian border that prompted Macedonia's leading politicians to honor the national August 2nd Independence Day that year at a major historic site of the First Ilinden rather than the monastery only an hour from the capital. They gathered in the more remote central Macedonian mountain town of Krushevo, a center of the rebellion of 1903. It was, no doubt, an important calculation to remind people at that particular moment of the rebels who had declared the formation of the Krushevo Republic at that time, although they had only managed to hold the town for ten days before it was retaken by an overwhelming Turkish force.

Some might wonder what the old rebels were thinking at the time, when simple arithmetic could have told them that a few thousand of them could not prevail against a Turkish army numbering in the hundreds of thousands. But Macedonians universally admire their courage. They went into battle under a banner that declared "Freedom or death." And many of them took those words quite literally. The rebel chieftain Pitu Guli with his forty men who had refused to withdraw from Krushevo when it was clear that the town could not be defended would forever after symbolize Macedonian courage and determination to be free. He and his small band had fought until they were down to their last bullet each. Then they had committed mass suicide rather than surrender to the Ottoman army. No doubt the present-day leaders wondered what tests of their own determination to hold on to their small Macedonian republic awaited them in the days and months to come.

The Macedonian nationalist party took the opportunity on that day in 1991 to call for the creation of an independent Macedonian national guard force, not unlike those that were recently formed in Slovenia and Croatia to defend the independence of those republics. Party spokesmen argued that in the absence of such a force, given the break up of Yugoslavia, Macedonia would essentially become a protectorate of Serbia.

The populace was also subjected to disturbing daily reports from the war zone. TV news journalists and photographers swarmed all over the battle zone and produced graphic visual reports on the carnage and destruction. Macedonians were, of course, most disturbed by accounts of their own young men dying in combat. Some wrote home begging their parents to get them out of this hell. They didn't know who the enemy was or what they were fighting for anymore. And suspicions were growing that soldiers from the ethnic minorities in the Yugoslav army were being placed in dispropartionate numbers in the front lines so that their Serb commanders could keep some guns at the backs of this increasingly unreliable element in the armed forces.

The reality of the war began to sink in as the first bodies of killed Macedonian soldiers began to arrive in their home towns and villages. Relatives and friends began to try everything they could to try and get their young men out of the army and combat. It must have been difficult, however, to persuade adventurous and perhaps traditional young men to avoid military service. After all, most of the nation's young men had looked forward to the day when they, like their fathers, uncles and grandfathers before them, would be honored with a "going in the army" party. It was an important rite of passage in their society, the day when they too would become one of the defenders of the homeland.

The Balkan Peninsula has long been the home of a number of competing tribes, and more recently, nation states that periodically encroach upon each others territories. The weak lose ground to the strong. This has created an almost permanent siege mentality among the populace.

Many people initially wanted to stress the peacekeeping role of the Yugoslav Army in 1991. The army was purportedly trying to separate the two warring factions. The fact that the commander in chief of the army was a Croatian had lent some credibility to this claim. Unfortunately, he and a number of high-ranking officers were later replaced by Serbs. But in August of 1991 many people in Yugoslavia believed that neo-fascists were behind the seccesion of Croatia. After all, many Croatians had collaborated with the Nazis during World War Two.

The funerals of their soldiers were a focus for Macedonian national attention at the time. Leading members of the government attended a number of the funerals and used the opportunity to speak through reporters to the entire nation. They expressed the growing concern that the deadly conflict to the north was fast becoming an all-out war that Macedonians wanted no part in.

No doubt the young soldiers who died that summer provided a most convincing argument for Macedonian withdrawal from Yugoslavia. On September 9, 1991 nearly 70 percent of the eligible voters, 95% of those who voted, chose conditional independence. Subsequent events would bear out the wisdom of that vote.

In September and October of 1991 there were a few attempts at cease fires that were followed by brief negotiations. None of these cease fire agreements lasted long enough for the ink to dry on the documents. In fact, the war expanded dramatically during those months. It was becoming ever more obvious that both the Yugoslav government and the army command were firmly in the hands of the Serbs. The Yugoslav Army expanded operations to include attacks on the Croatian capital, Zagreb, and there were indications that some of these attacks had targeted the leadership of that republic.

Western world opinion was slowly shifting in favor of the republican rebels. Yugoslavia had long been regarded as a source of peace and stability in a region historically torn by ethnic rivalry and conflict. But Serbian-dominated rump Yugoslavia appeared to be fighting break away Croatia in an increasingly agressive war of conquest, and it showed little interest in negotiated settlement.

One or two Macedonian soldiers died in the fighting every day that fall. The Macedonian parliament worked on a draft of a new constitution, and they voted to withhold their republic's share of the Yugoslav federal tax revenues. This was both an assertion of their independence and a protest against the fact that much of this money would be used to conduct war in Croatia.

The Yugoslav army continued, but with diminishing returns, to conscript draft-age youths in Macedonia. At the same time the army began to slowly remove military supplies and equipment from Macedonian bases. The high command could read all of the signs of increasing rebelliousness in the republic, and the Yugoslav army responded by increasingly behaving as if it were a foreign army on hostile territory.

The signs of organized government resistance were indeed obvious. First there was the overwhelming vote for independence. Then there was the withholding of funds to the federal treasury. Then there was an open call for Macedonia's young men to disregard draft notices sent out by the federal government. And finally there were meetings between Macedonian and Turkish government representatives in an obvious bid for outside support for an independent Macedonian state.

Yugoslav government leaders and the army high command were meeting late into the night during November of 1991 in order to formulate their response to events in all of the breakaway republics. The army with the aid of Serbian paramilitary units now occupied a third of Croatia. By no coincidence these territories roughly coincided with those regions where many Serbs lived. Serbian mini-republics were declared in eastern and southern Croatia. Although the Croatians were not militarily strong enough to prevent their formation, they certainly put up strong resistance. And as important, these moves by the Serbs, the agressive seizure of territory of a neighboring republic, further united all of the non-Serbs of former Yugoslavia against the federal government.

The Albanian Moslem majority in the southern Serbian province of Kosovo, who had been living under military occupation for several years, declared their independence after a clandestine referendum vote and essentially established a state within a state, with its own system of courts, schools, hospitals and a government assembly with their own president, Ibrahim Rugova. During this same period Bosnians also voted, two to one, for independence, and Moslem leader Alija Izetbegovic was elected president.

With so many mutinies to contend with all at once, the Yugoslav leadership had to establish their priorities and engage in a bit of triage, if they hoped to salvage anything out of the wreckage of their state. One could argue in hindsight that negotiated settlement would have been the wisest course. But the inheritors of the considerable resources of the Yugoslav army didn't see it that way at the time. They had chosen the military option, but they weren't foolhardy enough to risk war on several fronts, and certain regions were of far more interest to them than others.

Slovenia and Macedonia proved the lucky ones in these calculations. Both had less than two percent Serbian populations and both were located at the far north and south ends of former Yugoslavia, far from Serb centers of power and influence. Croatia, on the other hand, with some twenty percent Serbs in its population, and Bosnia, with close to thirty five percent Serbs, were another matter. And even Kosovo, with its ten percent Serbian population and its historical significance as a center of medieval Serb power and glory, was also considered worth fighting over. While Macedonia, predominately non-Serb and economically marginal, with only ten percent of the former Yugoslav economy, was not considered worth much of a fight.

Of course, a few of Serbia's radical right-wing militants, such as Vojislav Sheshel, tried to convince their countrymen otherwise. He argued in debates in the Serbian parliament that contrary to census figures that showed only 40,000 Serbs living in Macedonia, there were, in fact, 300,000. He also claimed to have evidence that they were being mistreated. And he assured his colleagues that the military occupation of Macedonia could be accomplished in as little as six hours!

Fortunately, more sensible voices prevailed. Macedonia was the least of Serbia's troubles. The Macedonian government was in the hands of a moderate multi-ethnic socialist coalition. The president, Kiro Gligorov, had lived and worked for many years in Belgrade. He was a former Yugoslav socialist government colleague of Serbian President Slobodan Miloshevich and a respected economist. He was careful and measured in his criticism of the Belgrade regime, something that had earned him the label of "Serbo-communist" by the more militant and right wing Macedonian nationalists.

However, President Gligorov, with the accord of the Macedonian parliament, made a formal request for foreign recognition of the independence of the Republic of Macedonia on December 4, 1991. This request was prompted by a European Community decision to consider all requests for recognition by former Yugoslav republics prior to a January 15, 1992 deadline.

Macedonia's cautious and moderate leadership was probably aware of the hostility such a request would provoke among some of their neighbors. Serbia's radical nationalists called for the opening of a southern front of the war, in Kosovo and Macedonia. The aim would be similar to that of Serb occupation of Croatian territory - to seize regions with predominantly Serbian populations. Proponents of this course of action pointed to the northern half of Kosovo and the northeastern part of Macedonia.

Would the Macedonians resist? Undoubtedly some would. The Yugoslav army could probably easily occupy the major towns, but the mostly mountainous surrounding regions could once again become the haven for a guerilla resistance movement that would probably draw its recruits from the 20,000 Macedonians on active duty in the Yugoslav Army and some 30,000 reservists. Although the Macedonians had little access to artillery, tanks or planes, they had their territorial defense forces, established years before as part of a Titoist Yugoslavian strategy for deterrence of outside agression. This force reportedly had enough rifles, ammunition, grenades, mortars and machine guns to equip a force of 100,000 soldiers. Macedonians had resisted outside agressors or occupiers of their land many times in the past. Tens of thousands had risen up against the Turks in 1903, and as recently as World War Two many thousands of Macedonians had joined the Partisans to wage war against the Axis Power occupation of their land. So there was indeed a history and tradition of resistance for them to draw upon.

Former Yugoslav professor of Slavic Studies in the US, Davor Kapetanic, remarked at the time that "Macedonians are not quick to anger or a fight, but if they are pushed too far, they will fight." Unlike the Bosnian Serbs and Croats, who have had a long-established tradition of service in Austro- Hungarian armies that kept the Turks at bay in that border region of the empire, Macedonians learned a certain patient endurance from centuries of life with little hope of successful rebellion against the Ottoman Empire. However, when they were pushed too far, they traded the saying: "The bowed head is never cut off," for: "Freedom or death."

Macedonian responses during these critical days in the late fall of 1991 reflected this consciousness. No one called for surrender to those who threatened them, but proposals at the time ranged from calls for a neutral and demilitarized Macedonia, under UN protection, to calls for the formation of a Macedonian army.

Serbia, however, was not the only threat to Macedonian security. Bulgaria had a large Bulgarian nationalist "IMRO" movement of its own. However, this IMRO's avowed aim was to reunite Macedonia to its "Bulgarian homeland." Most Bulgarians have been schooled into an abiding belief that Macedonia is historically a Bulgarian land, and that the Bulgarian population has in recent times been forced against their will to renounce their Bulgarian identity.

The Bulgarians can point to two periods during the Middle Ages when Bulgarian Empires ruled over Macedonia. However, during other periods native kings, Serbian and Byzantine Empires controlled Macedonia. More troubling for Bulgarians was the Great Power denial of Macedonia to them at the Congress of Berlin, after the Russians had prepared to hand it to them as part of the Treaty of San Stefano which concluded the Russo-Turkish War of 1878.

Bulgarians had then used their close ethnic ties to the Macedonians to promote rebellion against Turkish rule there. Bulgarians joined both the Razlovtsi Uprising of 1876 and the Kresna Uprising of 1878 and the Ilinden Uprising of 1903. The first Balkan War in 1912 had pitted Serbia, Bulgaria, Greece and Montenegro against Turkey for control of Macedonia. After their victory Bulgaria had made a terrible error of judgement that has only served to further whet the Bulgarian appetite for Macedonian land. Dissatisfied with their share of partitioned Macedonia, the Bulgarian Army staged a surprise attack on their former Serbian ally. After initial success, the Bulgaria was overwhelmed by the combined forces of their former allies and Rumania and even Turkey. In the end they were forced to accept an even less favorable partition that granted them only 17 percent of Macedonia, that part known as Pirin Macedonia.

The Bulgarians, however, never forgot their humiliating and unjust, to their minds, loss of Macedonia. In both World Wars One and Two Bulgaria allied itself with the enemies of Serbia and Greece and proceeded to reoccupy those lost territories of Macedonia, only to have to return them at the end of the war, because they continued to be on the losing side.

Bulgarians point to ethnic and linguistic studies that show strong ties between Macedonians and Bulgarians. There are also a number of 19th century teachers and writers from Macedonia who called their language Bulgarian. However, there are nearly as many Macedonians who identified with Serbian culture during the 19th century. Macedonia has long been a disputed border zone between Serbian and Bulgarian societies and cultures. However, the Macedonian language and culture has enough separate and distinct features to fuel a separatist movement at the beginning of the 20th century. That was a time when nearly all

Macedonians began to feel like pawns in their neighbors' struggles for territory and influence. Thus, they were able to rally around a separate Macedonian language and culture, neither Serbian nor Bulgarian, which was the basis for their separate nation state.

Although this Macedonian ideal was finally realized in the formation of an autonomous Macedonian Republic within the Yugoslav federation after World War Two, it has never been fully accepted by neighbors. The part of Macedonia that had been declared South Serbia after World War One became the post-World War Two Republic of Macedonia. But both Bulgaria and Greece have continued to insist that no such Macedonian people or nation exists. This position was taken mainly in order to prevent the next logical step, which would have been the reuniting such a people across borders, meaning reuniting the Macedonian populations in present-day Bulgaria and Greece.

The breakup of Yugoslavia, which prompted the former Yugoslav Republic of Macedonia's declaration of independence, gave new life to old claims on the land and people of Macedonia. There were Serbs who again began to talk about a South Serbian ethnic identity among Macedonians. Bulgaria's response was rather unique. Their government was the first to recognize the independence of the Republic of Macedonia, but they refused to recognize the existence of a separate Macedonian nation, with its own language and culture. This has continued to be a source of conflict between the two neighbors. The Bulgarians don't want to sign agreements that use the Macedonian language. They continue to regard it as a "mongrel" dialect of Bulgarian that continues to be unpleasing to Bulgarian ears.

Their neighbor to the west, Albania, showed a willingness, after the fall of communism there, to ally itself politically and economically with its Macedonian neighbor. But Albania has also been reluctant to fully support the new Macedonian state. Nearly a quarter of the population of the Republic of Macedonia according to recent census figures is Albanian. Most of those people live in close proximity to the Kosovo or Albanian borders. This has prompted calls for a greater Albania, or an autonomous Albanian province within Macedonia, or at the very least, equal status for Albanian language and culture in public life. Essentially this would mean the acceptance of official state-sponsored bilingualism of the sort that exists today in states such as Canada. A number of militant Albanian nationalists in western Macedonin were amnestied in late 1991 for the possession of substantial quantities of illegal weapons and ammunition. But Albanian calls for equal language status are no less threatening to the Macedonians.

However, the Greek response to the Macedonian bid for independence was certainly the most hostile of all their neighbors. This really should have been no surprise given their long history of bad relations, beginning with the ancient Macedonian conquest of Greece in the 4th century B.C. Macedonians, under an evolving identity as a Slavic people, again pressed the Greeks beginning in the 6th century A.D. The Byzantine Greek Emperor put an end to their incursions at the beginning of the 11th century when he captured a Macedonian army of 15,000 men. He had every 99 of 100 men blinded, leaving one eye per 100th man to lead his blinded comrades, and he sent the entire army back to Tsar Samuel in his fortress at Prilep in central Macedonia.

When the Greeks occupied half of Macedonia as their share of the spoils in the Balkan War against Turkey, they dealt harshly with the native Macedonian population. They banned the public use of their language and denied them the full privileges of Greek citizenship. Therefore, in the Greek Civil War that followed in the aftermath of World War Two, Macedonians joined the communist Partisan guerilla movement en masse, and when the war was lost, they fled north to the Yugoslav Republic of Macedonia, Eastern Europe and the wide world beyond. Greek policy towards the remaining Macedonian populatton in Greece has remained harsh and repressive to the present day. But so long as the Macedonians of Yugoslavia had remained Yugoslavians, the Greeks had welcomed a certain neighborly contact with them. Thousands of Macedonians crossed over into Greece every year to shop and to recreate. All of that changed as soon as the Greeks had to contend with an independent Macedonian state.

Greeks began to hold huge rallies proclaiming the eternal Greek character of Macedonia. Over a million Greeks attended one rally held in Salonica (Thessalonika) in 1991 in order to proclaim that Macedonia had always been Greek, and only Greek, and that they opposed any move by their neighbors to create an independent Macedonian state.

Exclusive Greek claims to the history and name Macedonia would have been more convincing if there had not been such a long history of Greek hostility for all things Macedonian. For most of Greek history Macedonians have been regarded as those unruly barbarians on their northern border. Even when the Greeks acquired their region of Macedonia in 1912, they quickly abandoned the name Macedonia, calling the newly annexed territory Northern Greece.

The first softening of this position came in the nineteen eighties, when Greek archaeologists uncovered some rather impressive artifacts of gold and silver in the tombs of ancient Macedonian kings. These treasures became the centerpiece in an impressive display in the city museum in Thessalonika that draws visitors from around the world. As the movement to adopt Macedonia as Greek gained momentum, there was a certain amount of scrambling to rewrite the history books. But the movement really took off when Greek politicians discovered that support for this position was quickly becoming a litmus test for Greek patriotism . It wasn't long before leading politicians from every party and political leaning were competing to see who could be the most proactive in declaring that "Macedonia is Greek."

The political leadership and the population at large of the Republic of Macedonia had never imagined that their cautious assertions of independence would provoke such an outpouring of passions among their neighbors to the south. Nor could they have imagined the pressure that the Greeks would eventually bring to bear on the Macedonians in order to try and prevent their international diplomatic recognition. The Greeks objected to the constitutional name - Republic of Macedonia or as the Macedonians prefer to say it - Republika Makedonija. They also objected to the new Macedonian flag, that bore an ancient Macedonian sun symbol, and concerns for the fate of the Macedonian minority in northern Greece that the Greeks interpreted as evidence of territorial pretensions.

The Greeks soon demonstrated both their power and resolve on this issue. As a member country of NATO and the European Community, they had veto power over EC recognition of Macedonian independence. The Greeks also had enormous influence in American politics. The large Greek emigre population in the US has succeeded over the years in building itself a considerable power base in both major US political parties. A number of senators and members of congress are Greek-Americans, as well as important federal administrators, presidential advisors, and even one former Vice President. The Greek lobby in Washington is considered second in power and influence only to the Jewish lobby.

Tensions along the Greek-Macedonian border grew throughout the month of December 1991. Macedonian visitors to Greece increasingly met hostility there. Greek military aircraft would occasionally violate Macedonian airspace in an obvious demonstration of their neighbor's helplessness to do anything about it.

Meanwhile, Macedonians in the Yugoslav army were finding conditions unbearable. Their Serbian commanders were treating them with increasing contempt. They were frequently given the dirtiest or most dangerous tasks. Over one thousand soldiers deserted and made their way home during the fall of 1991. And it wasn't just the troops who were feeling the heat. The highest-ranking Macedonian among the Yugoslav military command at the time, Vice Admiral Botsinov, was arrested and removed to a Belgrade prison to await trial on charges of insubordination or worse. He had refusedto order naval forces under his command into combat against the Croatians along the Adriatic coast.

January and February of 1992 passed without any decision on recognition of Macedonia by the EC, the pre-condition to UN membership. Slovenia and Croatia did, however, receive recognition that winter. This was despite the fact that the Badenterre Commission, set up to evaluate the break away republics on the basis of their adherence to international standards on human rights, principles of democratic governance, and economic reform, had ranked Macedonia highest of the four candidates. (Bosnia also had a request in.) Several factors apparently influenced the EC at the time. Greece had no objection to Slovenia's and Croatia's recognition and Germany strongly supparted it. Plans to send a UN peacekeeping force to Croatia also infuenced their decision.

The Greeks also extended their campaign against Macedonian recognition worldwide. Lobbying efforts occurred in nations around the globe. They also imposed the first of a series of economic blockades against their landlocked neighbor. Much of Macedonia's trade with the rest of the world was flowing at that time through the nearby Aegean port of Thessalonika. Normal land routes to Western Europe were blocked by the war, and no easy trade routes via Albania or Bulgaria existed. The Cold War had discouraged the construction of decent roads or rail connections with these neighbors. This meant that the Greeks had a powerful weapon that could cripple and perhaps even destroy the Macedonian economy.

The Greeks couldn't have done much more damage if they had launched a military attack. It could be argued that this was an act of war, a violation of international law, that clearly states that no nation will deny a landlocked neighbor access to sea routes. But the Greeks knew very well that their neighbors could not retaliate very effectively. It was a demonstration intended to make it clear that the Macedonians would have to live on Greek terms or risk disaster.

Almost immediately Macedonians began to feel the effects of the blockade. Disruption of oil shipments from from the Near East crippled production and transport and caused misery for many city dwellers when power plants curtailed production, leaving customers in the cold and dark at times that winter. A shortage of medical supplies put some people, mainly the elderly and children, at increased risk from normally treatable illnesses.

At the same time the Greek propaganda machine cranked out false reports of international mafia-like criminal activities coming out of the Macedonian Republic. They accused the Macedonian government of gun-running and drug trafficking. Anything seemed fair game in their campaign to convince the international community that Macedonia did not deserve recognition. Large ads were published in newspapers of record such as the New York Times, explaining Greek arguments for exclusive use of the name Macedonia.

US election campaigns for congress and the presidency had

already begun that winter, and Greek lobbyists succeeded in inserting a plank in the national Democratic platform opposing US recognition of Macedonia. They also succeeded in getting many members of Congress to sign a petition to that effect as well. Their influence in the Republican Party was demonstrated by the selection of the head of the Greek Orthodox Church in the US to open the national convention with a prayer of blessing. So Republican President George Bush was in no better position than his Democratic rival to defy the Greeks on the issue of Macedonian recognition.

The Serbs had not remained idle during these months either. By early February it was clear that the Yugoslav army was stripping Macedonia of weapons and materiel, including military hospitals, communications networks, radar and air traffic control equipment, and the like, that could even remotely be of use for military purposes. A steady stream of trucks and other military vehicles could be seen daily leaving Macedonian military bases and heading north on highways that led on up into Serbia.

During these operations all local Macedonian Yugoslav army personnel were ordered off the bases, and strange officers and soldiers, often sporting the old Serbian chetnik insignia favored by Drazha Mihailovich's royalist guerilla's during World War Two, would arrive with trucks which would be loaded with supplies and driven back to Serbia. It would later be learned that these transported supplies included everything right down to light fixtures and plumbing works. What couldn't be removed was often damaged or destroyed.

The Macedonians and their military and political leadership did not react at first. However, once the extent of Yugoslav army pillage became clear, pressure mounted for them to do something. After all, it was pointed out in the press, Macedonian funds had paid for at least ten percent of all the materiel in the Yugoslav army's substantial arsenal. The Serbs had no right to grab everything in sight. It was clear that they would soon leave the Macedonians utterly defenseless. This was not an appealing prospect for a people surrounded by hungry wolves, who would just as well carve up their territory and wipe the little Macedonian Republic right off the map.

Tense showdowns occurred during the final days of the Yugoslav Army's exodus. Macedonian state police armed with submachine guns stopped trucks trying to transport equipment and supplies from a military and veterans hospital in the capital Skopje. Similar armed troops took up positions of guard over armories that held the weaponry of the Macedonian Territorial Defense Force, exclusive property of the Macedonians. That was about all the Macedonian authorities could do at the time, unless they wanted to risk plunging their people into war similar to that in Croatia at the time.

Macedonian President Gligorov, a seasoned political veteran, as well as a former Partisan combat veteran of World War Two, put the best possible face on events. He suggested that it was not all bad that Serbia had taken those weapons. The maintenance and supply of such armed excess was an economic burden their people could ill afford. And as subsequent events have shown, those armaments did not serve the Serbs well. They were used in a campaign of ethnic cleansing, terrorism and even mass murder of civilians in Bosnia. While they allowed the Bosnian Serbs (who were supplied and resupplied by the Yugoslav army for several years of war) to run riot across the Bosnian countryside and win a series of military victories against the Bosnian Moslems and Croats, these actions earned the Serbs such worldwide condemnation that the world community eventually sided against them. The UN imposed harsh economic sanctions that literally destroyed the Serb economy, and in the end UN sponsored NATO airs strikes destroyed most of the Bosnian Serb military stockpiles.

The Serbs of the Croatian Krajina region fared even worse than their brothers in Bosnia. They also were the recipients of a substantial stockpile of Yugoslav army weapons. Apparently these allowed them to initially declare their independence from Croatia and deny the Croatians access to that territory for several years. Eventually, however, after three years of Serbian economic decline, there was little fuel available for tanks or trucks, nor resources for maintenance and resupply of armaments, and when a renewed Croatian army backed up by a reviving economy eventually rose to face them, the Krajina Serbs fled, and a quarter of a million Serb refugees followed on the heels of their army into an uncertain future in Serbia.

A credible defense analyst estimated at the time that Serbia and Montenegro (the last vestiges of a Yugoslav state) spent the equivalent of $20,000 per year to maintain each of the 188,000 soldiers in their armed forces. Approximately 10.8 percent of the federal budget was required for defense. The Macedonians during the same period, on the other hand, invested the equivalent of $5000 per soldier per year on a 10,000 man army. Defense during this period required only 1.6 percent of the Macedonian Republic's annual budget. In hindsight, the Macedonian president was probably right on the mark with his comment about the pointlessness of Macedonia owning and maintaining their share of the Yugoslav Army's arsenal.

Ironically, Greek attempts to influence world opinion against Macedonian recognition actually served to alert much of the world for the very first time to the republic's existence. Before the costly Greek advertising campaign, if the average American, for instance, were asked if he knew of the existence of Macedonia, he would have answered - "Weren't they an ancient people in Greek history?" Now, if you ask the same question, most will respond - "Aren't the Macedonians those people who are in some sort of dispute with Greeks?"

If the Greeks could not make a very convincing case for their position on Macedonia, they still wielded a hefty club to threaten those they could not convince. The timidity of most Western European leaders on this issue can only be explained by their desire at the time to see the Greeks sign the Maastricht Treaty on European Community economic union. But it was a temporary weapon, at best, that certainly created resentment and anger among Greece's EC fellow members that will not serve Greek interest well in the long run.

The Greek blockade of Macedonia did not have the desired effect either. It did not destabilize the country. It did not bring the Macedonian people to their knees begging for Greek mercy. While it caused a good deal of economic hardship, over the course of two years it resulted in the loss of billions of dollars to the Macedonian economy, it also taught the Macedonians some valuable lessons. If indeed they could not prosper under ecomic embargo and blockade, they certainly had the resources to survive. Trucks began to ply the tortuous back roads to Bulgaria or through the rugged mountains of Albania to link Macedonia with the outside world. It hastened the development of new infrastructure. Work began on a rail link to Bulgaria, and a natural gas pipeline inched its way toward Macedonia from far away Russia.

Eventually, in April of 1993 the Greeks could no longer deny Macedonia entry into the United Nations. Slowly the list of nations that recognize the Republic of Macedonia has grown. First was Bulgaria, then Turkey, followed by several of the successor states of the former Soviet Union, until today some 120 nations have defied Greece and established diplomatic ties with Macedonia. Greece was, however, able to impose a humiliating (to the mind of most Macedonians) set of conditions on its neighbor's entry into the world body. The Republic of Macedonia was not allowed to use its constitutional name, but was instead designated FYRO M, Former Yugoslav Republic of Macedonia. The new nation also was not allowed to fly its flag alongside those of other nations of the U N. until a new flag, acceptable to the Greeks, was adopted.

This was an arrangement without precedent. There were those in Macedonia who urged their government to reject this outrageous set of conditions. But it fulfilled the most critical condition for the state - it recognized the Macedonian right to exist as an independent nation.

It also allowed Macedonia to begin to participate in programs of the world body. One of the most critical of these was the UNPROFOR program that sent US and Scandinavian military observers, some 1000 eventually, under UN command, to monitor Serb military activity along the Macedonian border. This meant that an invasion force would likely have had to face UN ordered NATO airstrikes.

Greece predictably objected to the implementation of such a UN observer force. Serbian President Miloshevich met with President Gligorov at the time, apparently in a vain attempt to try and persuade him that such a move would do severe harm to Serbian Macedonian relations. However, any such concerns were overshadowed by growing Macedonian concern that the unstable situation in neighboring Kosovo could at any time erupt into large-scale violence that could easily spill over into Macedonia. It had not helped matters that it had been made public that Miloshevich had foolishly hinted the year before during a visit with Greek diplomats that they might divide Macedonia between them. And a number of tense stand-offs between Serbian and Macedonian border troops, when the Serbs decided to test their neighbor's resolve, hadn't helped matters much either.

Perhaps one of the finest hours in Macedonia's recent history was Macedonian sponsorship of UN General Assemby Resolution number 48-84 B on the 16th of December of 1993. That resolution proposed the creation of a Balkan zone of peace and cooperation, to be intiated through voluntary arms reductions by all the Balkan states.

Once again irresponsible and even criminal Balkan leaders chose to advance their careers by pandering to the lowest form of nationalism - one people advancing themselves at the expense of their neighbors. This has led to years of senseless, terribly destructive warfare at the end of the 20th century in the Balkans. Tens, perhaps, hundreds of thousands have died, many more have been maimed and crippled in body and spirit. Millions were made homeless, historic treasures were damaged and destroyed. Lovey cities and countryside were laid waste.

The Greeks finally agreed on September 13, 1995 to a 'peace' accord with their Macedonian neighbors. The accord signed at the UN in New York between representatives of Greece and Macedonia represented a compromise by both sides that again opened their border to trade and renewed diplomatic relations. One step often leads to another. One can only hope that these first steps will eventually lead to the full implementation of the dream of peace and cooperation among the Balkan peoples embodied in UN General Assembly Resolution 48-84 B.

Leshok church destroyed in the conflict in 2001 (photo by M. Georgiev)

Chapter Fourteen

Macedonian Wedding in a Time of Blood, the Conflict of 2001

Osman Beg: Come, you, with me, I'm taking you to my estate. As my guest. (To Tsveta) Would you like that, eh, infidel girl?

Tsveta: How? I can't be a guest of a Turk!

Blaguna: Aga, what are you saying? Let the child go!

Osman Beg: You'll hand over the daughter, infidel.

Tsveta: (Frightened, crying) Mother!

Rasim: You'll be an honored wife of Osman beg, what are you afraid of?

Duko: (Angrily) What! Aga, be sensible!

Blaguna: (To Duko) Quiet, son. Be good.

Shefkija: You'll be an honored wife, you'll eat and drink and sleep as you please.

> *Tsveta: (Cries) I'm a Christian, I won't join you!*

(from the play *Macedonian Blood Wedding* by V. Chernodrinski, from the period of the Ilinden Uprising)

Everyone - guests, family, the bride and the groom – knew that a storm was raging around them as they gathered for the wedding. Summer can be a time of storms in their mountains, when according to legend the prophet Elijah rides across the sky in his chariot bringing lightning, thunder, wind and rain. But this was not nature on the rampage. This storm was man-made, which meant that it was potentially far more deadly and highly unpredictable.

The wedding, on the other hand, was quite the predictable event. Weddings, in general, are highly ritualized, traditional celebrations. They are an ancient and essential element in human society everywhere. The wedding ceremony formally establishes the marriage that is the basis for nearly all family life.

This particular wedding took place in a small village at the foot of a great mountain range called the Shar Planina and on the edge of a fertile river valley known as the Tetovo plain in the Republic of Macedonia, an independent Balkan state of southeastern Europe since 1991. The wedding of Angelina and Vasko Mihajlovski took place on the weekend of July 21st of the year 2001 in their home village of Neproshteno.

Their wedding probably began some time before that weekend in July with a traditional Macedonian engagement party on a Sunday evening at the bride's home. Members of the groom's family arrived at the house bearing gifts. First there was the offering of the ring and several silver and gold coins and one very old coin to the bride, and then gifts were distributed to every member of the bride's family. The bride gave gifts as well to members of the groom's family.

Once the exchange of gifts and tokens was done, the engagement party was served various appetizers and rakija brandy and the bride served everyone coffee. Then, after all of the cups were empty, the groom placed gold coins in his cup. And when the party rose to go, the bride bid them all goodbye with a ritual kissing of their hands, and they responded by giving her money.

A week before the wedding there was another gathering at the bride's home. This time the groom served meat and bread to the guests and again gifts were given to the bride. This time they mainly consisted of ornamental items such as a necklace and a scarf adorned with silver coins for the bride to wear.

The wedding weekend ceremonies began with another meal on Saturday afternoon and an evening meal of all of the immediate family members. Then, the next day, Sunday, the groom and the best man approached the bride's house accompanied by musicians and asked the family to bring the bride out to them. In keeping with tradition, everyone but the bride's mother came out to greet them.

As her future in-laws approached the house the bride sat at the window and gazed at them through her ring and a household flour or grain sieve. Once again gifts and ritual tokens of money were offered. And the bride was served a cup of wine and coins were placed on her shoulders.

Then the family brought the bride out of the house and into the yard, where everyone danced several traditional oros or circle dances. And after further rituals the party proceeded on to the church for the marriage ceremony.

After the traditional Eastern Orthodox marriage ceremony in the church, the wedding party proceeded on to the groom's home. Further rituals took place at the threshold, where the bride made an offering to her new father-in-law of candy and grain and she then scattered handfuls over the assembled crowd. The bride and groom also shared at that time three traditional sips of wine, and what remained in the cup was sprinkled over head by the bride. Further rituals involved handing the bride a male baby to lift and carry and to give a small gift.

When the bride finally entered the house her new mother-in-law greeted her there with a loaf of bread, again accompanied by gold coins, and the bride bowed three times to her and offered her own gift in return.

The ritual wedding bread, wrapped in a colorful cloth, was later broken up and distributed among the guests. This is a custom described in accounts of Macedonian weddings going back to ancient times.

The wedding rituals ended with the bride's salting of the wedding stew and then casting salt in the stove. The groom then invited everyone to the table where they ate chicken, bread and wine for dinner. After the meal the bride distributed more gifts among the guests, this time provided by the groom's parents.

The next day, Monday, after the wedding is traditionally a time when young people join the bride in a gathering at the bride's house for small treats and gifts once again. And the day after that the young women would meet again, and a week after the wedding the two families would get together again for a dinner.

But as mentioned earlier in this story, Angelina and Vasko's wedding took place while a great storm was gaining strength all around them. I do not know for certain that they observed all of the rituals and customs I have described here, but I do know that being a village family surrounded by old familiar ways and traditions, they certainly observed most of these customs traditionally practiced in their community. But then, something went terribly wrong. The gathering storm broke over them with its full force just one day after their wedding.

On July 23rd unknown gunmen abducted Cvetko Mihajlovski from a wheat field near his home. At the same time they took his son Vasko and an elderly neighbor, Krsto Gogovski, from their homes. They were led at gunpoint in some unknown direction and have never been seen again.

The term "ethnic cleansing" first gained widespread usage in the English language by way of Serbo-Croatian during the time of the war in Bosnia following the break up of Yugoslavia in the mid 1990s. It might be defined as a systematic campaign of terror waged by one ethnic group in a region in order to drive out another group that makes its home there.

The victims of ethnic cleansing in the Balkans belong to nearly every ethnic group, as do the perpetrators. Serbs have ethnically cleansed Bosnian Muslims from villages in eastern Bosnia. Croats have ethnically cleansed Serbs from the Krajina region of Croatia. Albanians have ethnically cleansed Gypsies and Serbs from Kosovo and Macedonians from western Macedonia. Greeks have for over a hundred years been engaged in a campaign of ethnic cleansing of Macedonians from northern Greece. And Macedonians are also responsible for a recent incident of ethnic cleansing, when a Macedonian mob in the central Macedonian town of Bitola burned down the shops and homes of Albanians there in retaliation for the murder of Macedonian soldiers from Bitola by Albanians in the western Macedonian town of Tetovo.

The fact that members of nearly every ethnic group have at some time victimized their neighbors has provided outsiders with an easy rationale for ignoring desperate pleas for help from individuals and communities under attack. "Those people have always been killing each other" is a mantra that is often used to drown out the cries of the victims.

For those who choose the lovely simplicity of this response, there is little that one can say or do that would stir them to action on behalf of the victims of ethnic cleansing. It is responses such as this that allowed a ship filled with thousands of Jews to be sent back to Germany from a U.S. port of entry during the height of the Holocaust. This is why 6000 unarmed men in Srebrenica, Bosnia could be slaughtered by Serbian soldiers while U.S. jet fighter planes sat idly nearby in 1995.

This is why nearly a million people of Rwanda, men, women and children, could be slaughtered by their raging neighbors while the world looked on.

Yet, no doubt, there are those who would, in the name of justice, bear witness to such crimes against humanity. To them are offered the following documented accounts of the brutal campaign of intimidation and murder of Macedonians in western Macedonia by organized Albanian groups. In the absence of widespread public knowledge and condemnation of the ethnic-based violence committed against these people, their suffering will only serve the aims of their tormentors. It will only serve the forced eviction of the minority ethnic Macedonian community in western Macedonia from ancestral homes in thousand-year-old settlements.

The fighting in western Macedonia began as isolated attacks in the early spring of 2001 by armed and uniform wearing Albanian insurgents who claimed that their quarrel was with the government and its forces in Macedonia.

They also claimed that their goal was to achieve more equal rights for the Albanian minority population of Macedonia. However, in July of 2001 after achieving a sufficient mobilization of the local Albanian population, they began the conquest of territory where the Albanian population formed the majority.

Western journalists have continued to portray this insurgency as some kind of armed civil rights movement, but the reality on the ground is quite different. The insurgents, in fact, achieved a semi-permanent occupation of territory through an on-going campaign of ethnic cleansing. It is now clear that in July of 2001 there was a sudden shift in the focus of their movement from conflict with police and army units to systematic terrorization of the civilian ethnic Macedonian minority in the occupied territories.

One of the first documented cases of such terrorization in occupied western Macedonia occurred on July 8, 2001 in the village of Neproshteno, about 7 miles north of the city of Tetovo. Thirty year old Darko Boshkovski was alone, unarmed and in civilian clothes when he was abducted from his car at a road block near his home that day. He reported that it was about 6:30 in the evening when a group of about 150 men in Albanian National Liberation Army NLA uniforms stopped his car and forced him at gun point to accompany them first to the nearby village of Poroj, and then to Drenovec 2, and finally to the village of Gjermo.

There he was locked in a horse stall with two horses. He was blindfolded and questioned about his father, a retired policeman who had worked on drug-related crimes, and his possible family connection to Interior Minister Ljube Boshkovski. Then his arms were stretched and bound behind him with a rope that also bent his back to the point where breathing was made difficult. He was then repeatedly beaten over the course of the evening by a series of men, some with fists, others with clubs or shovels. He was also tied to a horse and dragged around the barn and later force fed horse urine and dung.

About 1:30 in the morning NLA commander Avzi came and told him that they were releasing him. They then took him by car to the city of Tetovo and delivered him to his waiting family, his wife and parents, who had paid a ransom for his release. He was warned not to reveal what had happened to him under the threat of further violence.

He was later treated for numerous wounds, including serious internal injuries, at the local hospital and later at a sanatorium in Serbia. When his family was finally able to return to their home in the village months later they discovered that their house, shop and outbuildings had all been looted and burned. Darko's automobile, a tractor and all of the goods from their building supply business had been stolen.

A year later the family remained homeless and destitute. All that they had slowly built up or acquired over the years was gone. And visits to the village or nearby town are made all the more painful by the open presence, after the public amnesty of the rebels, of those who tortured him and destroyed his family's home and livelihood in western Macedonia. It wasn't just the Macedonian authorities and press who were reporting such incidents either. According to a report issued on July 26 by the Organization for Security and Cooperation in Europe, their mission human rights specialists found evidence of numerous human rights violations by the rebel NLA forces. Their report on their meeting with three young Macedonian men who were being treated for injuries at the hospital in Tetovo on Friday, July 20, 2001 is typical of what they found during their investigation.

Although the young men refused to participate in a formal interview, the Mission report states that they were able to learn the following: "These persons appeared extremely fearful of Mission's presence, but ultimately consented to showing their injuries to the investigator. There were chafing marks on their wrists that appeared consistent with their hands being bound. By observing the pattern of the bruises and abrasions, it appeared they had been beaten whilst their hands were bound behind their backs. From the appearance of their injuries, it appeared they had been struck with rifle butts and wooden or metal rods, objects typically associated with the kinds of deep bruising observed on the subjects.

One person stated briefly that a particular pattern of injuries had been caused by being struck with a wooden broom handle and a police baton. All had been beaten on the soles of their feet as well as on the back of the legs. One had reduced kidney function upon admission, but was improving. These impressions were later confirmed in conversations with the attending doctor. It was also discovered that the three young men had attended an engagement party and were standing outside the house of one of them when a car with three armed NLA members drove up and accosted them. They were roughed up, blindfolded, and driven to a location where the beating was administered."

These two incidents were among the first of what soon proved to be a series of abductions and beatings of unarmed individuals or small groups of Macedonian civilians in the western part of the country. By July 23, the OSCE Mission had received credible information that at least 25 people had been abducted at gun point in the Tetovo region.

The ethnic cultural basis for these attacks can be seen in the case of Macedonian Orthodox Christian priest Perica Bojkovski. He was first threatened by an Albanian armed group on July 14, 2001. At that time he was pulled out of his car by an armed group that blocked the road at the village of Odri. At that time men dressed in the black uniforms and wearing the insignia of the Albanian NLA beat the priest and told him not to come back to his parish.

Three weeks later on August 9 Father Bojkovski was stopped again during a visit to one of the mountain villages that were his responsibility. At the time he was riding in a car with Pero Marchevski on the way to the village of Dobroshte. They were both dragged from the car by armed men wearing NLA uniforms. They were taken by car to the village of Djepchishte, where they were put in a barn. There they were questioned about the names of reserve policemen and the location of army and police units in the villages they visited. When their interrogators didn't receive the answers they sought, they began to beat the two men with guns and fists. They also put a gun barrel in the priest's mouth during the interrogation.

Their captors then drove them to another location in the village where about fifteen young men in civilian clothes awaited them in a cellar. This new group continued the beating, which included demands that the priest sing Albanian nationalist songs and the call of the Moslems to worship.

Eventually the priest lost consciousness and was revived with cold water. When it was discovered that he was coughing up blood, he and his companion were driven back to the village of Dobroshte, where they were again beaten and then released at their car. Father Bojkovski was later treated at the Military Hospital in Skopje, where doctors found injuries over the entire length of the priest's body.

This maltreatment of a cleric who carried no weapons and traveled openly in his religious dress on his priestly duties was clearly intended to intimidate the Christian Macedonians in that parish. It was meant to teach the lesson that no one from their ethnic religious cultural community was safe there any longer. Ethnic cleansing in western Macedonia by organized Albanian armed groups took on a truly mass character on the 23rd of July 2001. At that time the NLA launched a series of attacks on the mixed Macedonian-Albanian villages of Tearce and Neproshteno and the all-Macedonian village of Leshok in direct violation of a cease fire that their leadership had signed on to the preceding week. Poorly armed policemen and a few local reservists tried to defend the villages, but they were overwhelmed by the sudden onslaught of hundreds of heavily armed NLA fighters.

The NLA soldiers went door to door rousting people from their homes, from the smallest child to the oldest grandmother. Several thousand people were driven out with little or no time to gather any possessions and with little hope that there would be anything to return to later. Long lines of people, many hundreds, were forced to make their way on foot to the nearby Macedonian hamlets of Ratae and Zhilche.

Some did resist. Men who had invested years of their lives in the creation of a home, and those who could not bring themselves to abandon homesteads and communities with over a thousand years of family history in them. Some defended their homes with guns. Many resisted the invaders until it was clear that they could not win, and then they retreated along with their families.

Others resisted until they were wounded or killed by the NLA.

About a dozen men of Leshok and Neproshteno were wounded that day and one, Gjoko Lazarevski, died from his wounds. He was 30 years old. He had just completed construction of a new home, and he was soon to be married.

The NLA aggression and ethnic cleansing of Leshok, Gjoko Lazarevski's home village, was among the most indefensible acts of the recent conflict. The aggression took place in direct violation of a cease-fire agreement signed by the NLA with NATO mediation. It involved the occupation of a village that had never had a single Albanian inhabitant in its several thousand year history. It resulted in the criminal looting and destruction of the lifelong personal possessions and property of all of the residents.

The NLA or an allied group would later, completely outside the military conflict, set explosive charges under the foundation of a Macedonian and world cultural monument in Leshok, a beautiful Orthodox church, first built in the 14th century and expanded into a cathedral in the 20th century, reducing the Church of St. Atanasij to a pile of rubble. And one young man who tried to resist this ethnic cleansing was made the ultimate example of what resistance would bring, when he paid with his life.

The campaign of ethnic cleansing at that time also included one of the worst crimes of terror imaginable, the abduction that ends in the "disappearance" of individuals from a community. It was on that day, July 23, 2001, that the terrible crime that is at the heart of this story occurred. It was on that day, as described earlier, that NLA gunmen abducted 52 year old Cvetko Mihajlovski from a field near his home in the village of Neproshteno. At the same time they took his 37 year old son Vasko, whose wedding had taken place the night before, and an elderly neighbor, 69 year old Krsto Gogovski, from their homes in the same village. They were led at gunpoint in some unknown direction and have never been reliably heard from since.

That same day 62 year old Dimo Dimoski, who was visiting his wheat field in the neighboring settlement of Djepchishte, was also taken by NLA gunmen. And the next day 60 year old Sime Jakimovski was literally taken off the street of a suburb of Tetovo called Drenovec

One. The day after that, July 26, 2001, in that same northern suburb of Tetovo, where a number of fire fights between NLA and government troops would occur, 47 year old Gjoko Sinadinovski and 28 year old Bobi Jeftimovski were taken. Elsewhere on that same day the NLA apparently also took 48 year old Ilko Trajchevski and his 25 year old son Vasko Trajchevski. Two weeks later, also in the vicinity of Drenovec, two brothers, 59 year old Slavko and 42 year old Boshko Dimitrievski were taken by the NLA.

The families and friends of these 12 men have endured a number of years now of agony-filled uncertainty concerning the fate of their loved ones. NLA commanders claim no knowledge of these men. Swedish Ambassador to Macedonia Lars Wahlund recently headed an international commission to determine the facts of some 20 cases of unsolved abductions during the time of the conflict last year. His commission concluded that NLA commanders probably know the fate of the Macedonians abducted, and Macedonian officials may know the fate of several missing Albanians and a Bulgarian, but no one will reveal what they know.

Angelina Mihajlovska waited for over a year for news of her husband Vasko. As described earlier, the day after their wedding she and her husband and most of the guests at their wedding were kidnapped by the NLA. She and some others were released after three days. But there is a rumor that she received her husband's ear and a hand later from local NLA commander Leka. This was said to be in retaliation for Vasko having pulled a gun on Leka when he and his men appeared at their wedding. The commission concluded that it was likely that Leka, in particular, does know the fate of eight of the Macedonian men seized in his district of operations in July of 2001. Several bodies exhumed from a site near Neproshteno, according to the commission report, may yet prove to be some of the missing. But people like Angelina Mihajlovska have no choice but to continue a campaign of public protest before the public, the government and the international community in Macedonia until the fate of her loved ones is resolved. And to this day they must occasionally pass amnestied NLA leaders such as commander Leka on the streets, men who probably know of their missing men even if they are not directly responsible for their fate.

During the six months of the open conflict 15 civilians from the Tetovo region are known to have been killed and many others injured. The dead included Natsa and Petar Petrovski, a mother and son whose car hit a land mine set by Albanian rebels on the road between Leshok and Zhilche in mid July of 2001. It also included the particularly gruesome murder of two night custodians at the Hotel Brioni in the village of Chelopek. One night late in August Albanian gunmen appeared at this Macedonian-owned business. They took the two hotel employees present at the time prisoner. They were Svetislav Trpkovski and Bogoslav Ilievski. They then mined the premises with explosive charges and blew up the hotel, at the same time killing the two workmen, whom they had tied up and left inside the building to die.

Other grisly crimes committed against Macedonian civilians by armed Albanian groups during this period included the abduction and torture on August 8, 2001 of four construction workers from a site on the Tetovo-Skopje highway.

These four men, who were later released, reported to authorities that in addition to beatings, they were subjected to sexual abuse by their Albanian captors, and in a final act of barbarism before letting them go, they carved the initials of the rebel group into the living flesh of the backs of their captives with knives.

Abductions, robberies and brutal beatings of unarmed civilians in the Tetovo region continued after the open conflict ended in the fall of 2001. On the 3rd of November 2001, for example, 32 year old Cane Trpevski was returning to his home in the village of Ratae from Tetovo, where he had gone to pick up his monthly wages, when he was captured by an armed Albanian group. They robbed him and then held him for two days. During that time they beat him over the entire length of his body, while keeping his hands tied and with a feed sack placed over his head. He reported that the worst part of his ordeal had been the fact that during that entire time they had refused to give him a single drop of water to drink.

Reserve policeman Dushko Simoski received similar treatment as recently as April 14, 2002, when he was taken prisoner by an armed Albanian group in the village of Shemshevo. They also held him bound and blindfolded in a livestock stall, while brutally beating him for over two days, before he was finally released. Of course, hundreds of reserve and active-duty policemen and soldiers of the Macedonian army were wounded or killed by Albanian armed groups during the conflict in 2001, but at least their suffering came in the course of their sworn service, for which they are honored today for their sacrifice.

The ethnic cleansing campaign of terror, death and destruction included the looting and burning of over thirty churches in the Tetovo region and many hundreds of houses. The looting and destruction of Macedonian homes continued in outlying villages such as Otunje and Varvara after the military conflict ended. Even certain Tetovo neighborhoods continued to lose residents who found life unbearable there. Other communities, such as Arachinovo near Skopje, also fell victim to this ethnic cleansing.

It also included the destruction of many Macedonian-owned businesses, thus denying the people their livelihoods. These have included destruction of a textile factory and bakery in the village of Tearce, small shops, restaurants and gas stations in Tetovo, and the infamous destruction of the Brioni Hotel in the village of Chelopek. Of course, many thousands of people were denied their livelihood simply because they did not dare to go to work for extended periods. Farmers couldn't reach their fields and other workers couldn't drive the roads to various workplaces. And the Popova Shapka major ski center on the picturesque mountain above Tetovo had no tourist season.

American and French negotiators helped craft the Ohrid Accord of 2001 that ended the military conflict by granting Albanians in Macedonia rights and privileges that no minority in the Balkans has ever enjoyed to this day. It also altered the Macedonian Constitution so that it no longer refers to the Republic as the state of the Macedonian people, but as the state of all citizens of the Macedonian Republic, making it the first and only Balkan state to, at least in part, "denationalize" itself. The Accord was a source of terrible humiliation to the Macedonian people, but it put an end to the violent struggle that was tearing the country apart at a time when "only" hundreds had died in the fighting rather than the thousands who have been killed in the other wars that have accompanied the break up of Yugoslavia.

"Normalcy" has returned to daily life. Since 1991 all governments in the Macedonian parliament have been coalition governments comprised of allied ethnic Macedonian and Albanian parties. In fact, Albanian militants who only a few years before had led armed paramilitary units now sit in parliament as elected representatives of their people. Obviously, this is not a country where citizens are denied their democratic right to free association. This, however, cannot be said of their neighbors, Greece and Bulgaria. Macedonians who merely demand the right to self-identity as Macedonians and free association in organizations of their minority group are routinely harassed and intimidated by governmental authorities there. Both the Macedonian minority organizations OMO Ilinden in Bulgaria and Vinozhito in Greece have well-documented cases of violations of their rights. Human rights groups worldwide have come to their defense and issued reports on many of these violations. Human rights courts have also ruled in the Macedonian minority group's favor in cases brought before them..

The future of Macedonia, the Republic and the region as a whole, remains at risk. This is not, however, because Macedonians demand too much. They have made remarkable concessions in order to end inter-ethnic violence. It is because their neighbors have failed to make concessions. Macedonia's government has offered repeated public assurances that it has no territorial claims on any neighbor's territory. Certain national symbols were abandoned to placate the Greeks. The Albanian minority is granted rights that the Macedonian minority in neighboring states can only dream of someday having. In addition to free and open use of their language in public life, this includes the use of foreign Albanian national symbols, schooling in their native language, quotas in public institutions, and a degree of local government autonomy that is rare in Europe, and almost unheard of elsewhere in the Balkans. There is no further room for Macedonian concession, and make no mistake, this people will fight to defend itself. The history contained in this book clearly confirms that, as does the Macedonian response to the Albanian guerilla insurgency in 2001, and the more recent decision by the government to send troops to fight in Afghanistan and Iraq.

Conclusions

While the practice of ethnic cleansing is universally condemned as a crime against an entire people, it is rarely ever stopped or reversed once it begins somewhere. The fear and hatred that it creates only serve to accelerate the further division of the ethnic communities. It takes some enormous effort of public will and the expenditure of considerable resources by a society or state or the international community to halt the process.

Can the evil, barbaric process of expulsion of the Macedonian people from the villages and town of Tetovo, districts of Skopje, such as Chair, or the village of Arachinovo, or other villages north of the capital city ever be reversed, or at least halted where it stands? Likewise, can the worldwide campaign of Macedonians to challenge the denial of Macedonians' rights to self-identity, open practice of their language, culture and religion and to self-organization in Bulgaria, Albania and Greece achieve its goals?

Wherever there is life, there is also hope. For nearly every act of barbarism there is also evidence of acts of courage and compassion by members of all ethnic communities during these dark times. We can only hope that such acts might serve to guide these peoples out of their darkness and into a brighter future, a future where their differences are only played out on a friendly field for cultural competition, as the visionary Macedonian revolutionary Gotse Delchev once suggested back at the beginning of the past century.

Yes, the Balkan states are a terrible mess, but they will not make economic, political or social progress as a result of artificial population transfers in order to create racially pure states that would no longer need to grapple with issues such as laws to protect the rights of minorities, nor necessarily need to be held to any other standards of conduct. That is simply a prescription for further violence and lawlessness.

Consider if that had been the solution to the crisis in the U.S. following the American Civil War. Today there would be states wholly run by the Ku-Klux Klan and Black populations living in impoverished little Bantustans similar to those set up by the apartheid regime in South Africa. If everything should be on the table in some new international conference on the Balkans, as some have suggested, the old Macedonian Question must also be revisited in all its variations. This should no doubt include the possibility of a Greater Macedonia that would incorporate portions of Albania, Bulgaria and Greece into a state with the present-day Republic of Macedonia.

We should be concerned that any rewarding of recent ethnic cleansing in the Balkans will only serve as an open invitation for further such acts and the greater rise to power of the very worst elements in those societies. Vojislav Sheshel and his counterparts among Albanians, Croats, Macedonians and others may win a few seats in parliaments in the various states of the Balkans today, but I fear that they could become heads of states if enough people should decide that brutal ethnic cleansing gets rewarded with additional land for their favored ethnic group instead of a long stay in a quiet prison cell somewhere.

If the other Balkan states fail to follow in the progressive footsteps of the Republic of Macedonia, if they fail to now alter their own constitutions in order to create new rights and protections for the minorities living within their borders, they simply sow the seeds of the next Balkan war. Without justice there can be no peace.

Michael Seraphinoff

Further Conclusions

In 1903 Macedonia reached the crossroads of her destiny and failed to gain independence. Why? What else could have been done?

There are those who believe that the qualities that made the IMRO successful also made it weak. Instead of working with the bourgeois class of Macedonia, the IMRO aligned itself with the poor village peasants who did not have the finances or the means to support an armed insurrection.

Others believe that not enough lobbying was done to solicit outside (Great Power) help. If the IMRO had assured foreign investors that their investments would be secure, the outcome may have been different. It is true that the IMRO made little effort to solicit outside help.

I believe that after the 1878 Berlin Conference, Macedonia's fate was decided. First, Greece could not have survived economically without the Macedonian territory, Britain was well aware of that. Second, Britain at that time was not prepared to allow another Slav state to emerge in the Balkans. If Macedonia was not allowed to become an independent state, then she should have at least been allowed to merge with another Balkan state. Unfortunately, no Power wanted a large state in the Balkans that had the potential of overpowering the others and dominating the region. The balance of power was best assured with equal sized states.

Prompted by Italian imperial ventures, Greece, Bulgaria and Serbia expedited their own plans for conquest and in 1912 on the pretense of liberating the Macedonian people, declared war on Turkey and invaded Macedonia.

What was to be a liberation quickly turned to occupation in 1913 when the liberating forces set up the apparatus of government and, by legislative decrees, extended their own constitutions to the new Macedonian territories they occupied. Not only was Macedonia illegally partitioned by imposing artificial borders on its territory but worse than that, over time, the Macedonian people were either forcibly assimilated into the new folds or forcibly expelled from their own ancestral lands.

By the treaty negotiated in August 1913 in Bucharest, the map of Macedonia was redrafted ignoring previously agreed upon boundaries. Thus, the Bucharest delegates imposed an artificial sovereignty upon the Macedonian people.

With the exception of one minor change in 1920 in Albania's favour, these dividing lines have remained in place to this day. 34,603 square kilometers or 51% of the total Macedonian territory went to Greece, 25,714 square kilometers or 39% went to Serbia and 6.789 square kilometers or 10% went to Bulgaria. August 10th, 1913 became the darkest day in Macedonian history.

Macedonia's hopes were dashed again at the conclusion of the Great War (WW I) in November 1918, when Macedonians were not allowed to attend the Versailles France Peace Conference. Up to this time Macedonia's partition was illegal and not sanctioned by the Powers. With the stroke of a pen in 1919 by the Treaty of Versailles (Paris), England and France sealed Macedonia's fate by ratifying the principles of the Bucharest Treaty and officially endorsing the partition of Macedonia.

This, unfortunately, encouraged Greece to further pursue forced expulsions and denationalization of Macedonians, to begin mass colonization of Macedonia and by the Neuilly Convention, transplant "potential Greeks" into the Macedonian territories. About 70,000 Macedonians were expelled from the Greek occupied part of Macedonia to Bulgaria and 25,000 "so called Greeks" were transplanted from Bulgaria to Greek occupied Macedonia.

By the Treaty of Lausanne in July 1923, the Greco-Turkish war came to an end. Greece and Turkey signed a population exchange agreement. By a stroke of the pen some 380,000 Muslims were exchanged for something like 1,100,000 Christians. The total population in Greece, between 1907 and 1928, rose from 2,600,000 to 6,200,000. After the Greek occupation of Macedonia in 1912, for example, by their own accounts the Greek elements in Greek occupied Macedonia had constituted 43 percent of the population. By 1926, with the resettlement of the refugees from Asia Minor, the Greek element had risen to 89 percent.

The next major event in Macedonia's history started with

high hopes, but, unfortunately, ended with tragic consequences for the Macedonian people. While the Macedonians in the Vardar region of Macedonia had gained some concessions and were re-building their lives after the conclusion of World War II, the Macedonians in Greek occupied Macedonia were engaged in someone else's war. World War II rekindled Macedonian hopes for freedom, but the Greek Civil War shattered them. The oppressive aftermath was too much for most Macedonians to bear, so they abandoned their beloved ancestral villages and immigrated to Canada, the USA and Australia.

As mentioned earlier, throughout the 19th century the Western Powers, and Britain, in particular, were in competition with Russia for political and economic influence in the Balkan region. The Western Powers feared Russian Imperial expansion into the West and exercised every means to keep her at bay. Early in the 19th century, the southern Balkans, including Rumania, was dominated by Slavs. The Western Powers feared that with Russian influence, an Eastern Slav alliance (Panslavism) was possible, and they did everything in their power to prevent it.

To prevent the Slavs from uniting, the Western Powers encouraged the creation of "easily manageable Slav-opposing" states. These Slav-opposing states would not only counter Russian and Slav influence, but they would also remain loyal to their benefactors. And that is exactly why Greece and Albania were created. Being Christian Orthodox and loyal to Russia, Greece, perhaps under a different name, could have easily become a "Slav state".

Hellenism did not exist in the Balkans when the Kingdom of Greece was created for the first time in 1829. The idea of relating modern Greeks to those of 2,300 years ago came from Britain and France as a way of giving the newly created Greek nation a different "national character" from that of the Slavs to the north. This was a reliable way of ensuring Greece would not become a Slav state. Similarly, Albania was also a Western Power (Austro-Hungarian) creation designed to counter Russian and Slav influence in the Adriatic.

Not all people of newly created Greece were happy with the idea of becoming Hellenes. Many wanted to simply pursue their

Christian roots and maintain a "Christian character". Unfortunately, as nationalism gripped the Balkans, the Hellenic forces gained momentum and slowly extinguished the true multinational character of Greece. With the creation of Bulgaria, competition for influence in Macedonia intensified. By the turn of the 19th century Macedonia became the "apple of discord" between Greece and Bulgaria, two states with diametrically opposed national ideals.

Not to be outdone, Serbia too laid her own claims, insisting that the Slavs of Macedonia were Serbs and not Greeks or Bulgarians. So, were the 19th and early 20th century Macedonians "nationally" connected to the Greeks, Bulgarians and Serbians all at the same time?

In the 19th and early 20th century the question of what nationalities lived in Macedonia had little do with the real nationality of the Macedonian people and a lot to do with the Greek, Bulgarian and Serbian assertion of it. This was done purely for the purpose of laying claim to Macedonian territory. Attesting to her long history, Macedonia has always been and still is multinational and multicultural with a Macedonian majority. Greece, on the other hand, discarded her true national identity and opted for an ideal one.

Bulgaria and Serbia followed suit by claiming "homogeneity," but remained "Slav". In addition to claiming ties to ancient Greek ancestry, Greece went a step further and claimed "racial purity" and "homogeneity". By superficially connecting herself to the ancient people of the Balkans, Greece not only laid territorial claims to their lands but also intentionally excluded all others from making similar claims, including the "most recent owners." Additionally, without proof of "bloodline," Greece also claimed ties to ancient Macedonian ancestry and with that proceeded to take possession of Macedonian territory from its modern Macedonian owners.

Greece is occupying 51% of Macedonia's territory today, because, according to Greek claims, it belongs to the modern Greeks. Modern Greeks further claim that they are a pure race descended from the "ancient owners of the land," and thus the land is rightfully theirs by inheritance. Conversely, modern Greek claims that the 51% of Macedonian territory they occupy today does not belong to the Slavs (modern Macedonians) because the Slavs are newcomers who migrated to the region only 1,400 years ago. They also claim that today only "pure Greeks" live in "Greek Macedonia".

Let's put these assertions to a test. Is a modern Greek a "pure Greek with ties to the ancient Greeks" if he or she is a direct descendant of modern Macedonian, Turk, Albanian or Roma parentage?

If "yes", then modern Macedonians, Turks, Albanians and Roma must also have roots with links to the ancient Greeks and ancient Macedonians.

If "no," then modern Greeks are not "pure Greeks descended from the ancient Greeks" and, therefore, cannot exclusively lay claim to Macedonian territory on the basis of "inheritance by bloodline".

Let's take a look at some facts:

1. It is a well-documented fact that between 1907 and 1928 the population of Modern Greece grew from 2,600,000 to 6,200,000. Where did these people come from?

2. It is also a well-documented fact that any Christian Orthodox, be it a Slav, Turk, Albanian, Vlach or Roma, regardless of race, who assumed a Greek name and spoke the Greek language was considered to be Greek.

3. History has recorded that millions of people were assimilated and added to the Greek fold, regardless of race, some willingly some forcibly, between 1907 and 1928. Today Greece claims that these people are "pure Greeks, descendents of the old Greeks".

Based on the above facts does Greece have the following rights?

1. To discriminate against those who assert their non-Greek (Macedonian) identity?

2. To "exclude" Macedonians from "their own" heritage on the basis that they are Slavs and not "Hellenes"?

Here is a summary of what past Greek governments have done to the Macedonian people in the name of Hellenism:

1923. Greece and Turkey signed a population exchange agreement and by a stroke of the pen some 380,000 Muslims were exchanged for something like 1,100,000 Christians. Most of the Christians from Asia Minor were settled in Macedonia on the lands of those Macedonians killed or exiled in 1912-1913.

1926. Legislative Orders in Government Gazette #331 ordered the names of Macedonian towns, villages, mountains, and the like, to be changed to Greek names. The Macedonian people, under duress, were ordered to abandon their Macedonian names and adopt Greek ones assigned to them by the Greek state.

1927. Cyrillic inscriptions on churches, tombstones, and icons were destroyed or overwritten. Law prohibited church services in the Macedonian language.

1928. From 1926 to 1928, 1,497 Macedonian place-names in Greek occupied Macedonia were Hellenized.

English journalist V. Hild reveals, "The Greeks do not only persecute living Macedonians, but they also persecute dead ones. They do not leave them in peace even in the graves. They erase the Cyrillic inscriptions on the headstones, remove the bones and burn them."

1929. The Greek government enacted a law whereby any demands for national rights by Macedonians were considered treason.

LAW 4096 directive on renaming Macedonian place-names.

1936. From 1936 to 1940 fascist dictator General Metaxas created a reign of terror. Macedonians suffered state terrorism and pogroms. Thousands of Macedonians were jailed, sent to internal exile (exoria) on arid, inhospitable Greek islands, where many perished. Their only crime was being ethnic Macedonian by birth.

LAW 6429 reinforces Law 4096 on Hellenization of toponyms.

DECREE 87 accelerated denationalization of Macedonians. The Greek ministry of Education sent specially trained instructors to accelerate the conversion to the Greek language.

1938. LAW 23666 banned the use of the Macedonian language and strove to erase every trace of the Macedonian identity. Macedonians were fined, beaten and jailed for speaking Macedonian. Adults and school children were humiliated by being forced to drink castor oil when caught speaking Macedonian.

LAW 1418 reinforced previous laws on renaming.

1940. From 1929 to 1940 another 39 place-names were Hellenized.

1945. LAW 697 had more regulations on renaming toponyms in Greek occupied Macedonia.

1947. LAW L-2 decreed that Greek citizens suspected of opposing the Greek government during the Greek Civil War could be, arbitrarily and without due process, stripped of their citizenship.

1948. LAW M allowed confiscation of properties from Greek citizens who were accused of assisting the opposition or who fought against the Greek government.

28,000 child refugees, mostly from Macedonia, were evacuated to Yugoslavia, Czechoslovakia, Poland, Hungary, Bulgaria and Romania. To this day Greece denies their right to return.

DECREE 504 continued property confiscation of exiles and colonization of Greek occupied Macedonia with people from Turkey, Egypt and other parts of Greece. Parcels of land were given to colonists along with financial incentives.

1959. LAW 3958 allowed the confiscation of property of those who left Greece and did not return within five years.

Several Macedonian villages in Greek occupied Macedonia were forced to swear "language oaths" to speak only Greek and renounce their Macedonian mother tongue.

1962. DECREE 4234 reinforced past laws regarding confiscated properties of political exiles and denied them the right to return.

1968. The European Commision on Human Rights accused Greece of human rights abuses.

1969. The Council of Europe declared Greece undemocratic, illiberal, authoritarian, and oppressive. Greece was forced to resign from the Council of Europe under threat of expulsion. A military junta continued the policy of colonizing the confiscated lands in Greek occupied Macedonia. Land was handed over to persons with proven patriotism for Greece.

1979. 135 more Macedonian place names were renamed in Greek occupied Macedonia since 1940.

1982. The Greek internal security police urged an intensive campaign to wipe out the remaining Macedonian language and Macedonian consciousness in Greek occupied Macedonia.

LAW 106841 allowed political exiles who fled during the Greek Civil War and were stripped of their citizenship to return, providing they were Greek by ethnic origin. The same rights were denied to Macedonian political exiles born in Greek occupied Macedonia.

1985. DECREE 1540 stated that political exiles, provided they were Greeks by ethnic origin, who fled during the Civil War, were allowed to reclaim confiscated lands. The same rights were denied to Macedonian exiles born in Greek occupied Macedonia.

Human rights groups have documented the continuing violations of the rights of Macedonians and report in recent times that:

The combination, therefore, of traditional intolerance and the primitive nationalist resurgence in times of deep social and political crisis in Greece, spearheaded by an external stimulus (the issue of the recognition of the Republic of Macedonia) led to nationalist hysteria: as a result, not only any dialogue on minorities could not take place but, for the first time in the post-1974 democratic period of Greece, heralded as the most liberal in its history, people were prosecuted for their opinions on the basis of laws introduced by dictatorships but never repealed since. Within fifteen months, twenty Greek citizens were tried and fifteen of them convicted for voicing dissenting opinions on 'national' issues, and the prosecution appealed the acquittal of the remaining five. Eventually, an amnesty law swept away most of these convictions or pending trials, with only two still awaiting their appeals in 1996 (Helsinki Watch et al., 1993; GMHMR, 1994a: 3-6).

These trials have led to growing international reaction, reminiscent of the dictatorship years. Amnesty International has sent letters and published at least two special reports on the trials (Amnesty International, 1992 & 1993); likewise for Helsinki Watch & The Fund for Free Expression (Helsinki Watch et al., 1993). In addition, letters were sent by the Minority Rights Group affiliates in Flanders, France, Denmark, and St. Petersburg, as well as by the Norwegian Organization for Asylum Seekers, Article 19: International Center Against Censorship, International Pen: Writers in Prison Committee. The International Helsinki Federation for Human Rights, as well as its Balkan national committees, has also issued public appeals. Finally, proposals for motions were introduced by the Rainbow and the Green groups in the European Parliament, but were never passed, while in the US Congress, the Congressional Committee to Support Writers and Journalists, made up of 16 senators and 76 representatives, has sent a letter too. It is characteristic that the new socialist Minister of Justice promised, in the fall of 1993, to abolish or amend the articles which led to those trials and convictions; he subsequently never did, as he was reportedly told by his colleagues in the government that the major foreign policy problems Greece is faced with necessitate to keep those articles so as to quiet dissent.

In the 1990s Greece made every effort possible to block the formation of the Republic of Macedonia. It is time for the Greek people to accept the historical truth of the brutal and inhumane process of ethnic cleansing that that has been used in order to "build the nation." It is time to end the persecution of Greek citizens who wish to assert their true national identity.

The world is becoming a smaller place, and in order to achieve peace and harmony, exclusion, oppression and discrimination must end. I believe that Europe is on the right track in its support for human and minority rights. Greece must also recognize her past mistakes and make amends to the Macedonian people. If history has taught us anything, it has taught us that there is no peace and harmony so long as there is exclusion, exploitation and oppression.

For the skeptics among Greek readers , I offer you the following books, written in Greek by Greek authors:

1. If you wish to know more about Karavangelis's terrorist actions in Macedonia read his biography (the original version) "Arheio Makedonikou Agona, Pinelopis Delta, Apomnimoneymata, Germanou Karavangeli, Georgiou Dikonymou Makri, Panagioti Papatzanetea". By his own accounts and through his bragging you will learn what an upstanding religious figure, a Bishop no less, he was, and how many people he had killed for the good of his country and for Hellenism.

2. If you wish to learn what the Greeks did in Macedonia from 1903 to 1905 during and around the time of the Ilinden Uprising, read the book Ellinikos Antimakedonikos Agonas, Apo to Ilinten Sto Zangoritsani (1903 - 1905), Megali Popeza, 1998 by Dimitris Lithoxoou.

Chris Stefou (Risto Stefov)

Sources:

Association of the Macedonians in Poland. *What Europe Has Forgotten: The Struggle of the Aegean Macedonians*, A Report

Benefit Society Oshchima *75th Anniversary 1907-1982* Toronto-Canada

Bitoski, Krste. 1973. "The Course of the Ilinden Uprising", *The Epic of Ilinden*. Macedonian Review, Skopje.

Bogov, Vasil. 1998. *Macedonian Revelation, Historical Documents Rock and Shatter Modern Political Ideology*, Western Australia.

Brailsford, H.N. 1971. *Macedonia Its Races and their Future,* Arno Press, New York.

Chater, Melville. 1925. *National Geographic*, November.

Clogg, Richard. 1986. *A Short History of Modern Greece*, Cambridge.

Clogg, Richard. 1973. *The Struggle for Greek Independence,* Archon.

Dakin, Douglas. M.A., Ph.D. 1966. *The Greek Struggle in Macedonia 1897 - 1913*, Institute for Balkan Studies, Salonika.

De Camp, Sprague. 1963. *The Ancient Engineers*, New York: Ballantine Books.

Dnevnik, "They were beating me for two days, without even giving me some water" web posted: November 8, 2001, realitymacedonia.org.mk

Dnevnik, "Dene sozivot, noke - bez zivot!" 12/02/01 dnevnik.com.mk

Dnevnik, "Pogreban Gjoko Lazarevski - branitel na Lesok" 7/31/01 dnevnik.com.mk

Documents on the Struggle of the Macedonian People for Independence and a Nation-State, Volumes One and Two, The University of "Cyril and Methodius," Skopje..

Donski, Aleksandar. 2004. *The Descendants of Alexander the Great of Macedon: The Arguments and Evidence that Today's Macedonians are Descendants of the Ancient Macedonians (Part One - Folklore Elements)*, Shtip/Sydney.

G.A.L. 1966. I *Kata Tis Makedonias Epivouli*, (Ekdosis Deftera Sympepliromeni), Athinai.

Gilbert, Felix. 1970. *The End of the European Era, 1890 to the Present*, Norton, New York.

Holden, David. 1972. *Greece Without Columns, The Making of Modern Greeks*, J. B. Lippincott, Philadelphia & New York

Imber, Colin. 2002. *The Ottoman Empire, 1300-1650 The Structure of Power*, New York: Palgrave Macmillan.

Jelavich, Barbara. 1983. *History of the Balkans, Twentieth Century*, Cambridge University Press, Cambridge.

Karakasidou, Anastasia N. 1997. *Fields of Wheat, Hills of Blood, Passage to Nationhood in Greek Macedonia, 1870 - 1990*, Chicago.

Kushevski, Vojislav'. 1983. "On the Appearance of the Abecedar' *Istorija magazine*, No. 2.

Macedonia - Documents and Material, 1978. Sofia.

Macedonian Information Agency, "Terrorists demolished more than 30 churches and monasteries" web posted October 16, 2001 realitymacedonia.org.mk

Macedonian Review,. 1979. *A History of the Macedonian People, Institute of National History*, Skopje.

Mackridge, Peter. 1985. *The Modern Greek Language, A Descriptive Analysis of Standard Modern Greek*, Oxford.

The Marshall Cavendish Illustrated Encyclopedia of World War II Volume 4

Maticata na Iselenicite od Makedonia, spisanie *Makedonija*, Skopje.

McDermott, Mercia. 1978. *Freedom or Death*, Journeyman Press, London.

Misirkov, *Krste P. 1903. On Macedonian Matters*, Odessa.

Nova Makedonija, "Teroristite me kidnapiraa, me tepaa i me teraa da pejam kako odja!" 17 Avgust 2001, daily newspaper, Skopje

OSCE Human Rights Report, July 26, 2001 web posted: realitymacedonia. org.mk

Papagiannopoulos, Apostolos. 1980. *Monuments of Thessaloniki,* Thessaloniki: John Rekos & Co.

Popov, Stale. 2006. *The Legend of Kalesh Andja,* Sydney: Gr. Prlichev.

Quataert, Donald. 2000. *The Ottoman Empire, 1700-1922,* Binghamton University, Cambridge University Press, New York.

Radin, Michael. 1993. *IMRO and the Macedonian Question,* Kultura, Skopje.

Sapurma, Kita and Petkovska, Pandora. 1997. *Children of the Bird Goddess,* Pollitecon.

Saroska, Marina. *Sitel TV,* "All the Civilian Casualties" (transl. Ilievska, Aleksandra) web posted: December 11, 2001 realitymacedonia.org.mk

Shea, John. 1997. *Macedonia and Greece The Struggle to Define a New Balkan Nation,* North Carolina: McFarland.

Thomson, David. 1982. *Europe Since Napoleon,* Random House.

Toynbee, Arnold J. 1957. *A Study of History,* Oxford University Press, Oxford..

Trevelyan, George Macauley. 1927. *British History in the Nineteenth Century (1782 - 1901),* Longmans, London.

Vishinski, Boris. *Macedonian Vistas,* Yugoslav Review, Belgrade,

Wells, H. G. 1961. *The Outline of History,* Garden City Books, New York.

The Wold Book Encyclopedia

www.lib.msu.edu/sowards/balkans

Map

**Macedonia - its division into three parts
and its location in Europe**

Note on the authors:

Michael Seraphinoff, a US citizen, has Macedonian ancestry through his grandfather Mladen who was born in the Tetovo region of Macedonia and who was an immigrant to America after his participation in the unsuccessful pre-World War One efforts to liberate Macedonia from foreign rule.

Ph.D. Slavic Languages and Macedonian Studies, University of Washington, USA, he is author of the book, *The 19th Century Macedonian Awakening,* University Press of America, 1996, and *Macedonian Gold,* Literary Society Grigor Prlichev, 2005. Examiner Responsible for Macedonian for the International Baccalaureate Organization, Cardiff, Wales, UK

Chris Stefou, (Risto Stefov), born in the Macedonian village of Oshchima in the Aegean region of Macedonia, present-day northern Greece, emigrated to Canada in his teens. He and his family have maintained close ties to their fellow former villagers in Canada and he remains active in the on-going struggle for Macedonians to achieve human rights in Greece.

An engineer by profession, and a scholar of Macedonian history by avocation, author of the books: *History of the Macedonian People from Ancient Times to the Present*, R. Stefov, 2005, and *Oschima- The Story of a Small Village in Western Macedonia.* 2003